INGMAR BERGMAN'S
FACE TO FACE

INGMAR BERGMAN'S
FACE TO FACE

MICHAEL TAPPER

WALLFLOWER PRESS
LONDON & NEW YORK

A Wallflower Press Book
Published by
Columbia University Press
Publishers Since 1893
New York • Chichester, West Sussex
cup.columbia.edu

Copyright © 2017 Columbia University Press
All rights reserved

Wallflower Press® is a registered trademark of Columbia University Press

A complete CIP record is available from the Library of Congress

ISBN 978-0-231-17652-1 (cloth : alk. paper)
ISBN 978-0-231-17653-8 (pbk. : alk. paper)
ISBN 978-0-231-85121-3 (e-book)

Columbia University Press books are printed on permanent
and durable acid-free paper.
Printed in the United States of America

Cover design by Elsa Mathern
Cover image: Arne Carlsson © Cinematograph

CONTENTS

ACKNOWLEDGMENTS   IX

INTRODUCTION   1

PART ONE   PRELUDE: THE 1960s   5
    Under Fire   13
    Crisis   16

PART TWO   BERGMAN GOES TV   19
    Out of the Ivory Tower   28
    Mass-Market Bergman   33
    The TV Medium and Bergman's Style   37

PART THREE   BERGMAN'S MODERNISM   43
    Attack of Second-Wave Feminism   45
    The Strindberg-Ibsen-Bergman Connection   49
    Persona: War on Idealism   54
    The Making of Ingmar Bergman   59
    One Man, Four Women   65

PART FOUR   THE DJURSHOLM TRILOGY PLUS ONE   73
    The Lie: A Tragi-Comedy of Banality   77
    Scenes from a Marriage   85
    Life in the Beige Lane   91
    Cries and Whispers: Into the Belly of the Idealism Beast   99

PART FIVE *FACE TO FACE* 105

    To the Orgasm and Beyond: Ingmar Bergman and
       the Sexual Revolution 107
    Arthur Janov Conquers Sweden – and Bergman 112
    Workbook No. 29, Part I: Everything is a Dream 117
    Traum and Trauma 126
    Workbook No. 29, Part II: Jenny the Psychiatrist 130
    Workbook No. 29, Part III: The Primal Scream 141
    The Screenplay 149
    The Production 171
    The TV Series 177
    The Film 196
    Overture to the Release 199
    Reception 202
    A Success and a Failure 209
    Coda: The End of Art? 214

REFERENCES 217
INDEX 232

When I was a child I spoke like a child, thought like a child, reasoned like a child; but when I grew up I finished with childish things.
At present, we see only through a glass darkly, but one day we shall see face to face. My knowledge is now partial; then it will be whole, like God's knowledge of me.

– 1 Corinthians 13:11–12

FOR ISAK AND ISAAC

ACKNOWLEDGMENTS

For information and assistance, I thank:
Librarians at the National Library's Research Desk, Stockholm;
Jan Holmberg, CEO, Ingmar Bergman Foundation;
Rolf Holmqvist, Professor of Clinical Psychology, Linköping University;
Maaret Koskinen, Professor of Film Studies, Stockholm University;
Thomas Lindhé, Swedish Television Audience & Programming Analysis;
Librarians at Lund University Library;
Bengt Lorentzon, Archivist at Swedish Television;
Tomas Videgård, PhD in Psychology and psychotherapist.

For financial support of my work, I thank:
Gyllenstierna Krapperup Foundation;
Lars Hierta Memorial Foundation.

INTRODUCTION

Why another book on Ingmar Bergman? It is a reasonable question considering the extensive mapping of the director by critics and academic scholars (Steene 2005, pp. 879–1029). However, a pattern soon emerges to the reader of these works. Some films are canonised as the director's key works, frequently referred to as his 'masterpieces' and, hence, treated in numerous essays and books, for example *The Seventh Seal* (*Det sjunde inseglet*, 1957), *Persona* (1966) and *Fanny and Alexander* (*Fanny och Alexander*, 1982).

Others are dismissed as failures or simply ignored as of little or no interest, for example *It Rains on Our Love* (*Det regnar på vår kärlek*, 1946), *Dreams* (*Kvinnodröm*, 1955) and *The Touch* (*Beröringen*, 1971). The pattern largely follows Bergman's own sentiments about his works expressed in his books *The Magic Lantern* (*Laterna Magica*, 1987; English edition 1988) and *Images* (*Bilder*, 1990; English edition 1995), almost as if Bergman himself had directed the reception.

Possibly the most striking title in what we might call the Bergman Apocrypha is *Face to Face* (*Ansikte mot ansikte*), which premiered in a 135-minute cinema version on 5 April 1976 in the USA and on 28 April as a 177-minute TV series in four parts on Swedish Television.* At the time, it was generally praised by critics and received several important awards and nominations. Today, it is either ignored or dismissed as a minor work. Paramount's shoddy 2011 DVD transfer, released with no extras and accompanied by zero marketing, is a telling sign of the production's low status.

---

* Swedish Television was until 1978 a subdivision of public service company Sveriges Radio AB.

The few books that touch on *Face to Face* have largely followed Bergman's assessment. Both Peter Cowie's *Ingmar Bergman: A Critical Biography* (1982, pp. 300–303) and Mikael Timm's *Lusten och dämonerna: Boken om Bergman* (2008, pp. 457–459) include some quotes from Bergman to back up their summary dismissal. Frank Gado's *The Passion of Ingmar Bergman* (1996, pp. 440–454) includes the only extensive analysis of the production previous to this book. But his text is clearly based on the screenplay, not the much different filmed version of *Face to Face*, shot in the spring of 1975 and edited with some scenes reshot and some others added in the summer and autumn of the same year.

To learn about why it was such a praised production when it premiered more than forty years ago, and why it is treated with such disdain today, we must go back in time. *Face to Face* followed the successful TV series *Scenes from a Marriage* (*Scener ur ett äktenskap*, 1973), and again features Liv Ullmann and Erland Josephson in the leading roles. Bergman's work on the project began during the editing of his celebrated TV production of Mozart's *The Magic Flute* (*Trollflöjten*) in 1974:

> This should have been a happy period of my life. I had *The Magic Flute* behind me, as well as *Scenes from a Marriage* and *Cries and Whispers*. I was successful at the theatre. Our little company [Cinematograph] was producing films by other directors, and the money was flowing in. It was precisely the right time to tackle a difficult task. My artistic self-confidence was as high as it's ever been. I could do whatever I wanted, and anyone and everyone was willing to finance my efforts. (Bergman 1995, p. 77)

In his engagement planners and workbooks, Bergman not only noted his engagements but also what books and films he consumed. Frequently, there are reflections on his and others' artistry and sometimes even scribbled-down ideas captured in the moment. These scribbled notes therefore have the added value of being his diaries of sorts.

While writing the screenplay and working on the preproduction of *Face to Face*, he took an interest, the planner reveals, in feminist writing such as Erica Jong's classic book *Fear of Flying* and in pornography films, made chic by *Deep Throat* (1972) and mainstream by soft-core hit movie *Emmanuelle* (1974). The combination might seem curious today, but this was before the feminist movement against pornography got a wider public attention.

Most important, he read US psychotherapist Arthur Janov's bestseller *The Primal Scream* (1970; Swedish edition 1974), which made a great impression on him. Not only did he call his initial drafts of the *Face to Face* screenplay 'The Psychiatrist', but he continued to read other books by Janov and then met with the famed psychotherapist in Los Angeles with plans to make a film in collaboration with him. Janov's primal therapy was for many about psychosexual liberation as a stepping stone to personal freedom and empowerment.

Liberated from the lingering Victorian inhibitions and conventions, men and – even more so – women would be able to break away from social repression and psychological inhibitions to achieve a true free will, an authentic emotional life and self-realisation. Moreover, this process had political implications, as Bergman's old friend Vilgot Sjöman showed in his international hit film *I Am Curious – Yellow* (*Jag är nyfiken – gul*, 1967) by connecting Marx and Freud. Thus, *Face to Face* presents, in its early drafts, a vision of a political struggle through a psychological process. It was then gradually revised into a different tale as Bergman processed the drafts into the screenplay and finally the film.

Bergman was a man who revised his opinions over time, as we all do. My aim in this book is therefore to contextualise the production by trying to capture Bergman as he was at this point in his life and career – in the early to mid-1970s and under the influence of various people, ideas and issues. The reasons behind the project and the revisions that followed must be considered in relation to his personal history and body of work and in the context of the contemporary political and cultural debate. This is what I intend to do in this book.

I start with a prelude, a short portrait of Ingmar Bergman's cultural position in the 1960s, both as a much-awarded and praised artist at the top of the cultural establishment and as a controversial icon in the media and public debate. Then follows a section on the reasons behind Bergman's decision to write, direct and produce original works for TV and the consequences for him as an artist and commercial producer as well as his standing in the cultural debate.

In part three, I take a step back to look at Bergman's modernist roots and his many sources of inspiration, especially Henrik Ibsen, and I include some observations on the magic circle of family, friends and foes that was of great importance to Bergman's work in the 1970s. While working on *Face to Face*, Bergman also had a muse, who I will bring out from the shadows.

Part four elaborates on the discussion of Bergman's Ibsen-influenced, modernist aesthetics by analysing the two first TV productions in what I call the Djursholm trilogy – *The Lie* (*Reservatet*, 1970) and *Scenes from a Marriage* – and their connections to his film *Cries and Whispers* (*Viskningar och rop*, 1973).

Finally, in part five, I portray the production of *Face to Face* from start to finish. Beginning with Bergman's contemporary interest in the issues described above, I take a close look at his work: the notes in his workbooks, the writing of the screenplay, the making of the TV series and film version at his company Cinematograph and how he, by his contact with Dino De Laurentiis, got world distribution for the film at Paramount. I round off the book with the reception of the series and film and a discussion on why this generally well-received and awarded production fell so quickly into public, critical and academic oblivion.

PART ONE

PRELUDE: THE 1960S

The 1960s was the best of times and the worst of times for Ingmar Bergman. It began with him reaching the peak of his international fame, following a string of awards and honours bestowed on him after his breakthrough comedy *Smiles of a Summer Night* (*Sommarnattens leende*, 1955). In 1960 he made the cover of *Time* magazine, the first non-English-speaking filmmaker to do so since Leni Riefenstahl in 1936 (Balio 2010, p. 130). The following year his *The Virgin Spring* (*Jungfrukällan*, 1960) won an Academy Award as the Best Foreign Film, and another one followed for *Through a Glass Darkly* (*Såsom i en spegel*, 1961) in 1962.

As the poster boy for European art cinema, it seemed that his early days of financial insecurities in film production were over. Artistically, he had received just about every important award possible. Commercially, he was in the black. His films were inexpensive productions, costing on average about $160,000. In 1959, his US distributor Janus Films reaped the fruits of their efforts to build 'the Bergman image' with publicity firm

Fig. 1: Ingmar Bergman on the cover of *Time* magazine in 1960

Blowitz & Maskel by having five of his films playing simultaneously in New York. It was the year of the 'Bergman Boom', possibly earning more profits for Janus Films than all Swedish films shown in the US since World War II put together.*

Bergman should have been big business for his Swedish producers, Svensk Filmindustri (SF), but the times were troubled by dramatic changes in consumer habits. Audiences dwindled and the one that remained at the cinemas consisted largely of the young rock and roll generation born in the 1940s or later. Bergman's biggest box-office hit, *The Silence* (*Tystnaden*, 1963), seemed to dispel all fears when it sold close to 1.5 million tickets in Sweden alone. A staggering figure considering that the country then had a population of just 7.5 million people. In the USA, it earned over $1 million.†

Still, Bergman was not reassured since he thought that the overwhelming majority had come for all the wrong reasons, more specifically the censorship controversy about the film's sexual imagery. Though pleased with the attention, he saw it as a one-off affair that would not generate any interest for his films in the long run, perhaps just the opposite (Björkman et al. 1973, p. 180). He was right.

The strong Bergman brand abroad – mainly in the US – did not help his films commercially at home, and soon there would be trouble also at the box office across the Atlantic. On top of that, the Swedish reception of his films became critical at the end of the decade. For all the international acclaim, his deepest wish was to become a prophet in his home, not only winning over the reluctant audience but also his homeland critics (Sjöman 1963, p. 23; Steene 2008, p. 324).

However, to claim that Bergman had been misunderstood or abused by the Swedish critics over the years in his career, as one might think when reading interviews with the director, is an exaggeration. Already in the reviews of his first film, *Crisis* (*Kris*, 1946), he was recognised as a bold new film director with a vision of his own by important critics in leading newspapers such as Bang (pen name for Barbro Alving) in *Dagens Nyheter* and Filmson (pen name for Sven Jan Hanson) in *Aftonbladet* (Grönberg 1980, p. 513). There was, of course, the occasional scolding, such as Filmson's rage against *Sawdust and Tinsel* (*Gycklarnas afton*, 1953), beginning with "I decline an ocular inspection of the vomit Ingmar Bergman has left behind this time" – a line Bergman quoted from memory in countless interviews

---

* Janus Films earned about $1 million on Bergman's films in 1959; see Balio 2010, pp. 131–139 *passim*.
† Swedish box-office statistics from the statistics pages at the Swedish Film Institute's website: http://www.sfi.se/sv/statistik/ (accessed 31 January 2016). For US statistics, see Balio 2010, p. 144.

(as late as in a 2002 interview by Jan Aghed) and included in his book *Images* almost forty years after the fact (Bergman 1995, p. 188).

But in stark contrast to Filmson's review, *Sawdust and Tinsel* was lauded by distinguished critics, such as Mauritz Edström in *Arbetaren*, Nils Beyer in *Morgon-Tidningen* and future film institute founder Harry Schein in the prestigious literary journal *BLM*. Schein even declared the film to be one of the best he had ever seen (Geber 1983, p. 304). But that did not seem to matter to Bergman, who continued to be plagued by memories of reviews – good or bad, mostly bad – as something deeply humiliating (Björkman et al. 1973, p. 81).

Familiar to Bergman scholars are his caricatures of feared critics. A well-known case is his portrayal of Stig Ahlgren and his wife, actress Birgit Tengroth, as the mutually humiliating couple Mr and Mrs Alman (Gunnar Sjöberg and Gunnel Broström) in *Wild Strawberries* (*Smultronstället*, 1957). His anxieties also showed when American author James Baldwin came to Stockholm in 1960 to do an interview. Anticipating critical questions, Bergman opened with asking Baldwin if he was for or against him.[*]

This fighting spirit fuelled Bergman's own so-called anti-Bergman issue published by Sweden's then leading film journal, *Chaplin*, in the November issue of 1960 (see Forslund 1960). Under the pen name Ernest Riffe – Bergman's other first name was Ernst – he assumed the role of a fictional French critic and short-film director, leading a satirical attack on himself by heaping stereotyped remarks over his work, signing off by declaring the director as "an alarming evidence of the terrible decay of our film art" (p. 191). It was followed by three well-known critics, declaring him as "a spiritually completely empty human being" (Viveka Heyman; p. 192), "staggering between profundity and shallowness" (Erland Törngren; p. 192) and being "his own epigone" (Hanserik Hjertén; p. 194).[†]

Looking back, the anti-Bergman issue did not mark the end of Bergman's clashes with critics, as he might have hoped, but was rather the beginning of new attacks on him both at home and abroad. In France, auteurist Jean-Luc Godard's 1958 public love letter to Bergman was rebutted in 1960 by colleague Jean Domarchi's influential dismissal of the director and his "naïve metaphysics" as a fad (Domarchi

---

* Baldwin 1960, reprinted in Shargel 2007 (see p. 13 in the reprint for Baldwin's account of Bergman's opening remark).
† The translations in this paragraph are my own, as are all translations of extracts from and titles for non-English-language texts (i.e. those texts listed as non-English-language texts in the reference list) throughout the book.

1960, p. 7). Throughout the decade and well into the next, Bergman was locked into a series of fights with censors and the overlapping categories of young critics, the new generation of filmmakers and the New Left.

Possibly inspired by Domarchi, Swedish author Bo Widerberg wrote a manifesto titled *Visionen i svensk film* ("The Vision in Swedish Cinema", 1962). In the book, he accused Bergman of exporting exotic myths about Sweden and communicating only vertically – with God and his own soul. Widerberg countered with a vision of an artist that both could and would communicate horizontally with society and other people.

The book had a profound influence on the Swedish film debate and became a call to arms for the young generation of critics and filmmakers. Like the French New Wave and the West German filmmakers of the Oberhausen Manifesto (1962), the would-be director – making his debut in 1963 with two celebrated films: *The Pram* (*Barnvagnen*) and *Raven's End* (*Kvarteret Korpen*) – led a new generation that wanted to break with the past and its father figures, principally Bergman. His book would have a lasting influence on new film generations throughout the century.

The effects of Widerberg's manifesto are notable in the reception of *Winter Light* (*Nattvardsgästerna*, 1963). Several critics saw this as a prime example of the director's fixation with a bygone era and its concerns, signifying his lack of interest in contemporary social issues and failure to connect with the audience. Even veteran critic Robin Hood (pen name for Bengt Idestam-Almqvist) – usually one of Bergman's supporters – wondered if the director was of any concern to these modern and secular times (Donner and Nordin 1977, pp. 136–137). The tide turned for a time in Bergman's favour with the censorship controversy of *The Silence* in 1963 and the artistic triumph of *Persona* (1966). He was temporarily rehabilitated in the eyes of the critics, and until the mid-1960s he also acted as a mentor and an inspiration for several filmmakers.

In the 1950s, Bergman had collaborated with Lars-Eric Kjellgren on *While the City Sleeps* (*Medan staden sover*, 1950) and *Light of the Night* (*Nattens ljus*, 1957), leaving his artistic marks on both. The following decade saw new directors, such as actress Mai Zetterling and author-critic Jörn Donner, work in the artistic vein of Bergman's style and motifs with *Night Games* (*Nattlek*, 1966) and *To Love* (*Att älska*, 1964) respectively.

Zetterling got her international breakthrough in the Bergman-scripted *Frenzy* (*Hets*, 1944) and starred in his *Music in Darkness* (*Musik i mörker*, 1947) before taking her career outside Sweden. Donner had been an admiring follower of Bergman during the 1950s, and wrote one of the earliest books on the director – *The Personal Vision of Ingmar Bergman* (*Djävulens ansikte*, 1962; English translation 1964). He would later produce *Fanny and Alexander* and return to Bergman in interview films and books.

Bergman's closest ally in the 1960s was author-critic Vilgot Sjöman, a friend since the early 1940s whose career as screenwriter and director Bergman mentored. While working on his directorial debut, *The Mistress* (*Älskarinnan*, 1962), Sjöman documented Bergman's work on *Winter Light* in the behind-the-screen film *Ingmar Bergman Makes a Movie* (*Ingmar Bergman gör en film*, 1963) and the book *L136* (1963). He also served as an assistant director on the film.

In the cultural climate change at the end of the 1960s, as the protests against the Vietnam War escalated and gave birth to the New Left, Bergman's followers broke away from his shadow to explore new motifs, themes and aesthetics. Together with the new wave of young Swedish directors, they turned to politically outspoken and engaged films in a social realist tradition sprinkled with Brechtian *Verfremdungseffekts*: Sjöman with *I Am Curious – Yellow* and Zetterling with *The Girls* (*Flickorna*, 1968).*

At the Swedish Film Institute's new film school, founded in 1964, Bergman was to act as a lecturer, but there he was dismissed as yesterday's news by the students and thus rarely seen. Bo Widerberg and François Truffaut were far more popular as guest lecturers.† The neglect of Ingmar Bergman eventually became permanent. When I attended the international Ingmar Bergman Symposium in Stockholm in 2005, the film direction students at what was now called Dramatiska Institutet (DI) were to engage in a discussion with the visiting scholars. It turned out to be an embarrassing fiasco since the students had seen very few, if any, of his films and cared even less about them.

Consequently, his legacy is nowhere to be seen in Swedish film after the 1960s. As late as in 2014, director Roy Andersson, one of the students at the 1960s film school, spoke of his contempt for Bergman, calling him '"a hack" and "a stunted soul" (Andersson 2014). Bergman later commented on the 1960s as a cultural disaster in his book *The Magic Lantern* (Bergman 1988, p. 199):

---

* An exception was Donner, who stumbled into soft porn with films like *Sixtynine* – made, of course, in 1969.
† See the Stefan Jarl interview in Timm 2008, p. 367.

Today, frustrated revolutionaries still cling to their desks in editorial offices and talk bitterly about 'the renewal that stopped short'. They do not see (and how could they!) that their contribution was a deadly slashing blow at an evolution that must never be separated from its roots. In other countries where varied ideas are allowed to flourish at the same time, tradition and education were not destroyed. Only in China and Sweden were artists and teachers scorned.

At the end of the decade, Bergman was alone in all respects, also literally since he had moved in 1967 to the remote island of Fårö to continue making films in solitude with his own company, Cinematograph.

UNDER FIRE

When Bergman released *The Hour of the Wolf* (*Vargtimmen*) in early 1968, the artistic triumph of *Persona* was quickly forgotten and Widerberg's criticism returned with a vengeance. The film was received as an artistic regression. Again, Bergman was deemed a closed-off introvert – a solipsist in a time of social activism and political mass movements – rearranging old motifs and characters that were deemed as being of little significance to anyone but himself (Geber 1977a, p. 367).

Later in the same year, *The Shame* (*Skammen*) premiered. It seemed as if Bergman, at last, had taken notice of the call to political arms. Expressionist demons of the past were replaced by the topical horrors of war, more specifically the Vietnam War, which many critics saw as the film's obvious allegorical reference. Bergman confirmed this connection openly both in interviews made at the time of the film's release and in his reflections many years later (Björkman et al. 1973, pp. 228–229; Bergman 1995, p. 300).

At first, the reception was positive, celebrating a director revived by new ideas, new motifs (Geber 1977b, p. 400). Bergman had, according to the critics, finally raised his eyes from navel-gazing at a private hell to take a good look at the very real horrors of the contemporary world. Then a debate started that soon turned into a tidal wave of fury against the film.

Poet Lars Forssell's review in *BLM* was an omen of things to come. After calling the film "one of the most interesting and important" Bergman had made so far, he concluded with a speculation on what the left would do with the film's refusal to take sides (Forssell 1968, pp. 605–607). In *Aftonbladet* author and prominent antiwar activist Sara Lidman answered Forssell's misgivings by launching a series of attacks on *The Shame*, calling it a failure both artistically and politically. Bergman's non-commitment she saw as "propaganda for the American administration far better than they could ever dream of" (Lidman 1968).

In her 1996 reception study of Bergman's films, Birgitta Steene regarded the attacks on Bergman as a sign of the times, part of the zeitgeist. To the New Left intelligentsia and a wide spectrum of cultural journalists, debaters and reviewers, he was a belated echo of the nineteenth-century individualist artist: romantic and self-obsessed – that is, irrelevant to the cultural climate of the late 1960s (Steene 1996, pp. 111–13).

That Bergman was an outspoken supporter of the Social Democratic Party only added to the animosity against his films (Aghed 1969; Björkman et al. 1973, p. 178). Having been in government since 1932, they were the main enemy for the New Left, who saw them as traitors of the working class and even as social fascists (Tapper 2014, pp. 64–66). Moreover, the antipathy against Bergman was fuelled by his key positions in Swedish cultural life.

At the beginning of the 1960s he had become the undisputed leading director at the largest film company, Svensk Filmindustri. Behind the scenes, he also was the company's artistic advisor, controlling what new directors and screenwriters to recruit (Furhammar 2003, p. 264). Then, from 1963 to 1966, he was the director of the Royal Dramatic Theatre (Dramaten). Moreover, he was Sweden's leading auteur, that is, the standard against whom every director was measured. His creative freedom was envied by everyone, but many also saw him as the obstacle that blocked the new generation's claim for a place in the sun. In short, Bergman was "the centre of the bourgeois artistic establishment" (Bergom-Larsson 1978, p. 11), and this caused much resentment.

When Bergman's friend Harry Schein founded the Swedish Film Institute in 1963 it was to promote films with artistic ambitions. A jury of 'film experts' – mostly critics, but also some producers – administered 'quality points' that corresponded with the amount of governmental support a film would get from the Institute's funds. The jury also installed the Swedish film awards, Guldbaggegalan, in 1964. Needless to say, Bergman scored high both in quality points and in Guldbagge Awards during the first years. However, that changed with the controversy of *The Hour of the Wolf* and *The Shame*.

In 1968, the jury gave Stefan Jarl's documentary *They Call Us Misfits* (*Dom kallar oss mods*) a significantly higher score than Bergman's two releases, and the collective political documentary *The White Game* (*Den vita sporten*), helmed by a collective of filmmakers led by none other than Bo Widerberg, won the Best Film category at the Guldbagge Awards (Steene 1996, p. 111). The following year, Bergman's *A Passion* (*En passion*, 1969; aka *The Passion of Anna*) was snubbed, and the Best Film Award was bestowed on young directors Roy Andersson for *A Love Story* (*En kärlekshistoria*, 1970) and Lasse Forsberg for *The Assault* (*Misshandlingen*, 1969) – both politically engaged, both outspoken critics of Bergman.

Meanwhile, the Swedish film industry was in a state of crisis. Ticket sales continued to dwindle at the end of the decade; cinema theatres closed in alarming numbers. At the same time, new and alternative means of production and distribution challenged the dominating capitalist film industry.

In 1968, FilmCentrum was founded by Stefan Jarl and other young filmmakers as a distribution organisation primarily for documentary film, and in 1973 it hived off the alternative cinema theatre organisation Folkets Bio. Bergman tried to be part of the new cinema by having FilmCentrum distribute some of his TV productions, but that went largely unnoticed. To the new generation, he was still seen as the embodiment of the Swedish cinema establishment.* Radical new winds were blowing away the old to make room for the new, and although Bergman had a comeback in the 1970s, anti-Bergman sentiments lingered for decades (Steene 1996, pp. 112–114).

The early 1970s was an uncertain time in the film industry, as there was a change of generations in a period of social upheaval and industrial readjustment. It had a radical impact on Bergman personally and artistically, not the least since he had become financially vulnerable. In 1967 he had started the Switzerland-located company Persona AG 1968 (liquidated in 1974) for productions outside Sweden, and in the same year he founded Cinematograph for producing films at home – both his own films and works by others. To explore new commercial and artistic possibilities he had two bold strategies for Cinematograph: to make films in English for the foreign market, and to make films directly for TV (Vinberg 1968; Cowie 1988, p. 298).

---

* See the TV programme *Presskonferens*, broadcast 26 February 1971.

CRISIS

In October 1969, *A Passion* premiered. Ingmar Bergman later recalled the filming as "one of the worst I have ever experienced" together with a few other notable examples, one of them being the following production for the big screen, *The Touch* (Bergman 1995, p. 310). On a positive note, some Swedish critics defended Bergman's right to cultivate his own type of cinema, regardless of the political trends of the day. Several reviews also appreciated the use of colour (Eastmancolor), Bergman's first in a dramatic film.*

However, this response was more a reply to the overzealous attacks on *The Shame* than praise for *A Passion*. Even the most enthusiastic reviews could not find anything new and fresh about the film. Rather, it was regarded as yet another Fårö film, rehashing the same old motifs with the same set of actors in the same austere style and landscape.†

Meanwhile in the US, his most important market, the critics' love affair with Bergman continued. The National Society of Film Critics named him Best Director four times – for *Persona*, *The Hour of the Wolf*, *The Shame* and *A Passion* – and both Bibi Andersson (*Persona*) and Liv Ullmann (*The Hour of the Wolf*) were named Best Actress (Balio 2010, p. 284). Several of his actors had become stars in international productions, including Hollywood: Max von Sydow in *The Greatest*

---

* Previously he had used colour in his comedy *All These Women* (*För att inte tala om alla dessa kvinnor*, 1964; aka *Now About These Women*). Curiously, no review of *A Passion* mentions his use of the widescreen format, 1.66:1 – also a first for him.

† For an overview of the reception in the Swedish press, see Geber 1977c. Other notable reviews include Stig Björkman 1969 and Norström 1970 in Swedish film journals. Outside Sweden it was reviewed by Strick 1970, Dawson 1970 and others.

Story Ever Told (1965), Harriet Andersson in *The Deadly Affair* (1966) and Bibi Andersson in *The Kremlin Letter* (1970). The New York papers and journals in particular devoted much space to his films. Even *Playboy* had shown an interest in Bergman, publishing an extensive interview with the director by Cynthia Grenier in 1964.

In the late 1960s, Universal planned to make an anthology film with Bergman, Akira Kurosawa and Federico Fellini. Bergman wrote an outline to his segment called 'Rebecca' and reserved four weeks in his schedule to meet with his peers at Cinecittà in Rome. Either because Kurosawa got sick or because Fellini never finished his screenplay, Bergman decided to withdraw from the project.* By now there were also clouds on the commercial horizon.

Following Janus Films' successful marketing of Bergman in the late 1950s and early 1960s, United Artists had bought the rights to his films, starting with *Persona*. But the films all failed miserably at the box office despite the critics' passionate reviews. Following the flop of *A Passion*, they decided to drop Bergman altogether (Balio 2010, p. 284).

Bergman's prospects for an international career now looked grim, which would explain his decision to make a film in a language that was not even second to him. It would prove to be an even bigger failure. In both *Images* and *The Magic Lantern*, *The Touch* is only mentioned briefly and then as an instance of outright artistic failure, in stark contrast to his passionate defence of the film at the time of its release.† Since its initial premiere it has rarely been screened, and today it is one of few Bergman films unavailable in any video format. The dialogue was mainly in English, with only a few lines in Swedish. Newly formed ABC Pictures Corporation, a film-producing subdivision of the American television company, financed and distributed it.

The production cost was two million dollars, roughly ten million Swedish kronor at the time. Its budget was small by Hollywood standards, but corresponding to the cost of ten Swedish film productions on average budgets. In the male lead, Bergman had originally wanted Dustin Hoffman, who had to decline due to

---

* In the Swedish press the film has been described as a three-part anthology film directed by Bergman, Kurosawa and Fellini (see Anon. 1970a and Andersson 2007), while the Bergman interview in John Simon's 1972 book *Ingmar Bergman Directs*, pp. 21–22, and Peter Cowie's 1982 Bergman biography, p. 259, describe the project as being one of Bergman and Fellini alone, called *Love Duet*.

† Bergman 1988, p. 73, and 1995, p. 310. In a 1971 interview, he even singled it out as "one of my most interesting" (Sima 1971b).

other contractual obligations (Björkman 1970). Instead, the role went to Elliot Gould, fresh from his highly-praised performance in the countercultural hit movie *M*A*S*H* (1970). According to press reports, ABC Pictures Corporation had by its 110-page-long contract the exclusive rights to the film in all galaxies and planets (Sörenson 1970b). But alas, the intergalactic success passed Bergman by.

At the Berlin festival screening, where it got its world premiere, there were reports of a fiasco – the audience had booed during the screening. Bergman commented on the event with a stiff upper lip and some quips, and Bibi Andersson responded by writing an article in defence of the film in Sweden's leading morning paper (Andersson 1971; Mehr 1971). The Swedish critics were divided. In response to the hostile reception in Berlin, some took sides with Bergman. To them, it was a simple and perhaps even banal film but nonetheless beautiful and true (Bergström 1971; Edström 1971; Sima 1971a). Others just saw it as pointless and dull (Nordberg 1971; Olsson 1971; Schildt 1971). An open letter by a literary critic in film journal *Chaplin* asked rhetorically, "Is Bergman finished as an artist?" (Widegren 1972).

This time not even the New York critics made a collective rush to Bergman's rescue. In the *New York Times*, Vincent Canby wrote a respectful but nonetheless negative review (Canby 1971a), and when the advertisements for the film snipped out a piece that sounded like praise, he responded with an article in which he stressed the fact that he had found the film dull (Canby 1971b). The *New Yorker*'s two film critics found themselves on opposite sides. When Penelope Gilliatt praised the film, she was contradicted by her colleague Pauline Kael (Gilliatt 1971; Kael 1971b). In *Time*, the reviewer declared that the film was "disappointing" and "unsympathetic" (Anon. 1971a).

Bergman wrote in *The Magic Lantern* (1988, p. 228), "By the early 1970s, I had made some dubious films, but earned quite a lot of money." After the success of *The Silence* his films had failed, and in *Variety*'s box-office list of the all-time highest-grossing foreign films from World War II until 1973, his films are nowhere to be seen (Balio 2010, p. 9). At the top is Vilgot Sjöman's *I Am Curious – Yellow*, followed just a few entries down by Bo Widerberg's *Elvira Madigan* (1967). However, Bergman would make a spectacular comeback in just a few years, both at the cinema and more importantly in the new media for the masses that had stopped going to the movies: Television.

PART TWO

BERGMAN GOES TV

After a few years of test transmissions, Swedish public service TV was introduced in 1956 to an enthusiastic response. By 1963 1.8 million sets had been sold. During the same period cinema ticket sales dwindled from 80 to 40 million per year (Furhammar 2003, p. 249). At first there was only one TV channel, but in 1969 another was added – both administered by public service company Swedish Radio's television department.

By then most Swedes had access to a TV set, and this latest addition to post-war consumer life style changed the media landscape completely. The daily press and the weekly magazines soon jumped on the TV frenzy, and the celebrity glamour that once was associated with cinema now shifted to TV. That attracted talent and material previously monopolised by the film industry. Those who dared to go into the new medium soon learned of its public impact and the immediacy of the viewers' personal experience.

Ingmar Bergman became intrigued by TV while working at the Malmö municipal theatre in the mid-1950s. At a store, he caught a glimpse of a Danish TV transmission – Denmark had started public service TV in 1951 – and bought a set on the spot. In a 1957 interview, he described his infatuation with this new set of artistic tools. He was full of admiration for the Danish TV broadcasts, less so for the Swedish, which he described as "visually and technically poor" (Forslund 2006, p. 285). Still, he was full of enthusiasm for the new medium, which he regarded as something decidedly new and different from film, radio and theatre.

In 1957 he presented his first TV play, a production of Hjalmar Bergman's *Mr Sleeman Cometh* (*Herr Sleeman kommer*), to great acclaim, and until 1964 he regularly contributed to Swedish TV with new productions of classical and modern stage plays. That his output came to a halt in 1964 was due to the conclusion of his tenure as director of Dramaten followed by a decision to move to Fårö and found his own film company. Being his own master, he decided to no longer make adaptations of other playwrights but produce original works written, directed and produced specifically for TV.

His reasons were many. One is to be found in some personal notes in Workbook no. 24 (1967–68). Bergman writes about waiting alone at Fårö for the critical reception of *The Shame*, dreading the verdicts. He adds: "Would it not be better to go all into TV production so one could escape all these terribly sad and depressing experiences. And so humiliating."

Artistic and commercial reasons were also of importance. TV productions were relatively cheap and thus well suited to a small company like Cinematograph. With the rapidly growing international TV market and the rise of TV award galas such as Prix Italia, there was also much cultural prestige and a new audience of millions to be won now that the adults had stopped going to the cinema. While the film industry kept losing profits and audiences at an alarming pace, the TV industry was booming. TV was also a new and artistically largely unexplored medium.

This was the place for Bergman to renew himself creatively and to carve out previously uncharted artistic domains. His timing was perfect since former theatre director Lars Löfgren took over Swedish Television's theatre department in 1969 and became the driving force for introducing new playwrights with original dramas directly for the medium and often dealing with contemporary social and political issues. Löfgren and Bergman were close collaborators until Bergman's departure from Sweden in 1976.

The Rite (*Riten*; aka *The Ritual*) premiered on 25 March 1969 in a pan-Scandinavian TV transmission that attracted much interest. In Birgitta Steene's *Ingmar Bergman: A Reference Guide* (2005, p. 417), the debate following the premiere is summarised as "reserved and ambivalent", leading the reader to think of the play as a failure and the reception as tepid when, in fact, it was exactly the opposite. The debate was heated and the reception polarised, but that does not equal failure. Certainly not in Ingmar Bergman's book.

That I learned from my conversations with a close friend of Bergman's, director Vilgot Sjöman, during our guest lectures on Bergman at Gotland College Univer-

Fig. 2: *The Rite* (1969). (© Cinematograph AB)

sity in 2001 and 2002.* Back then, Bergman had yet again made headlines by talking about his fascination with Nazism in the 1930s.† When I wondered why he kept bringing up this subject already covered in previous interviews and in his autobiography, Sjöman laughed and said that it was one of Bergman's signature traits: he thrived on being at the centre of the media's attention.

Whenever he felt he had been left in the shadows too long, Sjöman continued, fear of being bland and insignificant struck him and he found one way or another

---

* Gotland College University is now under the administration of Uppsala University and has been renamed Uppsala University – Campus Gotland.

† Ingmar Bergman was interviewed about his Nazi sympathies by journalist Maria-Pia Boëthius for her 1991 book *Heder och samvete* ("Honour and Conscience"), about Sweden's collaboration with Nazi Germany during World War II. Bergman had already written about it in his 1987 book *The Magic Lantern* (see pp. 119–123 in the 1988 English edition), and it was then noted by the Swedish press. The subject came up again in 1991 when Boëthius' book was released. But the biggest headlines about Bergman's Nazi leanings were when Boëthius' book was rereleased in an expanded and revised 1999 edition, coinciding with articles on the subject in the foreign media (Anon. 1999, for example; see Steene 2005, p. 984, for an overview of the articles). She summarised the interview in a 2007 article (Boëthius 2007) about the obituaries in the press after Bergman's death.

to get back into the headlines. Bergman himself has reflected on the necessity of showmanship on numerous occasions. One instance can be found in the introduction to the screenplay of *Face to Face*, where he writes, "Ennui or indifference affect the film's originator in a terrible way, and it is only fair in that case that he should be put to shame, publicly mocked and the victim of thumping financial reprisals" (Bergman 1976a, p. 6).

The press clippings reveal that *The Rite* was saluted by banner headlines and followed by heated debates about the film's merits in the biggest newspapers. That must have reassured Bergman. Now he was back in the limelight after *The Shame* debacle and the lacklustre reception of *A Passion*. Yet again he had shown his opponents that he was an artist of significance, one that could stir intense feelings and provoke debates. He was pushing the envelope of his art with this provocative TV chamber play about a group of artists striking back at a repressive censor. The subject was clearly intended as a comment on Bergman's many clashes with Swedish head censor Erik Skoglund, perhaps most memorably in the 1963 case of *The Silence*.* Previously to *The Rite*, Bergman sent Skoglund his compliments by inserting an erect penis in the opening montage of *Persona*.

Looking back, one can see how he enjoyed preparing for the storm to come with the premiere of *The Rite*. Already on the day of the TV premiere, he made certain that interviews with him were published in several big newspapers. In them, Bergman declared that the TV audience always had the choice to read a good book or go to the cinema instead of watching his potentially disturbing film. The papers played along by publishing headlines such as "Bergman Cautions Against His TV Play Tonight" (Anon. 1969a) and "TV Shock Tonight!" (Bransmo 1969).

The media coverage of the play was boosted by the reports on the same day about Bergman being sued for assault and battery by *Dagens Nyheter*'s theatre critic Bengt Jahnsson. In her interview with the director shortly before the premiere, Marianne Höök, journalist and author of a 1962 biography on Bergman, even

---

* Erik Skoglund was the head censor of Statens Biografbyrå from 1959 to 1971. At the time of his resignation, he wrote an unintentionally amusing book, *Filmcensuren* ("The Film Censorship", 1971), in which he defended his authority to censor by arguing for "good taste" and "mental hygiene". He never wavered from his position that it was a breach of the censorship code to not cut some of the sex scenes in *The Silence* (pp. 164–166). However, *The Silence* was very consciously handed to his fellow censors and released uncut by them when he was on holiday. In an interview conducted at the time of Skoglund's resignation, Bergman commented on his years of struggle with Statens Biografbyrå, declaring his continued distrust of the institution even though it was under new management (Sima 1971c).

suggested that the connection between the two events was anything but accidental: "Hypothetically, one can see Ingmar Bergman's assault on Bengt Jahnsson as an exclamation point to *The Rite*. As a direct consequence of *The Rite*" (Höök 1969). Like August Strindberg, Ingmar Bergman had used his art as payback on his foes.* Moreover, the two coinciding events had propelled him into new fame with more efficiency than any marketing campaign.

On 26 March, headlines cried out "Stop Ingmar Bergman!" (Falk 1969) and "Nobody Understood Bergman" (Anon. 1969b). The following day, new headlines: "*The Rite* Got Rave Reviews in All of Scandinavia" (Anon. 1969c) and "Wonder and Admiration After *The Rite* on TV" (Anon. 1969d). Bergman had now been first-page news for three consecutive days. The angry audience response confirmed that he could still stir a controversy, and the reviews were on the whole positive and even passionate about the film. Notably, the few decidedly negative critics also wrote extensive reviews, thereby recognising both Bergman's artistic importance and the significance of his work.†

His next TV production, *Fårö Document* (*Fårödokument*), premiered on New Year's Day in 1970 and surprised both the critics and the audience alike. It was a small-scale documentary about the remote, small and sparsely populated island of Fårö on the eastern outskirts of Swedish territorial waters. The film portrayed the islanders and their economic and social needs forgotten or ignored by the prospering welfare state on the mainland. To make the film, Bergman had bought lightweight equipment that was a standard for 1960s documentary filmmaking: a 16mm Arriflex camera operated by Sven Nykvist and a Nagra tape recorder that Bergman handled himself when acting as a reporter and an interviewer.

The documentary was not as widely or as extensively reviewed as his feature films or stage or TV plays, but it was met by curiosity and respect. Film and TV critics alike appreciated meeting a "new aspect of Bergman – Bergman as TV

---

* This was not the first time Bergman used his art to get back at critics, censors and other enemies. I have already mentioned his caricature of critic Stig Ahlgren and his wife, actress Birgit Tengroth, in *Wild Strawberries*; see Björkman et al. 1973, pp. 140–141. In *Ansiktet* (*The Face*/*The Magician*, 1958), the Dr Vergérus character was widely assumed to be a caricature of critic Harry Schein (Björkman et al. 1973, p. 126), and the Schein reference would be present in Bergman's Vergérus characters also in the 1960s.

† Positive reviews by some of Scandinavia's most important film and TV critics include Jurgen Schildt (*Aftonbladet*), Gunnar Falk (*Svenska Dagbladet*), Niels Barfoed (*Politiken*, Denmark), Inge Dam (*BT*, Denmark), Leif Borten (*Verdens Gang*, Norway) and Anton Rönneberg (*Aftenposten*, Norway) – all published in 1969. For a summary overview of the reception, see unsigned 1969c and 1969d and Steene 2005, p. 417.

Fig. 3: *Fårö Document* (1970). Ingmar Bergman as socially engaged reporter. (© Cinematograph AB)

reporter" (Struck 1970), even a "master reporter" and "the best spokesman anyone could wish for" (Behring 1970). This was a 'Political Bergman' giving a voice to the everymen and women who lived far away from the corridors of political power but could still "express themselves in lively and temperamental manners" (Stenström 1970). "His final appeal for the people he had interviewed in the film came by its reserve to seem like a roar" (Edström 1970). In some interviews made shortly after the TV transmission, Bergman even hinted that he might go into politics to fight for the rights of his neighbours (Wester 1970, p. 25).

Fårö Document became Bergman's popular breakthrough. It was viewed by a mainstream audience of about two million on prime-time TV.* His newfound popularity got him a mass audience for his upcoming TV play *The Lie*, commissioned by Swedish Radio for the European Broadcasting Union (EBU, called Eurovision). Although directed by actor-director Jan Molander, the son of famous

---

* It was watched by 36 per cent of the audience aged from fifteen to eighty years old, or about two million viewers. Statistics from Audience & Programming Analysis, a department within Swedish Television in Stockholm, by email, 8 December 2016 from the head of the department, Thomas Lindhé.

film and theatre director Gustaf Molander and an accomplished TV director in his own right, the production was referred to in articles, interviews and reviews as a Bergman production.

The Lie was an expensive affair, with about thirty well-known actors in the cast of characters, and it proved to be a difficult production. The premiere broadcast was originally scheduled for 15 April but eventually postponed until 28 October (Sörenson 1970a). Works commissioned for the Eurovision could either be broadcast in the original version or adapted by each of the TV companies associated with the international organisation.

Only the British BBC chose the latter option, and their adaptation premiered on 29 October. Most likely the other Eurovision associates considered the Swedish production more suitable for catching the spirit of Bergman. Also, *The Rite* had been sold to many West European countries where it was met by rave reviews (Georgsson 1970). Three years later, an American version was broadcast by CBS.

In the Swedish press, the broadcast of *The Lie* was preceded by articles that emphasised Bergman's new and popular public image (Anon. 1970c; Anon. 1970d). In the press release, leading actress Gunnel Lindblom stressed that this was an accessible play – clear and straightforward – hence suitable for just about anyone interested in a drama about a modern-day, middle-aged couple faced with a crisis of love and trust. It got enthusiastic reviews; well, save for a predictably venomous dismissal by Bergman's archenemy Bengt Jahnsson (1970). The actors, and especially Gunnel Lindblom, were lauded as utterly credible and by some as genial (Branting 1970; Sten 1970).*

Bergman was by now referred to as something of a social critic, in complete contrast to the debate about his political non-commitment in *The Shame* (Perlström 1970). He was also a "genius dramatist" equal to Strindberg in his portrayal of the play's collapsing marriage (Beyer 1970). His dialogue was referred to as "natural, sparse and relaxed" (Donnér 1970). One of his "undeniable merits" was "that he did not get stuck in any fixed psychological set of values" (Janzon 1970). "Simplicity" was the key word in the reviews, as in the headline "Bergman with an Exquisite Simplicity in His Narrative" (Örnberg 1970).

---

* *The Lie* was watched by 22 per cent of the audience aged nine to seventy-nine, or about 1.2 million viewers. Statistics from Audience & Programming Analysis, a department within Swedish Television in Stockholm, by email, 8 December 2016 from the head of the department, Thomas Lindhé.

OUT OF THE IVORY TOWER

Reading Bergman's memoirs, *The Magic Lantern*, one gets the impression that the years 1971–72 were a dark and uncertain period in the director's life. However, his recollection of melancholia must be somewhat revised. At the 1971 Academy Awards, Liv Ullmann accepted the Irving Thalberg Memorial Award on Bergman's behalf. That same year he also received a Career Golden Lion at the Venice Film Festival, and the National Society of Film Critics Best Director award for *A Passion*. Other directors, such as Bo Widerberg and Jan Troell, had become international celebrities, but their list of merits and awards came nowhere near Bergman's. He was then – and still is – by far the most internationally celebrated and awarded director in Swedish film history.

However, Bergman's personal life was in turmoil, although that only lasted for a short moment and he was soon to be emotionally rescued by the security of a lifelong relationship. In 1970, his father Erik died and he separated from Liv Ullmann, though they continued to have an amiable relationship both privately and when working together. The following year, in November, he was married for the fifth and last time. After a brief affair with actress Malin Ek, his old relationship with Ingrid von Rosen rekindled.* They were wed in November 1971 and remained together until her death in 1995.

As for the career, Bergman's clichéd statement that film was his demanding mistress but that theatre was his wife again turned out to be a truism. While in disgrace with the former, he could always fall back on the latter, and now he had

---

* An autobiographical work referring to his relationship with Malin Ek is *After the Rehearsal* (*Efter repetitionen*, 1984); see Törnqvist 2003, p. 119.

also added TV as a new and exciting partner to his harem. In the spring of 1971 he received positive reviews for his staging of Lars Forssell's play *Show*,* a tribute to comedian Lenny Bruce, and a year later his stage production of Henrik Ibsen's *The Wild Duck* (*Vildanden*, 1884) was met with standing ovations (Steene 2005, pp. 634–635). With few exceptions, the Swedish critics lavished superlatives on Bergman's take on Ibsen, the audience came in droves and the guest performances in Florence, Berlin, Zürich, Oslo and Copenhagen were met with the same enthusiasm (Steene 2005, pp. 636–639).

The TV productions of *Fårö Document* and *The Lie* had made him popular by dispelling the myth that he was a difficult, even inaccessible, director. His newfound folksy image was cemented by his appearances on popular TV talk shows, such as *På Parkett* ('In the Stalls') on 12 June 1971. Its 75 minutes was devoted entirely to Bergman.† Apparently at ease, Bergman stands out as charming, witty and unassuming. To a captivated audience, he reveals his taste for mainstream cinema (Charlie Chaplin, Jacques Tati, Jan Troell's *The Emigrants*) and popular music (the Beatles, Povel Ramel), after which he strolls down memory lane with his first mentor Sven Hansson, who in 1938 installed him as a theatre director at Mäster Olofsgården in Stockholm. Towards the end, a few clips from *Fårö Document* are shown and Bergman turns into an engaged agitator, advocating for the rights of the islanders.

His ability to spellbind an audience was confirmed on a global scale when *The Dick Cavett Show* devoted an entire programme to an exclusive interview with him in a special broadcast from Stockholm on 19 January 1972. Cavett opens the show by introducing Bergman as "one of the most admired and certainly one of the most worshipped men in the movie world", then continues to be visibly awestruck before the Great Master throughout the one-hour-long programme.

---

*   Se Holm 1971, Janzon 1971 and Nilsson 1971.

†   An additional 45 minutes, titled *På Parkett Extra*, was transmitted on 14 August. The first programme had an audience of about 32 per cent of all aged nine to seventy-nine, or about two million viewers. Statistics from Audience & Programming Analysis, a department within Swedish Television in Stockholm, by email, 8 December 2016 from the head of the department, Thomas Lindhé.

Since *The Dick Cavett Show* was also popular in Sweden, it undoubtedly elevated Bergman's already high cultural standing at home, thus influencing the reception of his productions to come.

Despite the fiasco of *The Touch*, Hollywood's cheque book was still wide open to Bergman. He discussed his plans to direct a big-budget production of Franz Lehár's operetta *The Merry Widow* with Barbara Streisand in the leading role with a Swedish film critic in December 1972.* Although the plans for what would have been Bergman's Hollywood debut never materialised, the project still bore witness to his powerful position in the world of cinema.

Had *Cries and Whispers* been another flop and his company Cinematograph gone bankrupt, there would nevertheless be other options for him to make films, perhaps even on larger budgets, albeit at the price of a restricted independence. But he soon declared that he would never make a film in Hollywood (Matteson 1971). Instead, he took a gamble on his own low-budget Swedish production of *Cries and Whispers*.

From his private savings, he took 750,000 Swedish kronor – about $150,000 at the exchange rate of 1971 – and borrowed another 550,000 kronor from the Swedish Film Institute. Cinematographer Sven Nykvist and leading actresses Ingrid Thulin, Liv Ullmann and Harriet Andersson all agreed to work for a percentage, not regular salaries (Matteson 1971). The deal with the Swedish Film Institute soon turned into a new conflict between Bergman and the 1960s generation of filmmakers that lasted for weeks in the media.

Sweden is a small film nation with limited financial resources. Directors, producers and actors therefore objected to what they considered to be a VIP treatment of Bergman, resulting in budget cuts for their projects and perhaps even productions being put on hold or getting cancelled (Edlund 1971). Harry Schein counter-attacked with his usual mix of hard facts and sarcasm, arguing that Bergman's films were not only artistically qualified for special treatment, they were also profitable, thus a sound investment that would generate a profit from which new filmmakers would benefit (Schein 1971).

---

* Sörenson 1972; the plans were announced on 1 December by co-producer Svensk Filmindustri's CEO Kenne Fant. *The Merry Widow* had been a huge success for Bergman when he staged it in 1954 at Malmö City Theatre to celebrate its tenth anniversary. There are articles about his Hollywood production scattered between 1972 and 1974, the last one on 23 March 1974, declaring that "Bergman and Streisand Agree: We Are to Make a Film Together" (Nordmark 1974).

In an interview for *Aftonbladet*, Bergman, at first, responded with anger to the criticism: the attack on his film project was like a stab in the back. Then he turned to sympathise with the younger filmmakers' desperate situation. In yet another twist he counter-attacked by repeating a demand he had voiced for many years. "Socialise the entire film industry!" he declared in newspaper and TV interviews (Andersson 1971). His socialisation proposal never got any political response, not even from the New Left critics. But at least Bergman appeared to be more radical than them, and that seemed to have effectively put an end to the controversies about his loan.

However, Schein's promises of both artistic and monetary rewards to come did not reassure his opponents, and Bergman soon came to share their fears. In Sweden, he already had a distribution deal with the company for which he had done most of his work in the 1950s and 1960s: Svensk Filmindustri. But in the US, Bergman's agent Paul Kohner had a hard time finding a distributor for *Cries and Whispers*.

The Hollywood maxim "you are only as good as your last movie" also applied to Bergman – Oscars or no Oscars. Kohner and Bergman therefore decided to take a gamble on a minor distribution company called New World Pictures, which Bergman later described as "a small firm specializing in horror films and soft porn" (Bergman 1988, p. 229). The demeaning assessment of B-movie king Roger Corman's new venture would, however, be put to shame when it soon became the most important distributor in North America of world cinema.

In his memoirs (Corman with Jerome 1990, p. 189), Corman describes how he met with Kohner in New York to make the distribution deal. Kohner offered to screen the film, but Corman bought it unseen on the spot and released it just before Christmas 1972 to both cinemas in the art cinema circuit and the ones catering to the mainstream crowd. The result was Bergman's biggest box-office hit in America so far, and it established New World Pictures as a both adventurous and prosperous, if – as Corman put it – "schizophrenic", distributor of both lowbrow exploitation and highbrow art: "Who else could release *Cries and Whispers* in the same year as *Night Call Nurses*, or *Amarcord* with *Caged Heat*, two years later, or 1980's *The Tin Drum* and *Humanoids from the Deep*?"

Shortly before the American release of the film, the well-respected critic John Simon's book *Ingmar Bergman Directs* was published and reviewed. It featured texts on four films and declared Bergman to be "in my carefully considered opinion, the greatest film-maker the world has seen so far" (Simon 1972, p. 41).

In fresh memory was Pauline Kael's 1971 challenge of Andrew Sarris's opinions on the merits of *Citizen Kane* (1941), then hailed as the greatest American film ever. Fierce auteurist Sarris had claimed that the film's artistic qualities should be ascribed to director Orson Welles, while Kael argued for screenwriter Herman J. Mankiewicz.* In Bergman's case Simon solved the dilemma by arguing that the Swedish director was the superior example of an auteur owing to his combined roles as producer, screenwriter and director (Simon 1972, p. 41).

The *New Yorker* printed Bergman's 12,000-word *Cries and Whispers* scenario, followed by a review essay on the film by Kael. Her opinions were sometimes scathing: "there's a dullness at the heart of the movie". But for all her reservations, she was on the whole fascinated: "The movie is built out of a series of emotionally charged images that express psychic impulses, and Bergman handles them with the fluidity of a master" (Kael 1973). She even called him a "wizard", and the length of her text alone suggested the film's importance. The *New York Times* covered it even more extensively with a review full of praise by Vincent Canby, followed by several articles and letters to the editorial staff discussing the film plus a long interview with the director.†

The overwhelming response in the Bergman-cheering press of New York resounded elsewhere, often in words such as "awesome" (Cocks 1973), "hypnotic" (Ebert 1973) and "marvellous symphony" (Milne 1973, p. 61). The Swedish press also took notice. "A Very Great Bergman Film", shouted the headline of Jurgen Schildt's review on 6 March in *Aftonbladet* (1973a). Other reviews were published under superlative-heavy titles such as "A Difficult Masterpiece" (Olsson 1973), "The Most Exquisite Film Ever Made" (Hjertén 1973) and "One of His Richest Films" (Bergström 1973).

Gone were the demands for a commitment to the social and political issues of the day and for a horizontal communication with the audience and the world. Nobody wanted any answers from Bergman; everyone was happy with his provocative images and ambiguous endings. The failure of *The Touch* was completely forgotten – no review mentions it – and the director who made *Persona* had regained his full creative powers, making films with captivating, dream-like narratives. Ingmar Bergman, the film poet, was back.

---

* See Sarris 1971 and Kael 1971a.
† Canby 1972; Barrow 1973; Friedland 1973; Marowitz 1973; Richman 1973.

MASS-MARKET BERGMAN

Barely five weeks after the triumphant premiere of *Cries and Whispers*, Bergman was again making headlines with his six-part TV series, *Scenes from a Marriage*. The first episode was broadcast on 11 April 1973, and the series then distributed as a re-edited feature film to cinemas around the world, including Sweden. The US also showed the complete TV series, though not until 1977. Already in the summer of 1972 there were articles about Bergman building a studio on an old farm in the village of Dämba on Fårö for the production (Hellbom 1972). There, he shot most of the interiors of this six-act chamber play with his two main actors. The budget was a mere 1.2 million Swedish kronor, compared to 1.8 million for *Cries and Whispers* (Björkman 1973).

In the week leading up to the premiere, the mounting interest in the press revealed that international buyers were lining up outside Cinematograph's office to make a bid for the series (Big Ben, pen name for Uno Asplund, 1973). Some critics that had been allowed to preview the series in special screenings reviewed it on the premiere date of the first episode (Schildt 1973b; Swedberg 1973a). Others followed the series closely with reviews after each episode (Janzon 1973a–f). Some did a bit of both (Donnér 1973a–d, Edström 1973a–b, Swedberg 1973b–c).

What had been implied in the preview reports was spelled out in the reviews: the series was about a couple embodying the everyman and woman; thus, their problems were universal. The few who dared to say that they rather represented something else – well-adjusted upper-middle-class academics with high incomes and a sheltered life and who therefore had different problems than working-class people – were shouted down by the hallelujah choir.*

"Liv Ullmann and Erland Josephson Are Fantastic!" was the typical critical response (Behring 1973). There were appreciative comments about Bergman's "realism" and him showing a "more human" side (Edström 1973b; Swedberg 1973b). But more than spitting out superlatives, the reviews, columns and articles were busy discussing all the twists and turns in and between the episodes. Sympathies for one or the other of the two protagonists, Johan and Marianne, shifted over the course of the series. Most positive sentiments were directed at Marianne, possibly backed by Bergman's reputation as a 'woman's director'. In an interview, Erland Josephson therefore felt a need to emphasise that "Johan is no heel" (Baehrendtz 1973).

Towards the end of the series a media frenzy about the remarkable public interest – each episode had between two and two-and-a-half million viewers – and its effects ensued.† In an interview, Bergman hoped that everyone who watched the series would use it as therapy or at least as a starting point for discussing their own marriages (Edvardson 1973). His request was certainly granted by the media. Major evening papers *Aftonbladet* and *Expressen* both published extensive reports on their readers' mostly positive responses to the series, and the latter also started a series of articles about life after divorce (Anon. 1973a; Anon. 1973b; Gräslund 1973).

Following the end of the series, Bergman talked in interviews and talk shows about the many letters he had received from viewers (Sten 1973), and there were several articles about the rush to visit family guidance counsellors. One even declared that "Johan and Marianne Save Hundreds of Marriages!" (Larsson 1973). The interest in the series was so great that when it ran on TV again a year later, it was accompanied by more interviews and articles on the many debates and divorces triggered by the first showing in 1973 (unsigned 1974).

---

* There was, for instance, one viewer who responded to the first survey in *Expressen* (Anon. 1973a) by stating that he did not recognise himself in the series since the couple were of a different class than him. Author Britt West (1973) protested against what she considered to be marital problems as "upper-class amusements". In the debate about *Scenes from a Marriage*, the former debate about *Cries and Whispers* spilled over (see above). Most critics ignored the negative viewpoints; others dismissed them as irrelevant (Janzon 1973b; Strömstedt 1973).

† *Scenes from a Marriage* attracted 31–37 per cent of the audience or 2–2.5 million viewers. Statistics from Audience & Programming Analysis, a department within Swedish Television in Stockholm, by email, 8 December 2016 from the head of the department, Thomas Lindhé.

The re-edited cinema version of *Scenes from a Marriage* – cut from 278 minutes to 168 minutes, blown up from 16 to 35 mm and reframed from 1.37:1 to 1.66:1 widescreen – came about a year later. At first, Bergman considered editing the series into two films, to be shown either consecutively in one cinema or simultaneously in two adjacent cinemas. However, the US distributors balked at the idea.* The nearly three-hour-long feature was a compromise. In the meantime, the rumour of the Scandinavian success of the series fuelled anticipation elsewhere. When the cinema version was finally released, the reception was overwhelmingly enthusiastic. Like in Scandinavia, the voices of dissent were few.

Scenes from a Marriage, the film, opened in the US on 15 September 1974 and later in the autumn in the UK. Roger Ebert of the *Chicago Sun-Times* gave the film his highest marks, calling it "one of the truest, most luminous love stories ever made". Penelope Gilliatt followed suit in the *New Yorker*, claiming that "Bergman has never before made such an exhilarating film about grownup love" (Gilliatt 1974, p. 98). In *Film Quarterly*, Marsha Kinder found that "the acting performances of Ullmann and Josephson are so convincing, the dialogue so realistic, the conception of the relationship so subtle, that it is difficult to believe we are watching a theatrical illusion" (Kinder 1974, p. 49).

Only a few critics mentioned Bergman's TV style. After complimenting the director's artistic symbiosis with Liv Ullmann, *Sight and Sound* critic Julian Jebb found that the film was indeed an exercise in "simplicity of vision", though in his view simplicity "seems more to do with crudity and literalness than with purity and directness". To Jebb, *Scenes from a Marriage* was a sign that Bergman "has lost his true refinement of his art" (Jebb 1974, p. 58) These remarks could be read as a reply to the *New York Times*' chief film critic Vincent Canby, who stressed that the feature film version of the series was not like ordinary TV movies that "seem empty when seen in a theater"; instead he found that "the theater screen is bursting with information, associations, and contradictory feelings" (Canby 1974).

Bergman's next production was the realisation of an idea he had presented in a 1971 TV programme, namely to take a stage production at the Opera or the Royal Dramatic Theatre to a national mass audience by way of TV.† The reception of his staging of Mozart's *The Magic Flute* (*Die Zauberflöte*, 1791) was all pomp and

---

* Roger Corman was the first choice of distributor, but he lost to Donald Rugoff because Bergman originally did not want to cut the series. It was after buying it that Rugoff suggested cutting the series, which Bergman did. See Byron 1975, p. 27.
† *Presskonferens*, Swedish Radio, broadcast on TV1, 26 February 1971.

circumstance for "the magician". Indeed, already in the very first sentence of a location report from Drottningholm Castle he is referred to as a legend (Harrysson 1974, p. 4).

There was no shortage of superlatives for the production either. "The best musical in the world" (Hedberg 1975; Thoor 1975), "the most beautiful opera fairy tale in the world" (Åstrand 1975) and "a miracle" (Aare 1975) were just a few of the innumerable celebratory remarks. In *Aftonbladet*, even pop music critic Jan Andersson wrote a review in which he jokingly admitted to "almost becoming an opera buff" (1975).

The debate about the 2.6–4.3 million Swedish kronor in production costs that Birgitta Steene (2005, pp. 428–429) highlights in her summary of the Swedish reception was but a faint whisper in the unanimous roar of approval for Bergman's take on the classic from film, opera, theatre and TV critics.* It was also a dull repeat of the aforementioned debates about costs of *The Touch* and *Cries and Whispers* that only bore witness to a lingering animosity against Bergman's privileged place in Swedish cultural life.

Now that Bergman was both more popular and more profitable than ever, monetary considerations were of no great importance to most critics. As expected, *The Magic Flute* soon proved to be yet another one of Bergman's international hits. When shown on Swedish TV again a year after its premiere, quotes from rave reviews in the world press were printed in papers and magazines (see Anon. 1975). By then, Bergman was in preparation for the shooting of *Face to Face*.

---

* The reports on the budget varied; see Heurling 1988 for a summary of the debate about the production costs.

THE TV MEDIUM AND BERGMAN'S STYLE

What Bergman did for TV was not film for TV, but TV film.
– Sven Nykvist 1997, p. 101

In his foreword to Stefan Valmin's book *TV-Teater* ('TV Play'), the head of the theatre division at Swedish Television, Lars Löfgren, wrote about the strong impact and visible effects of the TV plays produced at Sveriges Radio (Valmin 1972, pp. 3–4). Ingmar Bergman was one who influenced his viewers both intellectually and emotionally, not least with the series *Scenes from a Marriage*. Valmin describes the political conditions and artistic prerequisites for Swedish TV plays in the 1970s, and by boiling them down to two points, we can discern how well Bergman and the new medium were suited for each other (1972, pp. 33–47).

1. POLITICAL CONDITIONS: A PUBLIC SERVICE TV MONOPOLY SERVING AN UNDIFFERENTIATED MASS AUDIENCE

From its start in 1956 until the late 1980s, Swedish public service TV had a market monopoly, which made it the national stage for TV plays. There were no commercial restrictions, censorship or artistic limitations, and no need for the producers to angle for popularity. Bergman could have continued to make plays for a small segment of the audience without the risk of losing future assignments. He was, of course, in constant need of securing financing of his projects so he could keep his independence, but then his choices were not primarily commercially motivated. They were fuelled by artistic curiosity and a desire to reach a new and wider audience.

TV was still an exciting new medium and the choice of programmes in the two public service channels was debated constantly in the press. With the combination of the media's interest in Bergman and his own flair for media hype, most, if not all, of his TV productions in the 1970s were almost certain to reach an audience of millions. However, Bergman also had social ambitions with his theatre productions, and that continued with his TV plays.

In a 1975 Dialogue on Film seminar at the American Film Institute, Bergman listed three things he considered to be absolutely necessary for making theatre: actors, a manuscript – or as he preferred to call it, a message – and an audience. The last element was crucial "because the performance is not here on the stage; it is in the hearts of the audience" (Anon. 1976a, p. 136). Connecting with the audience was essential to Bergman, although he did not necessarily seek its approval.

As noted above, any reaction besides indifference was what he looked for: "I want people to keep themselves busy with me, scream at me, scold me and then I will scold them back. [...] I want to touch people and I want them to touch me" (Sellermark and Sellermark 1974).

As the director of Dramaten from 1963 to 1966, Bergman changed the old and authoritarian organisation into a more democratic one. More than that, he diversified the repertoire to address a wider audience, for instance by staging plays for children and performing outside the institution (Bergman 1988, pp. 188–194). When presenting his first original TV play *The Rite* in magazine *Röster i Radio TV*, Bergman was interviewed in the middle of a stage rehearsal of *Woyzeck* open to the public. Interviewer Matts Rying describes how Bergman discusses the play with both the actors and the audience and explains that he tries out a kind of "theatre propaganda" to "help demystify and deglorify theatre work" (Rying 1969, p. 13).

A mixed blessing in his attempts to reach a new and wider audience with his TV productions was his cultural status as a 'highbrow' writer-director. Since the beginning of his career he had been regarded as 'difficult' or even 'inaccessible' for many, especially among the working-class viewers in the audience. Another mixed blessing was the aforementioned gender factor, that is, Bergman being perceived as a 'woman's director'. He thereby attracted cultural consumers that were then – and still are – mainly women, perhaps at the expense of the male audience (Jones 2016).

However, the huge response to his TV productions and *Scenes from a Marriage* in particular confirms that he had somehow managed to break through the class and gender barriers. Thus, he was able to largely demystify his own public persona as well as his work. Of the series, he said that his ambition was to make people discuss their marital problems unceremoniously, make them "talk over a beer and a sandwich", and that he did with a vengeance (Sellermark and Sellermark 1974).

To learn more about this, we have to look not only to Bergman's themes and motifs, but also to his mode of production and his search for a new narrative style suitable for the TV format. This was also of importance in his ambition to break away from his art cinema profile to achieve popularity with a mass audience.

2. ARTISTIC PREREQUISITES: TV DEMANDS AUDIO-VISUAL AND NARRATIVE SIMPLICITY

In the 1970s, TV was still a technically unsophisticated medium with low visual resolution and poor sound. Jamming and disturbance were not uncommon. The 1966 introduction of colour TV helped the image quality somewhat, and better speakers in the 1970s made for an improved sound reproduction. Still, buying a new colour TV set was an expensive affair for most consumers. Consequently, many kept their old and worn black-and-white ones well into the 1970s, and until the 1990s the screen remained in the 1.33:1 ratio.

Valmin (1972, pp. 37–43) suggests that these technical restrictions make for a number of artistic considerations that distinguish TV productions from the theatre stage or the film: TV emphasises script over visual design, telling over showing; psychological action and intimate drama are more suitable for the TV format than physical action and epic tales; close-ups are preferable to any other types of shots; interiors must be sparsely furnished, the production design simple and the frame uncluttered.

The restrictions were not to Bergman's disadvantage. On the contrary, they overlapped with the sparse palette of audio-visual techniques that he had refined in the 1960s, most distinctly in *Persona*. In his book *L136*, Vilgot Sjöman has elegantly described this development by quoting a scene from *Through a Glass Darkly*, in which the author David (Gunnar Björnstrand) struggles with his new book, becoming increasingly irritated by

> ...the winding sentences, the obnoxious words, the unbearable banality of the situations and the characters' poor lack of dimensions. He stares at the manuscript of his novel: *She came towards him, gasping with expectation, flaming red from the rough wind...* David groans. My God, did he really write that?

He clutches his pen and changes it to: *She came running towards him with her face flaming from the rough wind...* Does that sound any better? No. He tries out: *She came running towards him...* He sighs, crosses out everything to resolutely write: *They met at the beach.* That is a summary of IB's own stylistic development. (Sjöman 1963, p. 24; italics in original)

By the end of the 1960s, Bergman and Nykvist had stripped their films of many stylistic devices, such as extreme camera angles and expressive lighting. In low-budget TV productions like *Fårö Document* and *Scenes from a Marriage* he used a skeleton crew, one 16mm camera and long takes – up to twenty minutes – later to be trimmed and intercut with other shots (Nykvist 1997, p. 96). Bergman regarded his narrative style to be a non-style, an instrument shaped by and in service of the story:

> We have no camera style, Sven and I. What we are interested in is not a style for the camera because the solution of that is in the picture. What we are always interested in is the light or the shadows, the rhythm in the light and the shadows of the picture. [...] It's not an intellectual decision. It comes out from the whole thing. It's just natural. (Anon. 1976a, p. 137)

By the time of shooting *Cries and Whispers*, Bergman was promoting the idea of a static camera: "It would be the characters who would have to move in relation to the lens" (1995, p. 86). However, Nykvist undermined this aesthetic strategy slightly by also making use of a new zoom lens and the occasional pan (Nykvist 1997, p. 106). Overall though, he found Bergman's sparse techniques to be liberating and saw this style as a sign of professional maturity. In a published discussion with some of his colleagues in film journal *Chaplin*, Nykvist remarked:

> Most important for a cinematographer is to let his technique serve as a foundation. I therefore want to exploit the medium as much as I can to create the wonderful opportunities that exist, and above all to make the photographic work an integral part of the film itself. I guess we have all been through early days of creating beautiful images to get good reviews. It is wonderful to leave that behind. The screenplay and the director's intentions is what I consider to be of the utmost importance. (Anon. 1973c, p. 183)

Bergman claimed that he had also disposed of symbols: "those who have as their profession to hunt down symbols and interpret them more or less profoundly, they will find absolutely nothing of interest in *The Rite*. It is a thoroughly straight and pure performance" (Rying 1969, p. 14). He certainly strived for stylistic simplicity and a limited employment of symbols in his 1970s TV productions, most clearly in *Scenes from a Marriage*, but when he entered the realm of fantasy, as in *The Magic Flute*, or dreams, as in *Face to Face*, his lyrical impulses come to the forefront. Consequently, the production of *The Magic Flute*, with its use of saturated colours, symbols and physical action, was in many respects the opposite of *Scenes from a Marriage* (Nykvist 1997, p. 113).

Therefore, Bergman's claim to have "no style" must be taken with a grain of salt. His close-up techniques, zoom, framing, composition, lighting, production design, costumes, hair, make-up and manipulation of both black-and-white and colour film stock are notable. And there are some significant camera moves in his films and TV productions.

His framing techniques suggest an interest in visual arts, but in contrast to many other directors, he never had any great interest in painting or sculpture: "Art has, strangely enough, not had a strong influence on me" (Löthwall 1972, p. 91). There were other sources of inspiration, though, such as photography, an art form that got a cultural boost post-World War II from the Magnum Photos cooperative and journals such as *Life* and *Look*. And there were other filmmakers. Hitchcock is frequently mentioned in interviews:

> Thanks to Hitchcock, particularly, I'd long been intrigued by shooting long sequences in difficult and cramped circumstances, weeding out everything irrelevant – quite simply, in making things hard for myself. In *The Rite*, for instance, I've no décor, in the usual sense of the word: just blank walls, a curtain or so, and a few bits of furniture. It's a challenge, not having anything to play tricks with and get lost in. (Björkman et al. 1973, p. 67)

Likewise, his use of sound and music is also marked by sparseness and precision. He never resorts to standard symphony music or having non-stop musical accompaniment in his films. Every instant of sound and music has meaning, such as the recurring church bells that signal repressive idealism (see Part Three) and death.

He started to work on *The Rite* while shooting *The Shame* in 1967. When Erland Josephson read it, he wanted to make it into a stage play, but Bergman intuitively knew that it was better suited for television: "I wanted it in close-up" (Rying 1969, p. 14; Björkman et al. 1973, p. 237). Describing the opening scene in the script, he makes simplicity and sparseness into virtues:

> An interrogation room. Grey walls. Some pieces of office furniture. A general lighting without shadows, as on a hot cloudy summer afternoon. A clock strikes three blows. The quiet ringing of church bells. A door is opened somewhere and one can hear footsteps. (Bergman 1973a, p. 7)

Watching the TV production of *The Rite* after reading the script is a déjà vu experience for anyone familiar with Bergman's style. You sense the translation from text to images and sound in the sparseness of his stage directions. The choice to make it in black and white stresses the greyness of the setting and the atmosphere of the story.

Bergman's expressive or outright expressionist use of shadows and dramatic lighting effects in collaboration with cinematographers Göran Strindberg and Gunnar Fischer was by now a thing of the past. After teaming up with Sven Nykvist as director of photography in 1960, the films' cinematography changed with the use of diffused lighting, producing shades of grey with low contrast and almost no shadows (Werner 1973, p. 182).

Graphite, Nykvist called this soft grey tone, and it affected how he sculptured the actors' faces with light in Bergman's many close-ups (Nykvist 1997, p. 90). When the two protagonists in *Persona* have their dream-like night-time encounter, watching themselves in a mirror, the low contrast smoothens the individual features of their faces, making them look more alike and thereby stressing the film's motif of blurred identities.

In *The Shame*, the grey and grainy close-ups of the protagonists are part of the film's documentary look that stresses the parallel with contemporary news and films from wars in Vietnam and colonial parts of Africa. This continued in *Fårö Document*, Bergman's Direct Cinema-style production. Colour had different connotations than black and white at the time, especially on TV, and Bergman therefore hesitated to use it until *Scenes from a Marriage*.

PART THREE

BERGMAN'S MODERNISM

ATTACK OF SECOND-WAVE FEMINISM

Bergman's production is first and foremost a rehearsal of the subject of Bergman. He is intrusively autobiographical, one big me-drama, a monologue for many voices.

– Marianne Höök 1962, p. 16

Bergman always denied having any mouthpiece in his films. No character spoke for him.

– Ingmar Björkstén 1970, p. 27

That Bergman came under feminist attack was in part a consequence of the general criticism of him as, at best, politically naïve, or, in more sinister terms, as a conscious propagator of 'bourgeois cinema'. In the late 1960s, he could be dismissed as a relic, out of touch with the times and the general public. Not least, the poor box-office performances of his films at the Swedish cinemas seemed to confirm this. With the huge success of his TV productions and his comeback at the cinemas with *Cries and Whispers*, he was, however, back in vogue with the critics, and he had become a household name for an audience of millions.

By 1973, Bergman was a frequent guest on the radio and TV, on light entertainment talk shows as well as on serious programmes on human relations, existential issues, theology and philosophy. His public image had now changed into one of an artist very much in touch with the times and the mass audience, therefore to be analysed and criticised as a zeitgeist phenomenon. The film that for the 1970s second-wave feminists defined Bergman's misogyny underneath his media image of a director 'in touch with women' was *Cries and Whispers*, and here they could fall back on Marianne Höök's biography.

Höök describes Bergman as a man spiritually rooted in a bygone era, his attitude to women "hovering violently between symbiotic dependence and hatred" (1962, p. 13). The women might be "strong and maternally indulgent of the helpless and slightly ridiculous men", but in her view this is a scenario perfectly suited to his reliance on the old patriarchal gender myths. To her, Bergman's women are emotional, physical and closer to life, whereas men are the intellectuals with the big souls who ponder on existential issues such as God and death and the meaning of life. Though rarely referenced, Höök's views echoed in the 1970s debate.

Already before 1973 there had been occasional articles discussing Bergman's view on women. One example is a response to *The Touch*, posing the rhetorical question about the film's portrait of a woman having an extramarital affair: "Is it a sign of Bergman's covert hatred of women and hostile attitude towards sex?" (Klynne 1972, p. 29). However, *Cries and Whispers* stirred up angry feminist criticism like none of his previous films.

In one of Sweden's most prestigious cultural magazines, *Ord & Bild*, three notable feminists took *Cries and Whispers* as an example of Bergman's personal view on women. The film was deemed "static and ahistorical", ideologically set in Victorian times, propagating that era's myths about human nature. Bergman himself was summarily dismissed as an "ultrareactionary" filmmaker who "wraps pretentious crap in beautiful, obscure and haunting images that promote anxiety, not liberation" (Granath et al. 1973, pp. 13 and 15).

Across the Atlantic, Joan Mellen came to much the same conclusion when analysing the film in an essay published in *Film Quarterly*. She elaborated on her views in a 1974 book on women and sexuality in film, where she states that Bergman's women are "tortured, confused and incapable of rising above a repellent biological frailty".* Constance Penley (1976, p. 205) describes Bergman as a director with "near-morbid interest in the suffering of women", and the experience of *Cries and Whispers* as "one of being emotionally and physically raped as, once again, a man uses women driven to the edge of experiences as sacrifices for his own salvation and then calls it Art". She sums it up: "It is the filmic paradigm of woman as Other" (1976, p. 208).

---

* Mellen's essay "Bergman and Women: *Cries and Whispers*" was published in *Film Quarterly* (1973, pp. 2–11). It was then the basis of an in-depth study of Bergman and other filmmakers popular at the time in Joan Mellen, *Women and Their Sexuality in the New Film* (1974; quote on p. 16).

The 1970s feminists largely agreed with and renewed the 1960s criticism of Bergman's lack of social and political dimensions in his films. This issue was revived at the time of *Cries and Whispers*' premiere by two film students in the leading morning paper *Dagens Nyheter*.* A few years later, the two strands of criticism – feminism and Marxism – converged in Maria Bergom-Larsson's 1977 book *Ingmar Bergman and Society*.† Here, Bergom-Larsson elaborates on Höök's theories of Bergman as a cultural production imprinted by his upbringing: "He is ideologically tied to a traditional puritan Protestantism and a humanism with deep roots in Western bourgeois culture" (Bergom-Larsson 1978, p. 8).

Like Höök and Mellen, Bergom-Larsson considers Bergman an apt observer of the perverse male ideals of patriarchal ideology while at the same clinging to the same ideology's image of women. Men are violent, cold, rational, exploiting, juvenile and intellectual seekers – that is, 'culture'. Women are correspondingly 'nature': warm, intuitive, motherly, nourishing and mature. Their foremost property is having wombs. Hence, women's identities and meaning of life are closely linked to having children. Abortion is a catastrophe; sterility is a living death (Bergom-Larsson 1978, pp. 29–34).

His intellectual women are consistently masculine and sterile, as exemplified by Ingrid Thulin's characters in *The Silence* and *Cries and Whispers*. At the same time, the couples that do stay together and have children only pass on their own deformities to the next generation. In Bergom-Larsson's view, Bergman is certainly able to depict the tensions and anxieties of his gender and class with great accuracy, but he can never grasp the underlying social causes. Bergman might, in her view, rebel against the inhuman conditions of bourgeois society, but the rebellion is merely an individualist project aiming for a liberation of the mind only (Bergom-Larsson 1978, pp. 111–112).

Two decades later, feminist scholars such as Maaret Koskinen (1993) and Marilyn Johns Blackwell (1997) largely revised the anti-feminist mark on Bergman by pointing to his art cinema narrative techniques as disruptive of the hegemonic patriarchal gaze and ideology. But *Cries and Whispers* remained a problematic film:

---

* The two students, Ingmari Eriksson and Sölve Skagen, initiated the debate on 6 April (Eriksson and Skagen 1973a) and finished it with some closing remarks on 12 May (Eriksson and Skagen 1973b). Three other articles were published in the debate, one supportive of Eriksson and Skagen and two in defence of Bergman.

† The original title, *Ingmar Bergman och den borgerliga ideologin*, can be translated as "Ingmar Bergman and the Bourgeois Ideology".

> *Cries and Whispers*, while privileging female subjectivity and using many of the same disjunctive strategies that encourage a feminist reading of *Persona*, ultimately disavows the role of masculine ideology in the corruption of the self, locating that corruption instead in the female body and in the mother in particular and furthermore strives for precisely the kind of appropriation and false mergence that *Persona* rejects. (Blackwell 1997, p. 166)

Bergman never engaged in an open debate with his feminist critics. In interviews, he only expressed frustration with what he claimed to be attacks on issues irrelevant to the films. Responding to criticism of *Scenes from a Marriage*, he thought it was beside the point to accuse the series of not being about a "suburban working wife with her children at the day-care" or "the role of the children in a divorce narrative such as this"; instead, he pointed to what he saw as the "monstrous nineteenth-century corpse" (Sellermark 1974) still haunting modern life: women's anxiety to please men by keeping their mouth shut and generally being submissive. The cause of this conditioning he defined as a female tradition of education from mother to daughter: "the women's inner sabotage of themselves, the secret aggressions expressed in sexual aversion, the ambition to live up to a role created by their mothers" (ibid.).

A few years earlier, he had declared that his days of "political unconsciousness, unawareness and naivety" were overl; in the same interview, he rejected "leftists who lash out with their talk" but respected the ones "who make concrete and genuine work out of their convictions" (Aghed 1969). Clearly, there was a political gap between Bergman and his critics, but not necessarily one of position but one of aesthetics, one that his detractors could not or would not see. To locate Bergman's politics in the early 1970s, we must remember that he was a modernist artist under the influence of the pioneers of modernism in theatre.

THE STRINDBERG-IBSEN-BERGMAN CONNECTION

Our crusade was so stupid that only a real idealist could have invented it.
— Jöns the Squire in *The Seventh Seal*

There has always been a close connection between Bergman's films and his stage productions: "My films are only distillates of what I do at the theatre. Theatre work is sixty per cent, you see" (Sjöman 1963, p. 102). The major inspiration for his writing was August Strindberg, whom Bergman time and again recognised as his lifelong kindred spirit. He was particularly attracted to "the big angry pieces" and shared Strindberg's temperament: "Strindberg's aggressions – and my own – that's what made the deepest impression on me" (Björkman et al. 1973, p. 23).

Out of his seventy stage productions, forty radio productions and fifteen television productions, he undertook a total of twenty-eight by Strindberg – eighteen for the stage, eight for radio and two for television (Törnqvist 2009, p. 149). One example of a film that draws on Strindberg is *Wild Strawberries*, where he mentions influences from *A Dream Play* (*Ett drömspel*, 1902) and *To Damascus* (*Till Damaskus*, 1898–1904) (Björkman et al. 1973, p. 138). Another is *Persona*, with its close relation to – and possible subversion of – *The Stronger* (1889; see Steene 2000, pp. 24–37). The many connections between the works of Strindberg and Bergman have been thoroughly mapped by Egil Törnqvist (1995 and 2000).

This affinity with Strindberg, whom many feminists in the 1960s and 1970s regarded as the epitome of misogyny, most likely confirmed the critics' opinion that

Bergman possessed a hidden misogynist agenda, even though Strindberg's name was rarely mentioned. When asked about the discrepancy between Strindberg's misogyny and his own position, Bergman defended his fellow artist: "His psyche is fifty percent woman and fifty percent man. If anything, Strindberg's view on women is ambivalent, drawing no special distinction between male and female. Instead, the males and females often swap masks, as in *Miss Julie*" (Björkman et al. 1973, p. 18).

Bergman's Strindberg was thus radically different than many feminists' notion of their old adversary, and in the decades following the 1970s, Strindberg has been re-evaluated as more complex and ambiguous on gender issues. Margareta Fahlgren's analytical essay "Strindberg and the Woman Question", for example, points out that there are no winners, only losers, in his battles of the sexes and concludes, "Strindberg's literary works from the 1880s thus seem to contradict his articles on gender issues, which is what makes them so interesting today" (Fahlgren 2009, p. 30).

Bergman himself saw the differences between men and women as "astonishingly small", and applied his statement about mask-swapping between the genders to his own work: "I think that if I had made *Cries and Whispers* with four men in the leading roles, the story would have been largely the same" (von Essen 1973).

Strindberg might have been an "unconscious modernist", as one author has suggested,* but Bergman was very much a conscious one. Though feeling close to many of Strindberg's themes and motifs, Bergman was in his artistic practice closer to Strindberg's rival, Henrik Ibsen, perhaps the most important pioneer of modernist theatre. He brought the two together and added himself to make a trinity in the 1981 stage production: Nora (Ibsen's *A Doll's House*), Julie (Strindberg's *Miss Julie*) and his own Marianne (*Scenes from a Marriage*).

When looking closer at Ibsen's modernist project, there are striking similarities to Bergman's productions in the 1960s and 1970s. Strindberg and even more so Ibsen are most likely the artists he refers to in his comment on art and politics:

> Art used to be able to be an act of political incitement, it could suggest political action. Today art, in this respect, has completely played itself out. [...] Artists are hardly the social visionaries they used to be. And they mustn't imagine they are! Reality is running away from artists and their political visions. (Björkman et al. 1973, p. 210)

---

* See Göran Tockenström's essay "Crisis and Change: Strindberg the Unconscious Modernist" (2009).

In her book *Henrik Ibsen and the Birth of Modernism*, Toril Moi defines modernism as opposed to the idealism proposed by German authors and philosophers such as Friedrich Hölderlin, G. W. F. Hegel and F. W. J. Schelling (2008, p. 72). They celebrated artistic beauty as the highest expression of the Platonic aesthetic ideal of the beautiful, the good, and the truth.*

Alexander Gottlieb Baumgarten's definition in his 1750 book *Aesthetica* was the perhaps most quoted: beauty is the perfect (the absolute) perceived by the senses, truth is the perfect perceived by reason and good is the perfect attained by moral will (see Tolstoy 1897, p. iii). The idealists fused aesthetics with religion to create a programme for human perfection that reigned over the cultural canon of the nineteenth century and well into the twentieth.

To Friedrich Schiller, artistic beauty in this fashion was "the highest expression of human freedom" (Moi 2008, p. 78). Essential to his ideas was the distinction between actual/bad and genuine/good human nature, most specifically in sexual passion, which is always of an actual, thus bad, nature. Representation of sex therefore requires idealisation or it will be vulgar. Morality and duty must conquer material nature, and so the 'pure' woman must be ready to sacrifice her life for love – as a wife, as a daughter or as an artist's muse.

According to Moi, idealism's hegemony is exactly what Ibsen successfully attacked in plays such as *A Doll's House* (*Et dukkehjem*, 1879), thus hastening the de-idealisation of women and the demise of idealism as an aesthetic theory (2008, p. 81). Moi's assessment of Ibsen's key role in modernist theatre is shared by many, for instance Peter Childs (2008, p. 110) in *Modernism* and George Bernard Shaw in *The Quintessence of Ibsenism* (1891). Shaw's book became of key importance as a call to dismiss idealism as hypocritical, anti-artistic and conservative, and he would continue to propagate a modernist aesthetics that would grow to become the dominant intellectual movement in the arts after World War I.

A heterogeneous movement, modernism was at heart about the aesthetic autonomy from any commitment – social, political, moral, religious – although Shaw shared a Marxist strand with colleagues such as Bertolt Brecht and Erwin Piscator. They dismissed the artistic duty to produce works that promoted uplifting, positive and impossible ideals. Representations of women and sexuality were to be unbound, free from moral restraints. Moi lists the key features of Ibsen's modernism:

---

* A text titled *Das älteste Systemprogramm des deutschen Idealismus* ("The Oldest Systematic Programme of German Idealism", 1796) is usually credited to Hegel alone, but there have been suggestions that it was written collectively by Hegel, Hölderlin and Schelling; see Anon. 1796.

- There is a turn to realism and prose.
- Idealism is ironized or shown to be destructive.
- Scepticism is a central theme.
- The everyday is represented as a possible alternative to scepticism.
- Theatre as an art form is embraced and acknowledged.
- Antitheatricalism is rejected.
- Theatricality is criticized.
- Self-theatricalization in everyday life is a central theme.
- Love is shown to be destroyed by theatricality and scepticism.
- The situation of women is seen as the key social question of modernity.
- Marriage is a central theme, often used as a figure of the everyday.

(Cited in Moi 2008, pp. 9–10)

Bergman's interest in Ibsen probably began with the screenplay assignment of *A Doll's House* commissioned by Hollywood in the spring of 1948 (Björkman et al. 1973, p. 137). Bergman adapted the play, and introduced it as "a tale about the little doll wife Nora and her way out of dreams and lies to clarity and liberation" (Steene 2005, p. 80). The project was eventually dropped, and it took almost a decade for Bergman to try his hand at the playwright again.

Peer Gynt, staged in Malmö in 1957, was his first Ibsen production. It coincided with the making of *Wild Strawberries*, the director's celebrated study of a man confronted by his lifelong self-deception. 'Life-lie' or 'living a lie' is the key Ibsenian notion of idealist life in *The Wild Duck*.

In *Wild Strawberries*, protagonist Isak Borg (Victor Sjöström) travels from Stockholm to Lund by car for the celebration of his fiftieth anniversary as a doctor of medicine. The film is a prototype for the genre later known as the road movie, in which the protagonist also takes an inner journey, in this case to the past. For Isak Borg, that becomes anything but a pleasant stroll down memory lane as his flashbacks reveal the discrepancies between his sentimental self-aggrandisement and the sordid truth of him as a pompous and cold-hearted idealist much like Torvald Helmer in *A Doll's House*.

Bergman's next staging of Ibsen was *Hedda Gabler* (1890) in 1964, and this also became his first stage production outside Scandinavia – at the National Theatre in London in 1970. In 1972 he produced *The Wild Duck* (*Vildanden*, 1884) for Dramaten, declaring the play to be one of the ten best in world drama.* He later

---

* Ingmar Bergman in a 1972 interview with Elisabet Sörenson, quoted in Steene 2005, p. 634.

wrote, "I think Ibsen's *Hedda Gabler* was the only one of my productions that gave me any satisfaction" (Bergman 1988, p. 194). The timing of the two Ibsen plays in Bergman's career is interesting: *Hedda Gabler* just before the making of *Persona*, *The Wild Duck* at the time of shooting *Scenes from a Marriage* – a production that also explicitly references *A Doll's House*.

Ibsen's attack on idealism as living in illusions perfectly matched Bergman's own recurring metaphor of theatre and film as a world of illusions.* It is no coincidence that the family in his farewell-to-film-production *Fanny and Alexander* is named Ekdahl, just like the family in *The Wild Duck*. In theatre and film, as in the family, Bergman found a sanctuary to love and hate.

---

* See also Törnqvist 1995, p. 13.

PERSONA: WAR ON IDEALISM

Persona is a prime example of Ibsen's influence on Bergman. It is a film that in its metafilmic montage prologue proclaims the cleaning out of the old Bergman (iconography, themes, motifs) and the dawn of a director reborn. The boy in the prologue, played by Bergman-as-a-kid-lookalike Jörgen Lindström from *The Silence*, is an investigator not only into the minds of the film's two female protagonists but also into this new Ibsenian landscape of women struggling to break free of the idealist legacy.

He is Elisabet's rejected boy and Alma's aborted foetus, and his (and our) vantage point is from within their shared womb – that is, what patriarchy has defined as the core of the female mind. In his stage production of *Hedda Gabler*, Ibsen's study of the downfall of a woman poisoned by idealism, Bergman had shown the title character as pregnant and disgusted by the product of her unwanted sexual desires. She even tries to abort the foetus by her bare hands (Koskinen 2001, p. 54; Moi 2008, p. 317). In *Persona*, we get to see this inner struggle as a Bergmanian dream play set in the mind/womb of a woman, who is split into two entities locked in a power struggle.

Bergman regards art in the screenplay's 'foreword', "The Snakeskin" ("Ormskinnet"), as "free, shameless, irresponsible", something the idealist nurse Alma (Bibi Andersson) will learn from the modernist actress Elisabet (Liv Ullmann).* Alma considers art as therapeutic, edifying and comforting. Christo-

---

* "The Snakeskin" was originally Bergman's response to being awarded the Erasmus Prize in 1965; quote in Bergman 1966, p. 10. The text was, however, not coincidentally included as a kind of foreword to the *Persona* screenplay.

Fig. 4: Theatricality: audience as actor, actor as audience. Elisabet Vogler (Liv Ullmann) and nurse Alma (Bibi Andersson) in *Persona* (1966). (© Svensk Filmindustri)

pher Orr (2000, p. 89) regards her views to be an assessment of art as melodrama, a genre intended "to facilitate our adjustment to social reality".

At the beginning of the film, Alma is so well adjusted that she is almost an idealist prototype of the self-sacrificing woman, passionately clinging to utopian ideas about family life with marriage, a husband and children. In a monologue, she perceives her life as a wife and mother as her destiny – natural and predetermined – though her declamation betrays her idealist theatricalisation of herself.

Her patient, Elisabet, has done the very opposite: rejected her idealist imprint, thereby also rejecting that ideology's definition of her as a wife, as a mother and, indeed, as a woman. She represents the continuation of Ibsen's heroines and their troubled relationships with idealism in *A Doll's House*, *The Wild Duck* and *Hedda Gabler*. Bergman marries Ibsen with Carl Jung's persona symbolism – "a compromise between the individual and society as to what a man should appear to be"* – to stage women's "inner sabotage of themselves".

---

*   See Jung 1916, reprinted in Campbell 1976, p. 106.

The main part of the action in *Persona* consists of Alma trying to reprogram Elisabet to the social order in accordance with the dominant ideology. Elisabet refuses by maintaining an amoral and asocial stance, though she is clearly moved by images from the Vietnam War and the Nazi Holocaust. Aided by Bergman's modernist, disjunctive techniques of narration, the film becomes a symbolic defeat of idealism by modernism.

For all her efforts to get Elisabet back in the idealist fold of womanhood, it is Alma's own ideology that crumbles. Her initial monologue of trust in the role designated for her by the idealist hegemony turns out to be a persona which is at odds with her innermost feelings. Her sexual repression is highlighted by the scene in which she talks about the pleasures of a spontaneous orgy at a secluded beach, contrasting with her feelings of being "cold and rotten" when having marital sex as Elisabet's stand-in.

Likewise, her longing for children is called into question by the abortion that we learn of and by the twice-spoken monologue in which Alma presumes to speak Elisabet's mind only to express her own true sentiments. There she reveals that her longing for motherhood is all based on an ideological construction, not individual desire. Her true but repressed notion of being a mother is one of horror, disgust, guilt and self-loathing. At that point in the film, Alma and Elisabet are fused together in the film's emblematic shots of their complementary face halves.

The journey from their shared womb in the opening to their shared minds is complete, and the hypocrisy of idealism is exposed by Alma's confession while pretending to speak for Elisabet. Consequently, the language of hegemony that she has used throughout the film is revealed as corrupted, and it breaks down into meaningless phrases despite Alma's effort to restore social order by putting on her nurse uniform. As a last resort, she chooses to repress Elisabet and everything that has happened between them.

We are suddenly back at the hospital, where Alma urges Elisabet to repeat the word "nothing". When Elisabet does so, Alma is pleased. The only other sound in the scene is from church bells ringing, reminding us of the repressive structures foregrounded in several of Bergman's previous films: patriarchal Christianity. The scene ends in a Bergmanian white fade-out that corresponds with the white fade-in of the door at the end of the opening montage and the beginning of the main narrative. Perhaps all that we have seen has been but a dream, Alma's and ours.

At the end of the film, Alma and Elisabet go their separate ways, back to their old lives. The last glimpse of Alma is of her getting on a bus dressed in her old, drab and conservative clothes. Elisabet is seen making a film by Ingmar Bergman – we glimpse his director's chair in the shot where his camera crew are taking a crane shot – suggesting that she has been the director's agent in the narrative. In this context, the brief encounter between the women also becomes a metaphor for the reception of modernist art, more specifically Bergman's previous film: *The Silence*.

Appreciated 'for all the wrong reasons', *The Silence*'s reception is parodied in the opening montage of *Persona* by the flash images of an erect penis and of lips suggesting a vagina. But it is also mocked by Alma's efforts to apply her idealist model of melodrama in her responses to Elisabet. This time, Bergman's modernist film resists by returning the look. Elisabet the actor and Alma the audience switch places so that Elisabet is the one who watches in silence while Alma becomes the one who performs. Revealing her innermost secrets, Alma's sense of identity and ultimately her world-view are deconstructed as hypocrisy and self-deception – "a tangle of lies", as Karin says in *Cries and Whispers*.

Bergman's art cinema narrative does not end with a conventional melodramatic resolution that readjusts the protagonists and the audience to the social order. It has an open ending appropriate to Bergman's favourite saying that his job was not to provide the answers but the questions.* In other words, he was not political in the sense that he was making didactic films providing ready-made political answers, but his modernist strategies certainly have political implications. To summarise, we can apply Toril Moi's list of Ibsen's key modernist features to the film.

Persona is metafilmic in the same sense that Ibsen's plays are metatheatrical: it constantly reminds us that we are watching a film. Film form is thus embraced and acknowledged. The main story is about the clash between idealism and modernism, resulting in an ironic defeat of idealism as hypocritical and (self-)destructive. Although Elisabet is the theatre actress, it is Alma who theatricalises herself by inscribing herself in various scenarios of female sacrifice. This is foreboded in the overwrought radio play we hear at the hospital featuring a woman pleading for forgiveness.

For a start, the whole scenario – which could be interpreted as Alma's dream – with her dropping everything to be some sort of assistant or maid to an actress for months, is anything but realistic. At the summer cottage, she talks with enthusiasm about her self-sacrificing work, only to forget it in an instant when making a thoughtless comment on the heavy rain. Elisabet's hard look at her is telling

---

* See, for instance, the talk show *Kvällsöppet*, 9 April 1971, following a rerun of *The Lie*.

of Alma's poor theatrical performance. Already in Alma's aforementioned monologue we have become aware of her self-theatricalisation, and during the film we will see her utopian ideas of love collide with her stories about sexual affairs and infidelities.

In all this theatricalisation, her love for future husband Karl-Henrik seems to be of lesser, if any, importance. When she describes their relationship and forthcoming marriage it sounds more like an idealist construct – a kind of marriage out of convenience – than love. Her stand-in performance as Elisabet when having sex with the actress's husband becomes an omen of what lies ahead for her – a cold, perhaps even hateful relationship of the kind Bergman has depicted in previous films such as *Wild Strawberries* and would continue to explore in *Scenes from a Marriage*, *Face to Face* and *From the Life of the Marionettes* (*Aus dem Leben der Marionetten*, 1980).

Finally, the situation of women as the key to modernity is central. Bergman's notion of "the women's inner sabotage of themselves" locates patriarchal ideology not primarily as the outer repression of women by men, but as an imprint on the women's own minds – their inner police. If we take the main narrative as Alma's projection, dream or 'mindscreen', then Elisabet represents everything she has to repress in order to restore the presumed normality of her idealist frame of mind. Like Ibsen's Hedda Gabler, Alma chooses death, though not by suicide but by becoming a Bergmanian living dead. We will meet her sisters in the films and TV productions discussed below.

THE MAKING OF INGMAR BERGMAN

The only life that exists for me is this life, here and now, and the only holiness that exists is in my relations with other people. And outside, nothing exists. When I realized that, when I began to understand that everything happens here and now in the world around me, it gave me a marvellous feeling of relief and security. I found a new power with which to do my work, and there was a kind of new beginning for me. No, I don't believe in any afterlife because *this* life gives me everything I need; the cruel, beautiful, fantastic life. For me, the meaning of everything is life itself. I don't need any other.

– Ingmar Bergman interviewed by Charles Marowitz, *New York Times*, 1973

When summarising *Scenes from a Marriage* as the result of thirty years of experience, Ingmar Bergman spoke not only of his private life and experiences; he also spoke of impressions of other artists' works and of other people – parents, wives, lovers, friends, foes, colleagues – that his artistic imagination had processed, absorbed, split and recombined in his own work. This insight of being "a conglomerate of other people and the whole world" is also the great revelation his protagonist Jenny Isaksson experiences after her primal scream in *Face to Face* (Bergman 1976a, p. 7). The understanding of Bergman's "me-drama" must take these samplings and remixes of other people and the world, that is, the historical context, into account. His films could therefore best be described as a "monologue for many voices" in which everyone and no one speaks for Bergman.

Aesthetically and politically, Bergman was rooted in cultural radicalism, a Scandinavian intellectual movement that originated in the 1870s and included both liberals and socialists. August Strindberg and Henrik Ibsen were both at the fore of the movement, although the concept itself did not become widely accepted until 1910.* At its core it was a continuation of the ideals from the Enlightenment. It struggled for humanism and the natural sciences in opposition to irrationalism, anti-intellectualism and authoritarian institutions: idealism, religion, monarchy, totalitarian political movements, Victorian sexual morality and the bourgeois family.†

Cultural radicalism was essential to the introduction of modernism, and it dominated the Swedish cultural debate in the twentieth century. Between the world wars, when Bergman grew up, there was a culture clash mainly between the cultural radicals in the socialist student organisation Clarté and the Conservative Party's youth organisation Sveriges Nationella Ungdomsförbund, which in 1934 broke away from the mother party to become the Nazi party Sveriges Nationella Förbund. One member of SNU/SNF was Dag Bergman, Ingmar's brother (Pryser and Thunberg 2007). The culture war was not only close to home; it was very much raging within the family.

Bergman's reading, from pre-modernists such as Carl Jonas Love Almqvist to modernist Per Lagerkvist and feminist literature by Germaine Greer, must be understood against this intellectual background. The same goes for his musical interest in – and use of – composers such as J. S. Bach, W. A. Mozart and Tomaso Albinoni (uncredited in *Scenes from a Marriage*). It is no coincidence that Mozart's opera *The Magic Flute* – Bergman's only musical film, made in 1974, previous to *Face to Face* – is a celebration of the Enlightenment, in which the three messenger boys declare: "Soon superstition will die, soon the wise will prevail [...] Then the earth will be a paradise, and men will be gods" (Gutman 2001, p. 21).

Interviews in the 1960s and 1970s are packed with references to modernist filmmakers, from Robert Bresson to Alfred Hitchcock (see, for instance, Björkman et. al. 1973, pp. 27 and 43–44), and he is no stranger to referencing other artists' works. The most obvious reference is, perhaps, the one to Victor Sjöström's *The Phantom Carriage* (*Körkarlen*, 1921) in the opening of *Wild Strawberries*. Sometimes they are more indirect, such as Alma's brief account of her five-year-long and tormented affair with a married lover in *Persona* – a story close to Vilgot Sjöman's directorial debut *The Mistress* (*Älskarinnan*, 1962), in which Bibi Andersson played the title role.

---

* Historian Crister Skoglund (1993, p. 115) traces the notion of "cultural radicalism" back to a 1910 book by journalist Else Kleen, later a social debater and wife of social democrat minister Gustav Möller.

† For an overview of cultural radicalism and its changes from the 1870s until the 1960s, see Skoglund 1991 and 1993.

Then there are more convoluted examples, such as the ones Vilgot Sjöman noted when following the work process on *Winter Light* (1963, p. 37). Sjöman observes that the childhood trauma of Thomas (Gunnar Björnstrand) in the screenplay draft was perhaps not inspired by Bergman's own memories but by Pär Lagerkvist's short story "Father and Me" ("Far och jag", 1924). When he discusses this with Bergman, the story is quickly excised from the shooting script.

Later during the shooting of the film, Bergman analyses his claustrophobia as the result of a trauma when he as a child was locked in a closet as punishment. It is a story told in several interviews and frequently included in his works, also in *Face to Face*. Listening to Bergman's memory, Sjöman thinks to himself that it is a tale "straight out of Hjalmar Bergman's *Thy Rod and Thy Staff* (*Farmor och vår herre*, 1921)".*

When Bergman, using his Ernest Riffe pen name (1960, p. 189), wishes to be like one of the nameless builders of a cathedral, it is this intricate legacy of artistic sources he has in mind. Like all artists, he stands on the shoulders of artists that worked before him, and there is no clear distinction between Bergman's imagination and his artistic inspirations. Moreover, in Bergman's own personal universe of experiences, traumas, memories, fantasies and artistic impulses – his famous intuitive strategies – there are bits and pieces both of adult Bergman and of artistic works and people who for various reasons have made their imprint on him.

For instance, in the second episode of *Scenes from a Marriage*, Johan's (Erland Josephson) humiliation when a colleague criticises his poetry as bland and indifferent goes back to Bergman's own experience after the premiere of *A Lesson in Love* (*En lektion i kärlek*, 1954). Film critic and later Film Institute CEO Harry Schein had called his popular comedy "indifferent" and "so simple that a scolding would be out of place" (Heurling 1983a, p. 387). As we have seen above, that was the most damaging assessment Bergman could imagine.†

---

* Sjöman 1963, p. 161. The cupboard punishment story is told in numerous interviews, such as Jörn Donner's 1975 documentary *Tre scener med Ingmar Bergman*, part 1, and included in his autobiography (Bergman 1988, p. 9).

† Sjöman writes about Bergman's relations to his critics in his 1963 reportage book on *Winter Light*, titled *L136*, pp. 22–23, 212–213 and 235–237. Harry Schein has commented on Bergman's burning hatred of him as a critic in his autobiography *Schein* (1980, p. 115). Of note is that Bergman has commented very little about *A Lesson in Love*, despite it being his biggest box-office hit to that date. In *Bergman on Bergman* (Björkman et al. 1973, p. 79), he dismisses it as "only made for the passing moment". *The Magic Lantern* (1988, p. 171) refers to it once and incidentally. *Images* has no chapter on the film, and in the *Smiles of a Summer Night* chapter he only talks about some anecdotes related to *A Lesson in Love* (1995; see pp. 342–343).

But his fight against idealism also has important social institutions as its arena. Bergman mainly attacks the school system, the church and the bourgeois family and their repressive mechanisms of violence, rejection and, most powerful, humiliation:

> [T]he humiliation motif is of the very essence. [...] To humiliate and to be humiliated, I think, is a crucial element in our whole social structure. It is not only for the artist I'm sorry. It's just that I know exactly where he feels humiliated.*

When confronted by the possibility to stage the mechanisms of humiliation in a more overt social and political context, he retorted: "I stick to what I know. If I've objected strongly to Christianity, it has been because Christianity is deeply branded by a very virulent humiliation motif" (Björkman et al. 1973, p. 81). His argument for frequently making films about artists and artistry is the same. Artists were a kind of crystallisation because of their exposed position and because of their peculiar line of work. Not that he romanticised them: "It is just that this occupational group is the one I happen to know" (Henttonen 1969).

In Bergman's early films, artists are on the receiving end of the acts of humiliation, but from *The Magician* (*Ansiktet*, 1958) they also turn to humiliate others. Thus, the object of repression is not artists or artistry *per se* but rather what they represent: the female principle regardless of gender. To quote British author Quentin Crisp: "There's no sin like being a woman. When a man dresses as a woman everybody laughs. When a woman dresses as a man, nobody laughs."†

A biographical reference is Bergman's childhood memory of the punishment for wetting himself: he had to wear a red skirt all day to his parent's amusement (Donner 1975, part 1 of documentary; Bergman 1988, p. 8). It is a telling representation of femininity as Other – disgusting, grotesque, laughable.

In the 1950s, Bergman's feminine Other is mainly the artist, whose repressed position in society is underscored by cross-dressing or, in the case of men, female attributes such as make-up and jewellery. Prominent examples are the circus artists in *Sawdust and Tinsel* and Vogler's mesmerist troupe in *The Magician*. With their jet-black hair and the men's earrings and kohl-pencilled eyes, both groups are strikingly similar to travellers (Swedish: *tattare*) – an ethnic group subjected

---

* Bergman in Björkman et al. 1973, pp. 80–81. See also Björkstén 1970, p. 27; and *Filmkrönika* (TV programme), 4 March 1973.

† Quote from the documentary *The Celluloid Closet* (1995) about homophobia in films.

to social repression and racist stereotyping as beastly, deceitful, criminal and effeminate in Swedish popular culture (Wright 1998, pp. 95–147). *The Hour of the Wolf* even lets us witness the ritual construction of the Other, as clownish and feminine make-up is applied on the face of the artist Johan Borg so he can be properly mocked by the bourgeois demons.

Not until Vogler and Aman/Manda in *The Magician* and actress Elisabet in *Persona* remove their make-up to get the appearance of 'normality' and thus become indistinguishable from their bourgeois critics/audience are they are able to shift the power balance. The humiliation game comes full circle in *A Passion*, in which the cynical and exploitative architect and photographer Elis Vergérus (Erland Josephson) preys on the people he photographs. His world-view echoes Bergman's prominent strand of nihilism while at the same time illustrating Bergman's fear of a nihilist world:

[Elis Vergérus in *A Passion*:] It is hypocrisy to weep over the foolishness of the world. It is ridiculous to be horrified by human cruelty. It is emotional carelessness to call for justice or decency. My fellow human's suffering does not keep me awake at night. I am indifferent in my own eyes as well as in the eyes of others. I function. (Bergman 1973a, p. 179)

[Ingmar Bergman:] I've a strong impression that our world is about to go under. Our political systems are deeply compromised and have no further uses. Our social behaviour patterns – interior and exterior – have proved a fiasco. The tragic thing is, we neither can nor want to nor have the strength to change course. It's too late for revolutions, and deep down inside ourselves we no longer even believe in their positive effects. Just around the corner an insect world is waiting for us – and one day it is going to roll in over our ultra-individualised existence. Otherwise I'm a respectable social democrat. (Björkman et al. 1973, p. 18)

The author David's (Gunnar Björnstrand) use of his mentally disturbed daughter Karin (Harriet Andersson) as the raw material for a possible novel in *Through a Glass Darkly*, Elisabet's vampiric interest in Alma for the benefit of her acting in *Persona* and Elis making photographic art out of other people's misery in *A Passion* are all metaphors for Bergman's artistry as humiliating exploitation of others as well as himself. In the productions discussed below the artists are replaced by non-artists – what we for the lack of better words can call ordinary people – and the exploitation motif is replaced by one of idealist destruction by mutual deception and self-deception.

Most of Bergman's works have prototypes for his characters that are not so readily identifiable. Rather, his individual portraits are assemblages of many sources. Still, I want to pause to briefly introduce some people of importance to the works analysed below.

ONE MAN, FOUR WOMEN

Even though we will never know the complete list of people Bergman used as material, a few stand out from the crowd. First of all, his parents Erik and Karin Bergman, both dead at the start of what I refer to as the Djursholm trilogy in 1970. He would explore them more openly later in his career, particularly in *The Best Intentions* (*Den goda viljan*, 1992), but they are already present in his work from the very beginning in the 1940s. Then there are three women of his own generation whom I consider to be of special interest to this study: Karin Lannby, Ulla Isaksson and Marianne Höök.

ERIK BERGMAN (1886–1970)

Ingmar Bergman's many portraits of authoritarian patriarchs, such as the hateful priest in *It Rains on Our Love* (*Det regnar på vår kärlek*, 1946), were modelled on his parson father, Erik. In both Ingmar's autobiography, *The Magic Lantern*, and Birgit Linton-Malmfors' 1992 biography of his parents by way of their letters and diaries, Erik appears to be a patriarchal double personality. Publicly, he was a popular, forceful and successful spiritual leader of his congregation; at home he was a terrible and moody autocrat, whose demands for obedience and a respectable front were the family law, upheld by violence and humiliation. In the 1930s he, like many in the Swedish bourgeoisie, had a favourable opinion of Nazi Germany and its *Übermensch* ideals, though he was not a member of the Nazi party, as was Ingmar's older brother Dag.*

---

* Bergman 1988, pp. 7–10, 56–57 and 133–137. In one letter, Karin even suggests that Erik is insane (Linton-Malmfors 1992, p. 152). See also the first part of Jörn Donner's three-part documentary *Tre Scener med Ingmar Bergman*, 28 December 1975.

But Erik was also of a fragile disposition. He had frequent nervous breakdowns, and in time became more of a child in Karin's motherly care than a husband. In Bergman's 1950s films, the fearsome patriarch therefore turns into the fragile, infantile and ridiculed bourgeois husband: *Waiting Women*, *A Lesson in Love*, *Smiles of a Summer Night*. In all films, he was played by Gunnar Björnstrand, who continued as Erik's alter ego into the 1960s with the portrait of the existentially tormented parson in *Winter Light* and as Elisabet's needy, child-like husband in *Persona*. He reappeared, represented by other actors, in *Cries and Whispers* and perhaps most memorably as the demonic priest and stepfather in *Fanny and Alexander*.

KARIN BERGMAN (1889–1966)

Ingmar Bergman's mother is present in most of his work. He has referred to his "doglike devotion" to her and – stressing the oedipal angle – said that she was his "first love" (von Essen 1973; Bergman 1988, p. 3). In the Strindbergian sense, Karin was 'The Stronger' of the two parents: loving and caring, but also possessive, demanding and domineering (Bergman 1988, p. 3; Koskinen 2002, pp. 63–70). She was obsessed with truth and honesty. At the same time, she was living a lie.

Formally, she was the respectable parson's wife, but soon after their third child was born – Ingmar's sister Margareta – her intimate relationship with Erik came to a full stop. Karin had fallen in love with another man, Thomas. Still, she stayed for the remaining forty-plus years of her life due to social pressure and convention, comforting herself with the delusion that she did it for the welfare of her children. She saw her married life as a reflection of Strindberg's most scathing depictions of the bourgeois family (Linton-Malmfors 1992, pp. 29, 128, 133 and 151).

Sexual rivalry between father and son, a mother who kills her son's fiancée out of jealousy and a mother portrayed as an eerie, vampire-like creature of the night are some of the early stories that came out of Bergman's oedipal fixation on Karin.[*] Vilgot Sjöman recounts a dream Bergman told him during his work on *Winter Light* in which he meets with an old lover in his childhood nursery (1963, p. 134). In a second she transforms into his mother, then to his wife Käbi Laretei, then back to his mother again.

---

[*] Koskinen 2002, pp. 74–86. See also Thunberg 2008, pp. 248 and 256, for signs of Karin's possessiveness and/or jealousy.

The blurred borderline between mother and lover was staged in its most complex and brutal form in *From the Life of the Marionettes*. Protagonist Peter Egermann's (Robert Atzorn) mother (Lola Müthel) is an older lookalike version of his wife Katarina (Christine Buchegger). Failing to use his wife as a substitute for his sadistic sexual urges for his mother, he kills the prostitute Ka (Rita Russek) – Ka is short for Katarina – followed by an anal rape of the dead body. The logic of the cold womb comes full circle, a recognition that the child of the 'inner morgue' is destined to procreate death, not life.

Winter Light splits Karin into two: the priest's 'pure' idealised dead wife and his most alive but demanding and physically insistent mistress Märta Lundberg, played by Ingrid Thulin (Sjöman 1963, p. 47). Karin Bergman's inability to bring together her call for truth with living a lie is the inspiration for the two Anna Fromms of *A Passion* and *The Lie* respectively. Karin in *Cries and Whispers* manifests her repressed sexuality in haunting images of bloody genital mutilation that also echo the hysterectomy that nearly killed Karin Bergman in 1931 – a possible inspiration for the cold womb motif in several of Bergman's films (Linton-Malmfors 1992, p. 183).

Like Erik's admiration for an *Übermensch* man that he clearly could not live up to himself, Karin's life of discord, her utopian dreams clashing with her profane desires, illustrates the absurdity of idealism.

KARIN LANNBY (1916–2007)

In many respects, she was Karin Bergman's antithesis: politically radical, impulsive, sexually uninhibited, imaginative, temperamental. In the early 1940s, Bergman had an intense love affair with this communist, journalist, spy, translator, actress and artist.* Hers was a life of excitement, adventure and danger. Barely twenty, she ran away from her upper-middle-class family home to join the Republican side in the Spanish Civil War as an interpreter. Back home in 1939, she was recruited as a spy in the Swedish counter-intelligence during World War II, codename: Anette.

She published poetry to great acclaim, had a brief acting career in Swedish theatre and film and socialised with the crème de la crème of Stockholm. On a darker note, she suffered from traumatic memories of sexual abuse as a child and was briefly in

---

* For an extensive portrait of Lannby, see Anders Thunberg's biography *Karin Lannby: Ingmar Bergmans Mata Hari* (2008). Also of interest are Höök 1962, pp. 40–42, and Sjöman 1998, pp. 33–35.

1938 treated for schizophrenia. Although her diagnosis was incorrect, she had occasional difficulties in distinguishing between imagination and the real world.*

Bergman's affair with her ended in 1942 when Karin threw him out and Else Fisher entered Bergman's life, eventually to become his first wife. But although Karin would move to France and change her name to Maria Cyliakus, then Maria Bouyer, she would continue to haunt Bergman's films (Sjöman 1998, p. 33). In her Bergman biography, Marianne Höök uses "Rut Köhler" as a pseudonym for Karin Lannby (1962, p. 40). That was her first incarnation on the silver screen in Bergman's screenplay for *Woman Without a Face* (*Kvinna utan ansikte*, 1947), directed by Gustaf Molander.

Originally titled "The Puzzle Represents Eros", Bergman's 1946 prose outline for the script portrays a *femme fatale* stereotype. Though intelligent and imaginative, Rut is a tragic and doomed prostitute in accordance with a popular tradition from nineteenth-century dime novels to American film noir. Or, as Bergman described his Rut in an interview, "a woman with dangerous strains of a subhuman disposition, hysteria and erotomania" (Höök 1962, p. 40). She had a more innocent predecessor in the 1945 script "Marie", which would be revised five years later and made into the film *Summer Interlude* (*Sommarlek*, 1951), and she would also colour the portrait of the mother Jenny in *Crisis* (*Kris*, 1946).

In *The Magic Lantern* Bergman calls her Maria, which according to scholar Maaret Koskinen is not merely to protect her true identity. It is also because of her resemblance to many of the characters named Maria/Marie/Mari in Bergman's early stories.† Later in his career he transformed her into the schizophrenic and nymphomaniac Karin in *Through a Glass Darkly* and the sexual predator Veronica Vogler in *The Hour of the Wolf*, then returned her to the original name of Maria in the 1970s productions of *Cries and Whispers* and *Face to Face*.

ULLA ISAKSSON (1916–2000)

The only author besides early collaborator Herbert Grevenius and actor-friend Erland Josephson to write screenplays for Ingmar Bergman. She wrote *Brink of Life* (*Nära livet*, 1958) and *The Virgin Spring*, which gave Bergman his first

---

* See Thunberg 2008, pp. 20, 33, 39, 120 and 132. In Sjöman 1963, p. 30, she is described as a person who now and then fell under the command of inner voices.
† Bergman 1988, pp. 138–141; Koskinen 2002, p. 144.

Academy Award. They were in close contact from the late 1950s onwards, and in 1975–76 Bergman initiated the production of a film version of her 1973 novel *Paradise Place* (*Paradistorg*) – the 1977 film's English title was *Summer Paradise* – with actress Gunnel Lindblom making her debut as a director.

Isaksson had a religious and bourgeois background close to Bergman's, and in their respective works they touched on the same themes and motifs. Her 1962 novel *The Blessed Ones* (*De två saliga*) is about an insane woman pulling her lover into the world of passionate madness – a *folie à deux* – much like Karin in *Through a Glass Darkly* does to her brother Minus when seducing him into incestuous sex. Bergman would later be inspired by her Ibsenian novel *Paradise Place* while writing both *Face to Face* and *Fanny and Alexander*. It is, as we shall see, no coincidence that she lent her family name to the protagonist in *Face to Face*: Jenny Isaksson.

MARIANNE HÖÖK (1918–1970)

A sharp, witty journalist and fashion icon whose religious background was even closer to Bergman's than Ulla Isaksson's. She had a strict upbringing at her maternal grandparents' after her mother's suicide in 1919, and she shared Bergman's oedipal fixation although with a gender twist: she hated her grandmother and loved her grandfather with a sexual passion. Like no other of his biographers, her book haunted Bergman for years. It was the only full-length book she published.

Later in life Bergman admitted to Bergman scholar Maaret Koskinen: "For a long time I was mad at Marianne Höök. Now, finally, I realise that she was right about much."* However, things could not have been that bad between them since she interviewed him a few times after the biography's 1962 publication, for instance in 1969 at an informal rendezvous over dinner at a posh restaurant in Stockholm (Höök 1969).

In her 2009 Höök biography, friend and colleague Annette Kullenberg portrays a person who knew countless people, yet had very few friends, who had numerous lovers but never really loved anyone – including herself and even her children. Superficially, Höök's life was all song and dance, rubbing shoulders with important politicians and celebrities, being a natural at all the social and cultural events of importance in the Swedish capital. She also had the ambition to become an author of poetry and

---

* Koskinen 2002, p. 311. The Höök biography is the only Bergman book mentioned by him in Björkman et al. 1973, pp. 18 and 20. It is apparent that it struck a Bergmanian nerve.

novels, although she did not have the self-confidence to pursue this dream. Her forte was penning journalistic texts with style and punch – columns, reportage, interviews, causeries – and this was something she stuck to until the end (Höök 2008, pp. 7–8).

Marianne Höök was the career woman and the social focal point that Karin Bergman could have been if born a generation later. Yet she suffered severe depressions, was constantly guilt-stricken by her numerous marital transgressions and had a dark and cynical worldview that matched Bergman's own. She was marked by her parental or, rather, grandparental generation. All her restless adventures in sex, all her plastic surgery to stay young and all her psychotherapy sessions did not help according to Kullenberg (2009, pp. 158–174). The deep insecurities from never being able to make it into the intellectual salons as an equal – her Bergman book never got the recognition it deserved – was only matched by her horror of being old and losing her sex appeal (2009, pp. 345–347).

Some claim Bergman and Höök were lovers (see Thunberg 2008, p. 285), but it is undisputed that they became close friends and shared many values, such as being outspoken social democrats in an upper-class environment. In the 1960s, she lived at Blockhusudden on the island of Djurgården, close to the inner city of Stockholm. Bergman lived with Käbi Laretei in the more recently constructed Djursholm, the poshest part of the upper-class municipality of Danderyd just outside the capital. It was most likely from Höök that Bergman got the original Swedish title to the 1970 TV drama known in English as *The Lie*, namely *Reservatet*, which can be translated as "The Sanctuary", alternatively "The Preserve" or "The Reservation" – in the play's dialogue alluding to the feeling of living a life in a sanctuary of wealth and safety closed off from the rest of the world.

Originally, her remark referred to his upbringing in the "sanctuary" of a clergyman's home, a museum celebrating yesterday's ideals and social customs – in many ways mirroring her own upbringing. This, she explains, is why Bergman's stories about contemporary times always seem to be one step behind, always swept in "a soft atmosphere of unreality that has gelled into a style" (Höök 1962, p. 20). Bergman seemed to have come to the same conclusion. When writing and directing *Fanny and Alexander* – the grand finale to his semi-autobiographical film and TV projects – he set it in a time more than a decade before his birth, making his alter ego a generation older than himself. It was a representation closer to the social climate that formed him than the world in which he was born.

Her two autobiographical radio programmes from 1964 and 1969 are streams of consciousness with dream-like qualities much like Bergman's films of the 1960s.

In these journeys meandering through haunting childhood memories illustrating religious hypocrisy, class hatred and indoctrination in conservative family values, she attempted to explain the construction of a generation of repressed and false women anxious to please.* A key concept of hers that Bergman picked up and used in interviews and a film title shortly after her death was "the touch" ("beröringen"). In the years leading up to her death, she frequently talked and wrote about humanity's emotional perplexity and how people ought to touch each other more, both in the physical and spiritual sense of the word.†

Marianne Höök, another child of a cold womb, was one of the few who 'got' Bergman and who shared many of his dark ideas about the human condition. Not only that, she managed to articulate in words many aspects of the social conditioning they shared from their respective 'sanctuaries'. Outwardly, she kept an impeccable façade of success in both her work and her social career, but her inner life was in turmoil.

Reading Sylvia Plath's *The Bell Jar*, as Bergman did according to his 1974 engagement planner while working on *Face to Face*, he must have been struck by the many similarities between Höök and the novel's protagonist. After several suicide attempts, Marianne Höök finally succeeded in taking her own life on 17 April 1970 – close to the date of her mother's suicide fifty-two years earlier and just about the time when *The Lie* was originally scheduled to have its premiere. Perhaps that was the reason for the postponing of the TV premiere for more than half a year.

We know that Strindberg used fellow author Victoria Benedictsson's suicide in Copenhagen on 22 July 1888 as an inspiration for *Miss Julie*, and that he read Benedictsson's works while working on the play (Ollén 1984, p. 297). No doubt Bergman was likewise inspired to use Höök as the raw material for his portraits of modern women in his 1970s TV productions: *The Lie, Scenes from a Marriage, Face to Face* and *From the Life of the Marionettes*. In the introduction to the screenplay of *Face to Face*, he writes: "Another person's life story came to my aid; I could find similarities between her experiences and my own. The only difference was that her situation was so much clearer and more painful – more pronounced" (Bergman 1976a, p. 5). This other person was undoubtedly Marianne Höök.

---

* The two programmes have been transcribed and published in Höök 2008, pp. 813–832.
† Kullenberg 2009, p. 343. Her "emotional perplexity" became "emotional illiteracy" in his words, but the meaning is the same (see Bergman 1973b, p. 144).

PART FOUR

THE DJURSHOLM TRILOGY PLUS ONE

> I do understand the techniques used in both melodrama and soap opera quite well. One who uses melodrama as it should be can implement the unrestrained emotional possibilities in the genre.
>
> – Ingmar Bergman, *Images*, 1995, p. 278

In 1963, Bergman decided that *Though a Glass Darkly*, *Winter Light* and *The Silence* were a trilogy about the silence or, rather, the vanishing of God (Sjöman 1963, pp. 219–220). However, neither in his autobiography *The Magic Lantern* nor in *Images: My Life in Film* does he mention the films together as a trilogy. In *Images*, only the first two films are connected (Bergman 1995, p. 261). Still, this trilogy idea caught on.

Today we can read numerous Bergman books where the three films are treated as an integrated work, and we can buy them as such in a Criterion Collection DVD box set.

Likewise, some critics suggested that *The Hour of the Wolf*, *The Shame* and *A Passion* constitute a 'Fårö trilogy' (Geber 1977c, p. 493), although that never caught on. And in 1972 Bergman himself came up with the idea that there was a trilogy of works touching on common issues: *The Lie*, *The Touch* and *Scenes from a Marriage* (Hellbom 1972). But that idea for a trilogy did not stir anyone's imagination, not even Bergman's. He never mentioned it again, nor have any DVD box sets of this supposed trilogy or the 'Fårö trilogy' been released.

For this study, I propose a more productive Bergman trilogy: *The Lie*, *Scenes from a Marriage* and *Face to Face* – with strong connections to *Cries and Whispers* and *From the Life of the Marionettes*. The three main titles are all 1970s TV productions. The first two are set in the contemporary upper-class suburban district of Djursholm, north-east of Stockholm. Founded in 1889, it was part of a utopian garden-city movement that also swept over the United Kingdom and the United States in the last decades of the nineteenth century. Since then, Djursholm has been the home for many in the Swedish cultural, political and economic elite: heads of major industries, politicians, famous authors and artists.*

Bergman lived in Djursholm with his fourth wife, pianist Käbi Laretei, from 1959 to 1966. He had a parallel but secret relationship with one of his neighbours, Ingrid von Rosen, from 1957 onwards. She gave birth to their daughter Maria in 1959 – the year he married Laretei – and the relationship lasted through Bergman's love affair with Liv Ullmann in the years 1966–69 (Hagen 2004). After the divorce in 1969 from Käbi Laretei, Bergman and von Rosen married. Thus these three television productions, with their contemporary settings and intimate dialogues, are more personal – literally closer to home – than perhaps any of Bergman's other work.

All of them are soap-opera-like melodramas about the gaps between individual desires (love, identity, self-fulfilment) and social conformity of the idealist kind. However, instead of ending the series with the main characters' readjustment to the social reality of the ideological hegemony, Bergman breaks with melodrama genre traditions to close all three productions with art cinema open endings that suggest an ongoing struggle. Significantly, it is the women who for some reason cannot or will not adjust to a contentment with the state of things as they are at the curtain call.

Bergman's choice of genre attracted a mainstream audience, many of whom had never seen any of his works or would not readily seek them out. By denying them resolutions that reconciled the protagonists with the social order, he provoked a debate like few other films or TV productions. In the three works, Bergman portrays a small pocket of bourgeois life, isolated and sheltered from the rest of the world. The productions have much in common with the late-nineteenth-century plays of Henrik Ibsen and August Strindberg, portraying the lives of bourgeois families. Since Bergman only wrote the screenplay for *The Lie* and left the staging and filming to his friend and colleague Jan Molander, I will therefore focus primarily on the text when discussing it below.

---

* For the history of Djursholm and an analysis of its carefully protected social segregation, see Mikael Holmqvist's *Djursholm: Sveriges ledarsamhälle* ("Djursholm: Sweden's Community of Leaders") (2015).

THE LIE: A TRAGI-COMEDY OF BANALITY

The screenplay originated with a 1968 project titled "Annandreas: Scenes from a Marriage", which split into two: *A Passion* and *The Lie* (Geber 1977c, p. 493). Both feature a woman by the name of Anna Fromm, who is in a relationship with a man called Andreas. The couples live on islands – literally and figuratively – closed off from the rest of the world. They are living lies, deceiving themselves and each other.

A Passion is a tragedy, in which Andreas Winkelmann and Anna Fromm have scarred souls that reflect their troubled background and poor living conditions. The Anna and Andreas of *The Lie* are living a seemingly carefree and affluent lifestyle. The tone in the latter is lighter, sometimes one of outright comedy, but the mood turns decidedly darker and more tragic during the story. She is a university lecturer in Slavic languages. He is an architect in a governmental department. Home is heaven, or so it seems. Here, nothing bad really happens. Until it does.

The English title stresses the connection to Ibsen's *The Wild Duck*, and its central question of whether it is better to live in a lie or not. To underscore the connection, Anna and Andreas have a housemaid named Berta, the same name as that of the housemaid in Ibsen's play. In *Cries and Whispers*, Anna will assume the part of the selfless servant to her masters and a silent witness to their downfall.*

Typical of his new aesthetic strategies – celebrated as 'a new simplicity' by the critics – Bergman addresses his 'message' head-on in the Brechtian opening monologues by Mr and Mrs Fromm. Anna and Andreas are both educated and intelligent people, reflecting on the fact that they have a charmed but delusional way of

---

* See Bergman 1973a, p. 156, for a description of Anna in *Cries and Whispers*.

life. Their self-awareness, however, does nothing to free them from these delusions. It is all part of their self-theatricalisation as they actively choose to live the lie even as they recognise it as false.

Anna talks about short attacks of awareness about the world. This produces "a dizzy feeling of sickness as the news strikes me", but then her carefree everyday life comes to her rescue and the sickness fades away. Andreas is more aware of his fragile existence: "not many people have a life as good as mine". He sometimes feels that "it is almost a bit uneasy to have an existence protected from unpleasantness and real worries to such a degree".

Their 'sanctuary' could be a representation of the last days of idealism. We see it in a diluted and faded edition, much like the waning Christian faith in *Winter Light*. The inside is hollow, but the outer structures and rituals still go through the motions much like the snakeskin in Bergman's foreword to *Persona*. No one believes in it any more. Only old conventions, perhaps idle routine or perhaps not knowing any other way of life, keep everybody in their place.

Anna talks about her closest relatives and friends as "good, decent people, all completely normal except my oldest brother Albert, who is about to drink himself to death". Andreas occasionally thinks about when "the storm is going to change its course" and "come to this sheltered island", but these "are not exactly thoughts that keep one awake at night".* Their life and world Bergman summarised in the play's subtitle: "A Tragi-Comedy of Banality". Since it is not readily available for viewing, it is necessary to provide a brief synopsis.

The play opens at six o'clock in the morning on 5 April 1968. Anna wakes up, but lingers in "the big comfortable bed" to enjoy "a pleasant numbness" (Bergman 1973a, p. 60). Her eight-year-old boy Henrik, who has a cold, comes to her room to tell her about the murder of Martin Luther King during the night. We note Anna's momentary pang of discomfort before she sinks back into idle self-satisfaction. When Henrik asks to share her bed, she bluntly refuses him. Later Andreas notes that there is a lack of tenderness in his marriage, except for some fleeting moments during sex. This lack is also extended to the children, who "get all the fucking vitamins they should have, but no physical affection" (Bergman 1973a, p. 84).

What follows are glimpses from the lives of Anna and Andreas, two seemingly successful and happy people in a bourgeois family. Anna meets with her alcoholic brother, Albert, who is in a psychiatric hospital suffering from delirium. He is wearing make-up and we learn that he likes to dress up in women's clothing. After

---

* All quotes from the opening monologues of *The Lie* are from Bergman 1973a, p. 59.

his doomsday speech about the world being ruled by lies and destruction, Anna departs. She goes to a university library, where she is confronted by a bitter and angry colleague attacking her for being too beautiful, mannered and well-spoken. Her errands end in an apartment "in a quiet street" (Bergman 1973a, p. 70), where she meets her lover and neighbour, the cynical and distant Elis.

At the department, Andreas learns that his project proposal has been rejected and that he has been replaced by two younger colleagues. For the rest of his working day he is busy with unfruitful and rather pointless meetings.* On his way home he has an unpleasant incident with an angry stranger in the street, which leaves him upset. He makes a desperate visit to his doctor, but only Nurse Ester is on duty. She is forthcoming, and Andreas soon pours out all his anxieties of living a false and empty life. Afterwards he goes to a bar and writes a letter to Anna about everything he finds to be wrong about their marriage, but we never see him deliver it to her.

In the evening a few days later, Andreas and Anna are invited to a big dinner at a neighbour's house. Anna learns that Elis is going away for two months with his wife Eva and his secretary, who might also be his new mistress. Back home, Andreas comes to Anna's room in the middle of the night. He wants to confess that he has had a brief affair with Nurse Ester and talk about his longing for another kind of relationship, more truthful and intimate. Anna hesitates but then tells him about her eight-year-long affair with Elis. Their conversation ends in a quarrel and an ugly violent fight. In the closing image their future together is uncertain, as Anna suddenly says: "I don't want to. No, I don't want to" (Bergman 1973a, p. 99).

Anna and Andreas in *The Lie* are nothing like their namesakes in *A Passion*, but appear to have more in common with the other couple in that film, Eva and Elis Vergérus. They are successful, wealthy, modern, smug, carefree and comfortably numb, troubled only by the brief but alarming glimpses of the outside world. We are far away from the religious questions that haunt Bergman's characters in the 1950s and early 1960s.

The spiritual 'sanctuary' of Thomas's church rituals in *Winter Light* has been replaced by a profane one. This is signalled in the opening of the play when Anna emphatically turns off a religious sermon on the radio to enjoy the sensual

---

* The satire of the bureaucrats' self-importance and inefficiency at these meetings has much in common with Strindberg's portrait of the ridiculous government officials in his novel *The Red Room* (*Röda rummet*; see Strindberg 1879).

pleasures of dozing off in bed. Still, the closed-off world of the Fromms rests on the brittle foundation of the bourgeois family and its social conventions, upheld by lies.

The narcissistic and hedonistic Anna in *The Lie* is an inversion of Anna in *A Passion* in that she lives her lie with open eyes, even loving it. Her character is clearly inspired by Marianne Höök, and several of the play's smartest lines – like Andreas talking about how the children get all the necessary vitamins but no affection – could have been taken right out of an article by her. Like Isak Borg in *Wild Strawberries*, Anna Fromm is a product of the cold womb, uncaring for the ones who love her – the needy son, the infantile husband – and only in love with the one colder and more calculating than herself: Elis, who in Erland Josephson's persona is identical to his namesake in *A Passion*.

Andreas comes out as the weaker one, both as a Strindberg-Darwinian loser in the power struggle between the classes and genders and as an Ibsenian case of self-deceiving idealism. As soon as he wakes up in the morning and "in all modesty enjoys being Andreas Fromm" (Bergman 1973a, p. 61), we know that this smug self-theatricalisation will eventually lead to his downfall. Sure enough, at work he is outmanoeuvred by two younger colleagues, although we sense that there might be some truth to the management's assessment of his architectural designs as outmoded – which in turn is a euphemism for his lack of talent. At home, he is outmanoeuvred by his neighbour Elis, who is more skilled in satisfying Anna's sexual needs.

When his world of illusions is finally crushed, he reaches out to the ones who have assisted in its downfall – his boss, his colleagues, his wife – failing to see that it is his own doing by living a lie. Bergman's swapping of gender masks now becomes apparent; Andreas is designated the role traditionally reserved for women in melodramas and soap operas: that of the trusty, faithful, boring and naïve wife. With only slight adjustments to the plot and by changing his gender, he could easily be the female protagonist in a 1950s Douglas Sirk film.

Andreas is not only Anna's inferior in the gender power game; there are also indications of him being of working-class origin. One is, of course, that he is at a loss in the social games of his betters, both at work and at home as noted above. Another is the confrontation with the angry working-class man, who triggers him to take his marriage to task. Furthermore, he only gets sympathy from the play's working-class women: his secretary Miss Prakt and Nurse Ester at the clinic. Along with Berta, they are the silent witnesses to the fall of the Fromms.

Figs. 5 & 6: Living a lie. Andreas Fromm (Per Myrberg) and Anna Fromm (Gunnel Lindblom) in *The Lie* (1970). (© Sveriges Television AB)

Anna, on the other hand, has all the traits of a privileged male: money, success, looks, the envy of others and the possibilities of an international career. In a scene that seemingly has nothing to do with the plot, she visits her brother at the psychiatric hospital. Albert is an author, one of Bergman's effeminate artists. His place in the drama is to represent Anna's repressed female principle. Like Dr King, whose "I have a dream" speech on love and equality is faintly heard on the radio in the opening of the play, Albert's warnings of a world heading for disaster are an inner voice that gives her "a dizzy feeling of sickness" before the 'sanctuary' of her carefree everyday life comes to the rescue.

Anna's colleague Karin is yet another messenger from the repressed depths of her mind. Karin's unkempt hair, plain looks and ordinary clothes stand in stark contrast to the dashing Anna in her costly outfit, elegant make-up and hairdo. Karin talks about her impulse to hit Anna because of her perfect exterior – her beautiful face, clothes and her unfailing ability "to always say the right things" (Bergman 1973a, p. 69). As they part, Karin shows her ugly teeth to Anna and says they are like that because of laziness, reminding us of the opening shot of Anna's laziness both in mind and in body.

By the time of the closing scene in the early morning hours, both Anna and Andreas have been through pangs of existential angst and incidents of humiliation and shame. The violent ending is a striking contrast to the controlled manners they both have shown previously. It is as if their agents of repressed feelings – the angry working-class man in Andreas's case and Karin in Anna's – have finally surfaced. The quarrel is undoubtedly inspired by Edward Albee's play *Who's Afraid of Virginia Woolf?* – staged in 1963 by Bergman at Dramaten – when Anna and Andreas trade hurtful remarks, insults, moments of tenderness and physical assaults. Looking back, it is a rehearsal for the more (in)famous marital battle between Peter and Katarina in the first episode of *Scenes from a Marriage*.

Hints of Andreas's origins in a lower class than Anna lend something of Strindberg's *Miss Julie* to the finale as we note the condescending tone in Anna's attitude. Her comforting "My dearest, my dearest Andreas" is all theatrical, to which Andreas responds with irony: "Do not lower yourself in your boundless generosity and positive outlook on life." Anna retreats, "looks at her husband with cold eyes" and suggests that they have a sandwich, perhaps in the hope that the numbing comfort of their delusional life has the repressive power to shut out this unpleasant intrusion of true feelings and insights (Bergman 1973a, p. 98).

Even more striking are the similarities to Strindberg's *The Father* (*Fadren*) from 1887, for instance in the fragile patriarch's jealousy, violence, loss of self-esteem and ultimate mental breakdown. The corresponding scene to Captain Adolf's throwing of the lamp at Laura that marks his fall is Andreas's axe attack on the bedroom door – incidentally, a moment taken from Sjöström's *The Phantom Carriage* – and his subsequent beating of Anna. Like Strindberg's tragic protagonist, Andreas's 'sanctuary' collapses when he learns about his wife's true nature and feelings. Andreas's line "I am not even sure that I am the children's father" (Bergman 1973a, p. 97) mirrors the central question in Strindberg's play. Not only has he lost his social position at work, now his family might no longer be his.

The Lie – staged by Jan Molander with perhaps a few suggestions from Bergman – emphasises this association with Strindberg's play by using Gunnel Lindblom as Anna Fromm.* She played the captain's wilful and scheming wife Laura in Alf Sjöberg's 1969 film version of *The Father*, and her Anna Fromm is strikingly similar. Sjöberg was a mentor and teacher to both Bergman and Molander, and most likely Bergman wrote the play and then Molander staged it under the influence of Sjöberg's film and Lindblom's powerful creation of Laura.†

After the dialogue above, Anna has a short monologue about her ability to take care of herself and her children which echoes Laura in *The Father*. Andreas is now at a loss for words to respond and just lets out a meek "I do not know how it will be without you". Anna shakes her head "as if to silence him and stop him humiliating himself". When Andreas wonders how she feels, she responds: "It hurts" and then "I don't want to. No, I don't want to." Andreas wants to know what it is that she does not want, and the play ends with: "She does not respond, but keeps looking at him. He is about to say something, but hesitates" (Bergman 1973a, p. 99).

The lingering question is, of course, what Anna says no to. Her marriage? A divorce? In the TV show that followed the 1971 rerun, Bergman eventually gave in and made a few comments on the meaning of his work.‡ He had a bad prognosis of the marriage and declared Anna to be the stronger one – robust, brutal and ruthless enough to survive in the real world. She can take care of herself and her children but rejects the infantile Andreas. He concluded that she in the closing image sees Andreas for what he really is and finds him to be a complete stranger. Her life begins with her "no".

However, Bergman's assertions are unconvincing since there are elements of the play that contradict his reading. We learn, for instance, that Anna has been angry with Andreas because of his conventionality. Yet her relationship with Elis never suggests anything that breaks with marital conformity.

Rather, Anna and Elis act as the proverbial old couple. Their affair is utterly mundane and passionless, reflected in the bland apartment where they meet. When they finally get down to sex, Bergman's dry prose hardly stirs any hormones in the reader. Instead, Bergman inserts a discomfort in Anna that we associate

---

* Jan Molander made his film debut as an actor in Alf Sjöberg's *Frenzy* (*Hets*, 1944). Bergman wrote the script and was the film's assistant director. Molander later became one of the pioneering TV play directors in Sweden. He also worked in radio theatre, and was the head of Sveriges Radio's radio theatre department from 1969 to 1972; see Forslund 2003, pp. 278–294.

† *The Father* was Sjöberg's last film. He worked at the Royal Dramatic Theatre from his early days as an actor in the 1920s, then from 1930 until his death in 1980 (caused by a traffic accident on his way to work) as a director.

‡ *Kvällsöppet*, 9 April 1971.

with untold nightmares and daytime clashes with people who remind her of a chaotic world outside her 'sanctuary':

> Anna removes the bedspread and draws the curtains. There is a mild semi-twilight. She casts off her bathrobe and crawls into bed, lying there while watching Elis get undressed. When nude, he takes a sip of tea. Anna listens to this. The vague fear from the dreams of the night and the experiences of the day comes back. (Bergman 1973a, p. 74)

Furthermore, it is Andreas, not Anna, who has second thoughts about their family life in material affluence and emotional starvation. He talks about it at length in the scene with Nurse Ester at the clinic. Later in the bar, he describes it as a travesty when writing the letter to Anna that he never delivers (Bergman 1973a, pp. 82–85). Andreas is the one who initiates the talk about their inauthentic life, taking it to the point where he sees no other way out of their situation than a divorce. In fact, she is a complete stranger to him, while he is utterly transparent to her.

Anna does not want to get a divorce. On the contrary, she suggests that they postpone all further plans for a divorce while she goes away on a university grant for six months. Her only reason for staying married during her eight-year love affair with Elis is also utterly conventional: "I belonged to you" (Bergman 1973a, p. 95). Bearing that in mind, the final chord of Anna's "no" as her call for liberty and self-fulfilment rings false and this is confirmed by her disturbed look. It is in every way contrary to Nora's emphatically repeated "no" to the bourgeois family at the end of *A Doll's House*.

To sum up the play in accordance with Toril Moi's modernist scheme for Ibsen's plays, it begins with two metatheatrical monologues that emphasise the protagonists' self-theatricalisation. Love is destroyed at the end by this theatricality and the protagonists' mutual scepticism. Marriage is the central theme, but here the everyday is not an alternative to scepticism since it is imbued with what little remains of idealism. If that is what Anna says no to in her final line, then it might be a starting point for a new and possibly more authentic life, though her hearty embracement of living a lie throughout the play suggests the contrary.

SCENES FROM A MARRIAGE

In his second depiction of family life in Djursholm, Bergman continues the project from *The Lie*. It is a world close to the one in Ibsen's *Hedda Gabler* and other late works by Ibsen as described by Toril Moi: "Without the utopian energy of radical idealism, everyday life in modernity becomes incapable of generating meaning, energy, passion or hope" (2006, p. 319). However, the roles and shifting balances of power between Bergman's married protagonists are now more complex.

The married couple is Johan (Erland Josephson) and Marianne (Liv Ullmann) and the series' main reference is Henrik Ibsen's *A Doll's House*, which is discussed by the protagonists at the end of episode two. This time, Bergman downplays the presence of a class society to a minimum to make the protagonists representative of ordinary people. In *The Lie*, every household has a housekeeper, the reminder of nineteenth-century bourgeois Sweden fading away in the 1960s society of increasing class equality. There is also a hint of class differences in the final showdown between Anna and Andreas.

Three years later, in *Scenes from a Marriage*, all class markers are gone. The only clues to the social standing of Johan and Marianne are the dinner with married business partners Peter (Jan Malmsjö) and Katarina (Bibi Andersson) and some references to high society friends in episode one. We learn, for instance, that they have an invitation to "Egerman's at Högsätra" – Högsätra possibly being a countryside mansion – a line that will be repeated as a class reference in *Face to Face*. Other than that, their world looks like the abstract middle-class world that has dominated mainstream cinema and soap opera around the globe for the most part of motion picture and TV history. In a way, Johan and Marianne are the everyman and everywoman in a soap opera that consciously deconstructs the genre by ending in the joy of divorce and extramarital sex.[*]

The protagonists' home is "nice and tasteful but not expensively furnished", just like in Ibsen's play, and the two spouses seem perfectly matched.[†] Both of them are of the opinion that their marriage is nothing less than ideal, and their circle of friends agree. In *Scenes from a Marriage* the 'sanctuary' is even more narrowly defined, as the innermost circle of husband and wife in the bourgeois family.

There is a political satire at the heart of *Scenes from a Marriage*, since there are hints that the world it presents might be a snapshot from the future of the radical generation of 1968 turning old, grey and conservative. That could possibly explain the odd timeline, where the protagonists age ten years over the course of the series but largely remain the same – and so does their world.[‡] In episode two they recall their days as young radicals, when Johan with both nostalgia and a touch of irony describes Marianne as "sweet and ill-tempered" and "terribly attractive as a socialist". Bergman notes in the foreword to the screenplay that

> Johan and Marianne are children of fixed norms and the ideology of material security. They have never seen their bourgeois life style as oppressive or false. They have conformed to a pattern that they are ready to pass on. Their previous political activity is a confirmation rather than a contradiction of this. (Bergman 1973b, p. 5)

As with many in the New Left of the 1960s, Johan and Marianne are children of the bourgeoisie who, as Johan describes, "had the pleasure of annoying our

---

[*] When creating American TV soap *Dallas* in 1978, writer David Jacobs was inspired to break with the romanticism and happy ending formula by *Scenes from a Marriage*; see Bloom 2012.

[†] Quote from the very first sentence in Ibsen's *A Doll's House*, describing the interiors of Nora and Helmer's home; see Ibsen 1971, p. 197.

[‡] They have supposedly been married for ten years when the series starts, and at the end of it twenty years has gone by since their wedding but only seven years since Johan was last at the summer cottage. If this was the time when he told her about his elopement with Paula, three years are missing. But then some years pass between episode one and five, in which Johan is about to be forty-five years old – he was forty-two in episode one (Marianne was thirty-five). Still, there is a gap between the wedding and the birth of their daughters, who are eleven and twelve in episode one. Perhaps they were born out of wedlock. Even so, something is strange about the chronology since Marianne was supposedly only nineteen when they met. The confusing chronology also affects when we are in time in episode six: in 1975 or even further into the future from 1973? For this reason or maybe for reasons of censorship about children born out of wedlock, the French version moved back their wedding in episode one by three years.

Fig. 7: Metatheatrical staging: *Scenes from a Marriage* (1973). Johan (Erland Josephson), Marianne (Liv Ullmann) and the reporter Mrs. Palm (Anita Wall). (© Cinematograph AB)

parents". Sexual and political passions seem to go hand in hand, and when the latter come to a halt and even go into reverse, so does the love life. They are youth rebels that have regressed into becoming spitting images of their conservative parents. Nothing is changed, and correspondingly the world looks much the same during the twenty years since their marriage.

The same applies to the cancelled sexual revolution. After a short but bitter quarrel about the lack of sparks between the sheets, Johan makes some sexual advances but is promptly rejected. When in bed a few minutes later, Marianne says that he may have sex with her if he wants to. Her dispassionate, not to say ridiculously formal, offer is met by his equally formal thanks but no thanks before bidding her goodnight.

Most scenes in the first three episodes have a distinct theatrical quality, as if Johan and Marianne were marionettes mouthing lines rehearsed from a script rather than speaking from their heart. Bergman emphasises this by using a static camera, in front of which the actors perform. The opening scene of Johan and Marianne posing with their two daughters (whom we never see again) for some photographs for a glossy women's magazine is doubly metafilmic. We note that they are not only posing for the magazine's camera but also for Bergman's when we hear the director's familiar voice from behind the camera giving instructions to both the protagonists and the journalist. His voice also introduces episodes two to six of the series.

After the opening scene in episode one follows a metatheatrical interview in which Johan and Marianne in accordance with instructions from the journalist are expected to present themselves as the perfect bourgeois family: successful, happy, healthy and 'normal' (= conformist). Johan's self-congratulatory ravings about all his virtues as a husband and lover make him into an overwrought idealist patriarch much like the satirically portrayed Helmer in Ibsen's play. There is simply no way Johan can live up to his self-aggrandising persona.

He is perfectly matched by Marianne's self-effacing display of sacrifice when defining herself in one sentence only: "I am married to Johan and have two daughters." The only cloud on the horizon seems to be that, in Marianne's words, "the lack of problems in itself is a serious problem" – words that can only come from the 'sanctuary' of the wealthy Western world.

They round off by summarising their respective worldviews. The more cynical Johan aggressively upholds his right to live a secure life in the 'sanctuary' of the family by paraphrasing Voltaire's *Candide*: "The world goes to hell and I am in my rights to cultivate my garden." Marianne nurses an abstract and non-committal humanism: "I believe in a human feeling." Their performances verge on caricature, possibly an influence of Bergman's third household god besides Strindberg and Ibsen: Molière. Close to caricatures are also their matching opposites Peter and Katarina, the dinner guests from hell in one of the most memorable scenes in the series.

Even more than Anna and Andreas Fromm in the final scenes of *The Lie*, Peter and Katarina recall George and Martha in *Who's Afraid of Virginia Woolf?* – right down to Katarina's sexual humiliation of Peter. It is, of course, an omen of what lies beneath Johan and Marianne's 'perfect marriage' and by extension the bourgeois idealism imprinted on them. This "tangle of lies", as it is called by Karin in *Cries and Whispers*, will rise to the surface with a vengeance in episode five.

Formally, *Scenes from a Marriage* is a drama of two people and they both get their share of individual scenes, but while Johan stays in caricature mode, Marianne grows into a more complete human being. Earlier, I described a scene in episode two where Johan is visibly hurt by his colleague Eva's (Gunnel Lindblom) criticism of his poetry as bland and indifferent.* Up until then we would never have guessed that he wrote poetry, and this possible key to his emotional life stays hidden as we never hear or see a word of his writing.

Moreover, we never meet his mistress Paula nor his parents. It is not only Eva and Marianne who in episode six note that he has become shrunken. By then, we the viewers also realise that we have hardly learned anything about him.

At most, Johan borrows some traits of Bergman and his friends. The scene in which Eva criticises Johan's poetry, for instance, was partly inspired by Harry

---

* See "Part Three. Bergman's Modernism".

Schein's scathing review of Bergman's marriage comedy *A Lesson in Love*, partly by Bergman's dreams of becoming a recognised author and in part also by Marianne Höök's shattered hopes of becoming a recognised poet.[*] However, Johan is mostly what feminists say of many women in men's fiction: a stereotype projection and sounding board for the protagonist. See for instance his long, blunt and tiring anti-feminist tirade punctured by Marianne's ironical comments in episode two. During the series, he does not change significantly. He merely shrinks from life altogether.

Correspondingly, Marianne rises from being almost a non-person to become the most memorable character of the series. Therefore, the female is the one who takes the position as the representative of the universal human, not the male.

Marianne is a familiar name in the Bergman filmography and the character is described in his workbook for *A Lesson in Love* as "strong and independent, even downright wilful. Resolutely female in her responses, resolutely faithful until the day she realises the betrayal" (Koskinen 2002, p. 243). That might be true of Eva Dahlbeck's 'Battleship Womanhood' persona in that film, but not of the Marianne (Ingrid Thulin) in *Wild Strawberries*, nor the, at first, vulnerable Marianne of *Scenes from a Marriage*. The Marianne of *Scenes from a Marriage* will be a mix of the other two: at the beginning the *Wild Strawberries* take and at the end more of the *A Lesson in Love* variety.

Despite being described in the opening interview of *Scenes from a Marriage* as quick-tempered, the first four episodes present Marianne as selfless, supportive, timid, indulgent and even submissive. She is very much the exemplary idealist woman – the one Karin Bergman was modelled to be and whom Bergman depicted, played by Maj-Britt Nilsson, in *To Joy* (*Till glädje*, 1950) with added inspiration from his second wife Ellen Bergman (Bergman 1988, p. 159). What we hear and see in episode three, when Johan comes to the summer house to tell Marianne that he is leaving her for his new mistress Paula (incidentally a student of Slavic languages, just as Anna is in *The Lie*), is, according to Bergman (1988, p. 161), a replication of his own departure from Ellen.

We must wait until episode four for Marianne to come into her own by way of trying to find words to articulate the ideological imprint of her upbringing, always anxious to please, always being the one others want her to be. One could say that she writes herself into her own life, refusing to play an extra. The pictures from Liv Ullmann's childhood shown when she reflects on her background for

---

[*] Regarding Bergman's dreams of being an author, see Koskinen 2002, p. 307. A selection of Marianne Höök's poems is published in Höök 2008, pp. 775–781.

Johan suggest that her story might be Ullmann's own, but it also has very much in common with Marianne Höök's background.*

Some stills from Erland Josephson's early years are also included, indicating that Johan shared the same imprint. If so, he apparently does not take Marianne's story to heart. At the end of the episode, Bergman breaks momentarily from his rigid static camera technique to do a whip pan, revealing Johan sound asleep. A symbolic indication of his intellectual and emotional indolence, therefore his inability to evolve into a living human being in the full sense of the word.

In the fifth episode, the power balance shifts and Marianne becomes the Strindbergian stronger of the two. Although Johan abuses her in his office in episode five, this only confirms his loss of control over her. Defeated and humiliated by his final downfall as father, husband and patriarch, he signs the divorce papers she brought. In the final episode, it is she who initiates their renewed love relation.

Enjoying the pleasures of sexual freedom, she surprises both Johan and the audience by confessing some affairs with other men during the early years of their marriage. Also, she talks unashamedly about her intimate life with her new husband, who apparently is something of a sex athlete. These revelations seem to be at odds with Marianne's persona at the beginning of the series, but possibly Bergman wants us to see that the new Marianne is just the return of her former self, repressed by marriage. Marianne is based on Ellen Bergman in episodes one to three, then she transforms into Marianne Höök in episodes four to six.

In episode two we learned that she is the good bourgeois wife and the good and obedient daughter to her mother, as she cannot muster the strength to break with her mother's ritual Sunday dinner. Now, in episode six, she can finally get a grip on the repressive legacy by discussing her parents' sex life with her mother. Unsurprisingly, it is a story of the nineteenth-century idealist legacy of sex as duty, not profane pleasure, passing down through generations of women in the family. A bland life symbolised by the bland colour scheme of the film. With *Scenes from a Marriage*, Bergman finally mastered the technique of colour film.

---

* See Höök 2008, pp. 813–824, the text for a radio programme she made in 1964.

LIFE IN THE BEIGE LANE

Initially, Ingmar Bergman and cinematographer Sven Nykvist found colour film to be problematic. Like Alfred Hitchcock, Bergman got his early impression of colour from nineteenth-century stage lighting techniques and lantern slide shows. That colour symbolism influenced the tinting and toning of silent film and for a long time also in the colour sound film (Yumibe 2015, p. 35). Colours were often used for various physical conditions and/or psychological connotations, though silent film historians have cautioned about simplifying the practices (Usai 2000, pp. 23–27). Colour practices vary between nations and filmmakers, but there is a discernible pattern in the use of some primary colours.

Bergman's economic use of colour, making a few highlighted splashes of colour really matter, is possibly inspired by Hitchcock. Likely, he had read his British colleague's essay "Direction", originally published in 1937 and then republished in several anthologies and magazines (see Hitchcock 1937, p. 258). There are also numerous comments by Hitchcock on the use of colour in interviews published over the years (Chabrol 1954, p. 40).

At the start, however, the use of colour film did not seem to become Ingmar Bergman and Sven Nykvist. After studying other directors' use of the technique for years (Höök 1962, p. 167), their first attempt, *All These Women* (*För att inte tala om alla dessa kvinnor*, 1964; aka *Now About These Women*), was an outright fiasco. Bergman concluded, "I'll never use color again!" (Archer 1967).

When finally getting the courage to try again with *A Passion*, Nykvist recalled that Bergman wanted to do a "black-and-white film with some intense shades in a rigorously restrained colour scheme". Nykvist was of great help, having learned from John Huston's instructions to the film laboratorians how to manipulate the colours (Nykvist 1997, p. 103). The Fårö landscape was particularly suitable for their experiments "since it did not have much colour" (1997, p. 102).

Still, *A Passion* had to be processed at the laboratory for colour correction because "the images threatened to be too beautiful and brilliant" (ibid.). Bergman struggled with getting what he wanted in natural settings and light:

> We tried to get the landscape to look as it really does. You know yourself what it's like to shoot in colour in sunlight; how the colour can take on a sort of musical-comedy effect. It was a hell of a job to get the sun to function as I wanted it to. For example, there is no blue in the entire film. It all goes in greys, browns and greens. And then, this red scene [i.e. when Andreas and Eva meet in the sunset]. (Björkman et al. 1973, p. 264)

The Touch has a more conventional and beautified colour scheme as late summer turns into autumn and winter during the course of the story. Compared to the films and TV productions Bergman made before and after, its style is overall more mainstream, suggesting that he wanted to appeal to a wider, international audience. But even here there are interesting uses of colour, such as red, as seen in various garments worn by Bibi Andersson's character (a coat, a trouser suit, a sweater). Red comes back to dominate *Cries and Whispers*.

In contrast, the palette of his two TV series – *Scenes from a Marriage* and *Face to Face* – is dominated by sombre shades of blue, green, brown and, notably, beige. These are all colours associated with the profane, marking his continued departure from religious symbolism after the making of *Winter Light* (Pavey 2009, p. 63; Sjöman 1963, p. 219). But as we shall see, there are notable splashes of bright green, yellow and red at crucial points in the two series.

Before Johan and Marianne's role play finally breaks down in episode five to a showdown even more violent and crude than that between Peter and Katarina, Bergman uses colour to paint a picture of an alternative nightmare: what if Johan and Marianne manage to keep up the charade for so long that their masks get stuck to their faces – that is, they live in the "happily ever after" of the glossy magazine's design? By washing out most of the colours in the lab processing of the film and by the careful use of production design, costumes and make-up, he makes the de-beautified images suggest the drabness of the protagonists' lives in the first three episodes. The drab colour of preference – beige – dominates the

Fig. 8: Marianne's glimpse of a possible future self: Mrs. Jacoby (Barbro Hiort af Ornäs).
Scenes from a Marriage.
(© Cinematograph AB)

colour scheme of *Scenes from a Marriage* and *Face to Face*. Virtually everything Liv Ullmann's protagonists in the series wear is beige in various nuances. Even the house Marianne lives in is beige.

A possible future Marianne is represented by Mrs Jacobi (Barbro Hiort af Ornäs) in the second episode of the TV version. The grey-haired, black-clothed and soft-spoken woman has come to the lawyer's office where Marianne works to file for a divorce after more than twenty years of marriage. Mrs Jacobi has no serious complaints about her marriage. Her husband is good and they have lived a life in comfort and security. But already from the start in the marriage she found that she had no love for her spouse, nor did she feel any love for the children.

After talking with her husband, she agreed to stay out of duty until the children had grown up. Now she has finally become Nora in *A Doll's House*, rejecting her designated role as wife and mother to become a free individual. But she has done it late in life.

When reflecting on her state of mind, Mrs Jacobi feels that there is love somewhere deep inside her, locked in a small room. Now, her inner life does not in any way correspond with the life she lives. Senses have dulled. She is detached from the sensations of life. While she describes her condition, Bergman pans down to make a close-up of her hands. Then as the meaning fully penetrates Marianne, resonating with feelings within herself, Bergman makes a whip pan from Mrs Jacobi's hands to Marianne's shocked face. The words have touched Marianne deeply.

Mrs Jacobi is not only a future Marianne, she also resembles Bergman's previous representations of living death in the shape of older women such as the dying Mrs

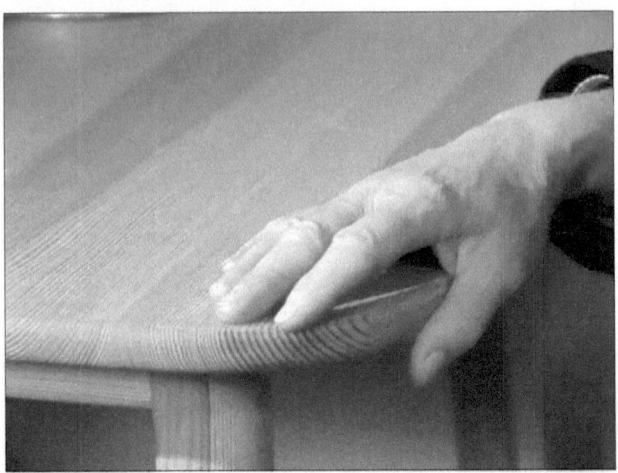

Fig. 9: Dulled senses. *Scenes from a Marriage*. (© Cinematograph AB)

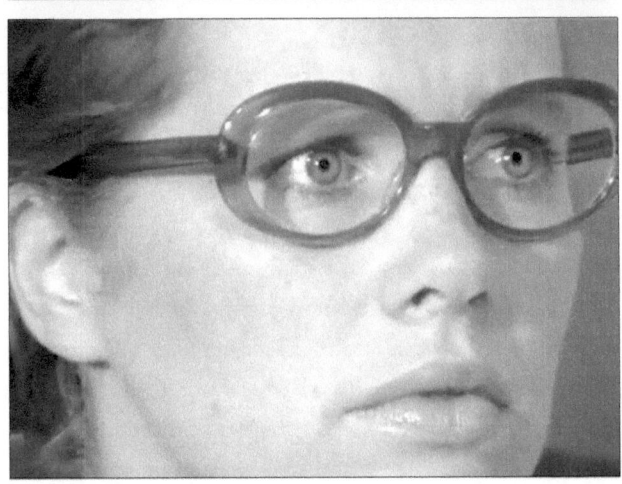

Fig. 10: Marianne's shocking insight. *Scenes from a Marriage*. (© Cinematograph AB)

Calwagen (Mimi Pollak) in *Summer Interlude* and the old and cold Mrs Borg, Isak's mother in *Wild Strawberries*.* Her story is close to Marianne Höök's fear of what she called "petrification", a condition in which all feelings are lost: "There is nothing left of the bleeding core" (Kullenberg 2009, p. 340).

This also echoes Isak Borg's nightmare in *Wild Strawberries* when Mr Alman declares that all painful memories have been surgically removed, leaving "nothing

---

*   Anna Calwagen was Ingmar Bergman's maternal grandmother's maiden name. The "cold womb" motif is more expressively elaborated in the character of Mrs Borg (Naima Wifstrand) in *Wild Strawberries*. There we also note Marianne's (Ingrid Thulin) concerned observation of her throughout the scene, suggesting the procreation of death might be a family trait continuing with Marianne herself.

that bleeds or trembles".* Moreover, Mrs Jacobi is Karin Bergman, considering divorcing her husband after her duties as a mother have been fulfilled. But there is still hope for Mrs Jacobi. A small sign of her possible rejuvenation is visible in the bright yellow scarf popping up from the neckline of her black coat.

Green is another colour of significance. Green was the colour of the velvet sofa where he was punished as a child, hence a place of horror (Sjöman 1963, p. 161). In *Scenes from a Marriage*, a green velvet sofa is where the family portrait is taken at the beginning of the series. The sofa returns in episode four as the place where Marianne digs into her past to settle the account of her upbringing. Green is also the colour of their family car, a Volvo estate favoured by many Swedish families at the time and prominent in many American films as a signifier of family safety and conformity. In magic lantern and silent film tinting, green was often used to signify ghostly apparitions and madness. Here, green is then associated with the bourgeois family as a deranged institution of the past haunting the present.†

Red is used by Bergman to indicate love and passion. The final scene in episode one features a big all-red kitchen lamp prominently framed and glowing reassuringly during Johan and Marianne's self-congratulatory talk about their perfect marriage while cleaning up after the terrible dinner with Peter and Katarina. When the kitchen lamp comes back at the end of episode two the context is different. We have now witnessed cracks of existential anxiety in the scenes of Eva's devastating review of Johan's poetry and Marianne's disturbing meeting with Mrs Jacobi.

In the following scene, Johan has crushed Marianne's dreams of a romantic trip abroad. Back home after an evening at the theatre, watching *A Doll's House*, Johan voices a long, bitter and bluntly sexist monologue that begins by declaring Ibsen's play old-fashioned since "Now women can do whatever they please. Sadly, though, they are too lazy." His torrent of sarcastic clichés on the topic is occasionally punctured by Marianne's ironic comments.

The static camera looks down a narrow hallway leading into the most intimate rooms in the house: the bathroom and the bedroom. Wearing nightclothes, Johan and Marianne pop in and out of the rooms, performing before the camera like in an old bedroom farce. It is another example of Bergman's metatheatrical strategies

---

* When waking up, Isak Borg declares that his dreams want to tell him something he does not want to hear: that he is dead, although still alive.

† This is how Hitchcock used green in the scene in *Vertigo* (1958) where Judy steps out of the bathroom remodelled as the dead Madeleine. Captured in soft focus and bathed in an eerie green light from a neon sign, we see Madeleine through Scottie's eyes as someone who has come back from the dead.

and one in which the protagonists' self-theatricalisation comes to the fore. When they leave for the kitchen, the two doors in the hallway are left opposite to one another, closing off the respective rooms from each other as a sign of Johan's and Marianne's inability to talk frankly with each other about their more intimate problems.

In the kitchen, the glowing red lamp reminds us of the false marital bliss of episode one. But now it is at the edge of the frame, indicating the waning of love in Johan and Marianne's relationship. His angry misogynist speech about women's intellectual and biological shortcomings could have been lifted right out of a play or an article by Strindberg, while Marianne's sarcastic rejoinders sound more like Ibsen's ironic takes on idealism. Bergman underscores the series' message: that we have come practically nowhere from the nineteenth-century doll's house.

Yellow signifies love and life revitalised, at least for Marianne, in the three final episodes. When episode four opens, some time has passed. Johan comes back to the family house, where Marianne and the children still live. While we recognise most of the interiors, some things have changed. There are yellow lamps in the hall, living room and kitchen, and yellow wallpaper indicating that life has begun anew for Marianne. Her hairstyle is different, looser and more youthful. We soon learn that she has a new lover, David. Johan, who so far has been dressed in dull grey and beige colours, now appears in a blue suit, preparing Marianne and us for his confession that his love for Paula has cooled.

Episode five takes place in Johan's impersonal office at the university's Institution of Psychotechnology and gives us a premonition of the self-delusion and rage that lurk beneath his controlled façade. We will be reacquainted with this trait of character when meeting Johan's psychiatrist colleague in *Face to Face*, the protagonist Jenny. Johan's room is all white and beige. It is undecorated and only has a desk with two chairs, and a small couch in the same sombre grey-blue tone as his clothes. He has almost become part of the furniture.

On his bookshelf two red binders seem lost in a sea of blue ones, a sign of his fading love life, and this is soon confirmed in words by Johan himself. The chill in his heart is heavily underscored by him having a cold. Marianne is dressed in beige as usual, but she has a gold and red scarf in her hair indicating her new and more colourful life. She is also notably lively and cheerful in contrast to the grumpy Johan.

They make love or, rather, Marianne seduces Johan for her own pleasure – the camera is fixed on her face, her pleasures. We see almost nothing of Johan. But the context of lovemaking in this naked room of cold colours tells us that the act is far from intimate. It is part of the couple's bitter power game, which will soon turn ugly. At the end of the episode, another representation of red comes in the form of blood running from Marianne's nose after Johan has beaten her. All their repressed feelings from the seemingly perfect married life in episode one have finally surfaced in mutual contempt: her manipulation, his brutality.[*]

The final episode takes place "a few years" after their divorce, more precisely at the twentieth anniversary of their wedding (Bergman 1973b, p. 165). Marianne still wears beige clothes, but she has a colourful scarf in gold and red on her head – the same as in episode five? – at her mother's (Wenche Foss) apartment. The old woman is dressed in black. Is she perhaps a resigned version of Mrs Jacobi?[†] Later, we meet with Johan, who breaks up a tired on-off affair with his colleague Eva. He wears a black sweater, an early sign of his petrification.

Here, Bergman make an amusing comment on the different conditions of Johan's and Marianne's new lives by way of their cars. She drives a shiny Volvo P1800ES, a family version of the sports car associated with glamour and action TV series *The Saint* (1962–69). We are not surprised to find that she lives with a man successful both in his career and in bed. Johan, however, drives an old, worn and rusty Volvo PV544. Still, they have one thing in common: both cars are blue, reflecting the cool emotions in their respective marriages.

The new arena for their resumed relationship is nothing like a doll's house. Like Nora finds freedom in her everyday clothes, Johan and Marianne's modest love nest in the cramped and untidy cottage echoes their now modest love ambitions. Marianne wears a red sweater, later a red nightgown. Over their small dinner table shines a bright yellow paper moon.

True romance or, perhaps, just another 'sanctuary' – a comfortable illusion, as in the jazz classic "It's Only a Paper Moon"?[‡] That we will never know. The series ends in the middle of the night, when Marianne wakes up from a disturbing nightmare, in which she cannot reach Johan because her arms have been cut off.

---

[*] Note that not all manipulative seductions in Bergman's works are the design of women. For example, in *Sawdust and Tinsel* theatre actor Frans (Hasse Ekman) uses seduction to humiliate Anne (Harriet Andersson).

[†] In her home, we witness the last remains of the old class society as the mother clearly has a housekeeper of her own (though the housekeeper remains unseen).

[‡] The song was written in 1933 by Harold Arlen and has been recorded by many artists, for example Nat King Cole, Frank Sinatra and Marvin Gaye. A verse from the song was famously used by Tennessee Williams in his play *A Streetcar Named Desire* (1947). Incidentally, Peter Bogdanovich's *Paper Moon* – another film about people chasing a dream – was released in 1973.

Ibsen's *A Doll's House* aimed to be more than feminist propaganda – Ibsen called its message humanist – but it was certainly received as an outright call for feminism (Moi 2008, pp. 229–230). Bergman likely anticipated the same with his series, and therefore ended with a riddle, just as he had done in *The Lie*. Thereby, he also suggested that the struggle for Marianne, as well as for Anna Fromm, was far from over. They were, after all, both products of an old and perverse social order that continued to haunt them. This ghost of the past was to be the subject of his next production, the feature film *Cries and Whispers*.

CRIES AND WHISPERS: INTO THE BELLY OF THE IDEALISM BEAST

> Presently, I am reading a female author named Germaine Greer. She has written an entertaining book called *The Female Eunuch*. It is a roaring contribution to the debate on women and gender. It is one of the soundest and most biting and best that I have ever read in this matter. I also read rather a lot on psychiatry. It is a hobby.
> – Bergman quoted during the shooting of *Cries and Whispers* in Löthwall 1972, p. 96

> Sometimes I think of myself as a lesbian man obsessed by other women. Sometimes I believe my impressions and feelings are extremely feminine and very little masculine.
> – Bergman in his screenplay draft for *Cries and Whispers*; see Workbook no. 26

> All our interiors [in *Cries and Whispers*] are red, of various shades. Do not ask me *why it must be so*, because I do not know. I have puzzled over this myself and found that each explanation has seemed more comical than the last. The bluntest but also the most valid is that the whole thing is something internal and that ever since childhood I have imagined the inside of the soul to be like a moist membrane in shades of red.
> – Bergman 1973a, p. 154; italics in original

In *Cries and Whispers*, Bergman dissects the "monstrous nineteenth-century corpse" of idealism that continues to haunt the present, as we have seen in the cases of Anna in *The Lie* and Marianne in *Scenes from a Marriage*. Here, he presents us with both a Strindbergian dream play and an Ibsenian feminist deconstruction of it. To quote Strindberg's introduction to *A Dream Play*:

> The characters split, double, multiply, evaporate, condense, dissolve and merge. But one consciousness rules them all: the dreamer's; for him there are no secrets, no inconsistencies, no scruples and no laws. He does not judge or acquit, he merely relates; and because a dream is usually painful rather than pleasant, a tone of melancholy and compassion for all living creatures permeates the rambling narrative.[*]

The dreamer in *Cries and Whispers* is Ingmar Bergman himself, just as the Poet in his 1970 stage production of *A Dream Play* was the dreamer and Indra's daughter – in human manifestation known as Agnes – was his dream within a dream.[†] The film is set in a 'sanctuary' out of time and place, though we can roughly date it from the clothes and furniture to his parents' formative years just before the turn of the century in 1900. It opens with beautiful shots of a landscape park with a manor house. These are exactly the kind of beautified images that Bergman wanted to avoid in the colour productions of *A Passion* and *Scenes from a Marriage*, a stylistic hint that we are looking at a romantically idealised exterior masking an ugly "tangle of lies".

Inside the house, we hear clocks ticking. They suddenly stop to let us know that we are caught with the cast of characters in a limbo between then and now, life and death. They remind us of the world of clocks without hands present in Isak Borg's dreams and childhood home in *Wild Strawberries*.

The stylised red scenery and the actors' choreographed movements in colour-coded dresses – white in the first half, black in the second – heighten the theatrical quality of the drama and emphasise the characters' carefully choreographed self-theatricalisation. Bergman saw the red interiors as a representation of the soul, but they also suggest inferno and Germaine Greer's pathologised wicked womb of hysteria and menstrual blood (1970, pp. 53–59). Like Jean-Paul Sartre's inferno play *No Exit* (*Huis clos*, 1944; aka *Behind Closed Doors*), which inspired Bergman's *Prison* (*Fängelse*, 1949), hell is other people in *Cries and Whispers*, though the characters also do horrible things to themselves.

At the centre of the story is the thirty-seven-year-old virgin Agnes (Harriet Andersson), pure of sin, sexless, saintly, innocent, religious and dreamy. Darkly

---

[*] Strindberg 1907, reprinted in Strindberg 1988, p. 7.
[†] See Steene 2005, pp. 622–623, for a description of the production, based on a radio interview with Bergman.

ironical is her cancer in the genitals and the womb.* In rejecting the 'low' impulses of the flesh, Agnes has become the sister of Ibsen's title character in *Hedda Gabler*. Like Hedda, Agnes is destined for death. She does not kill herself, not directly, but her ideas do the job, as idealism's cancerous growth – the cold and wicked womb in its most poisonous representation – destroys her from within.

Agnes's condition is also a grotesque parody of the Annunciation of Mary since she is blessed by higher, cruel powers to give birth to her own death. But the suffering in what looks like a grotesque parody of childbirth also recalls the Passion of the Christ in her *pietà* scene with the maid Anna (Kari Sylwan), shown twice in the film. The film performs an ironic profanation of Christian symbolism to illustrate the tragic consequences of its ideas as Agnes's sacrifice does not bring life. Rather, we can imagine her inside as the landscape of the morgue-womb in the opening of *Persona*, not only populated with unborn children but with all the unborn possibilities of life killed by the restrictions of her beliefs.

Agnes cherishes a painting. It is never seen in the film, but mentioned in the screenplay (Bergman 1973a, p. 184). It depicts the same hymn we heard Isak Borg recite in *Wild Strawberries*, a few lines of poetry about the longing for God's grace that in Bergman's now fully profane universe has been replaced by the yearning for a human touch:

> Where is the friend I seek where'er I'm going?/ At the break of dawn, my need for him is growing./ At night he is not there to still my yearning. (Hymn text by Johan Olof Wallin, 1818)†

The twice-depicted *pietà* scene in which the maid Anna becomes Mary to Agnes's Christ, nursing her at the bosom as if breast-feeding a child, is the film's emblematic shot. But it is not the film's true representation of "the touch" since the scenes are tarnished by the master/servant relation between the two. We must

---

* The Swedish word "underlivet", which Bergman uses in the screenplay, is unspecific. It refers to both the womb and/or the genitals. Perhaps Bergman was aware of George Drysdale's influential 1854 book on sexual health, published in a Danish translation in 1879, the same year as the premiere of *A Doll's House* (see Ferguson 1996, p. 261). See also "To the Orgasm and Beyond: Ingmar Bergman and the Sexual Revolution" in Part Five.

† Bergman 1973a, p. 184. The translation is from the English subtitles to Criterion's Blu-ray edition of *Wild Strawberries*. The original Swedish text of the first verse: "Var är den vän som överallt jag söker?/ När dagen gryr, min längtan blott sig öker;/ När dagen flyr, jag än ej honom finner,/ Fast hjärtat brinner" (Bergman 1973a, p. 184).

remember that Anna is employed to serve Agnes, and there are hints that she might not be the life source that her soft and buxom body leads us to believe she is. When we learn that Anna's daughter has died, the child-like Agnes could very well be a substitution that Anna again nurses to death. In her function, Anna rather becomes a Bergmanian Reaper in female guise and a silent witness to the decay of the bourgeois doll's house and the values it represents.

The film's fleeting moment of "the touch" is instead located in a flashback scene of the three sisters' unnamed mother (Liv Ullmann), a dead ringer for Karin Bergman and significantly without a husband (a virgin mother?). Agnes remembers or fantasises about her childhood, describing her mother much like Bergman describes Karin Bergman in *The Magic Lantern*: beautiful, warm and loving but also capable of being distant, cold and cruel. We see her mother engaged in an intimate conversation with little Maria during a magic lantern show. Karin and Agnes are clearly not invited into their magic circle. Only when Agnes and her mother have a moment alone does there seem to be a connection. Or is there?

During the film, we realise that Agnes's memories and notions might not be real, but carefully doctored wish-fulfilments of her skewed worldview. That becomes even more clear when we see her fantasies about her sisters Karin (Ingrid Thulin) and Maria (Liv Ullmann) in the light of the overall narrative. The two scenes of love and harmony between the three sisters are so out of step with the rest of the film, in which we learn that Karin and Maria only feel horror and disgust for their dying sister, that we must take the two instances of bliss as products of Agnes's delusional mind.

In the nineteenth-century fairy tale – a narrative cherished by the bourgeoisie and referenced in the magic lantern scene – Agnes would be the innocent and good-hearted princess, locked away in a golden cage to die but ultimately rescued by Prince Charming. Bergman's tale is the negative, one in which the princess is rescued and rewarded for her good heart by no one, deluded to the bitter end into thinking that her sisters care for her.* But are Karin and Maria wicked for trying to break free of idealism's chains, rejecting its representation in the dying Agnes?

At crucial moments in the film, all four women look straight at us, the audience, in acts of defiance. They not only challenge us to judge them just as 'bad girls' in the way Monika (Harriet Andersson) did in *Summer with Monika* (*Sommaren*

---

* One could easily see it as a variation of the play within the film in *Through a Glass Darkly*. In the play, Lars Passgård's Linus in the role of the Artist promises Harriet Andersson's Karin/the Princess that he will follow her in death but fails to fulfil his promise.

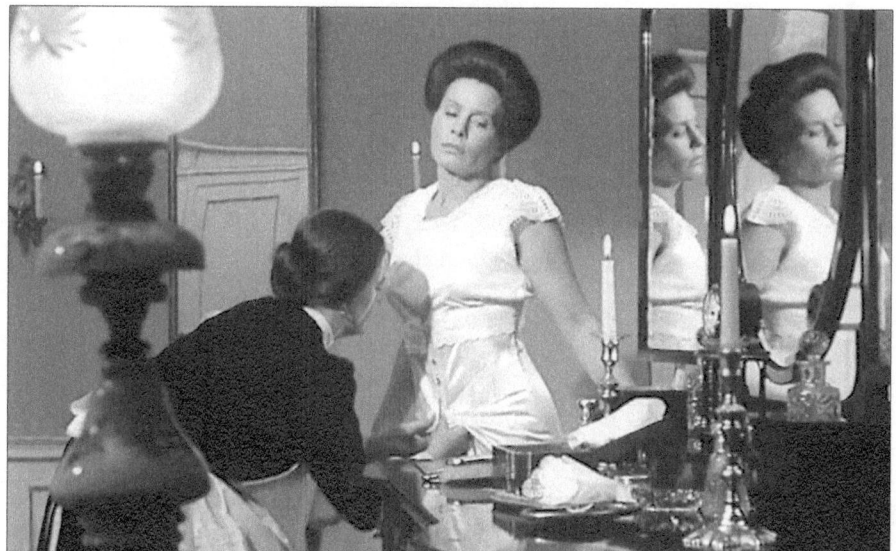

Fig. 11: The intellectual corset comes off. *Cries and Whispers* (1973). Anna (Kari Sylwan) and Karin (Ingrid Thulin). (© Cinematograph AB)

med Monika, 1953), they invite us to contemplate what they represent. By the film's *Persona*-like images, in which the four women's faces are split in light and darkness, it is suggested that they are complementary impressions of one person. While Anna and Agnes are featured as idealised self-sacrificing women, Karin and Maria represent the dark and repressed feelings of hate and sexual desire.

As for the sketchy portraits of the film's men, they are Bergman's father Erik split into two, one strong, one weak. Karin's husband Frederik (Georg Årlin) is the stern, almighty and punishing Old Testament Father, while Maria's husband Joakim (Henning Moritzen) is the fragile, child-like neurotic. Erland Josephson repeats his role as Bergman's voice of misogyny in David, the family doctor and Maria's lover.

The manor is a doll's house in which the women live in a state of regression, also literally since they stay in their respective childhood rooms. One image shows us Maria lying in bed with a doll, sucking her thumb, looking at the doll's house of her childhood. Like the cold womb of *Persona*, the manor is marked by petrification and destined to breed a living death of neuroses and sexual perversion.

Agnes is 'pregnant' with cancer; Anna's daughter is dead. Both are victims of this unsound environment, their situation only made worse by doctor David's cynical uselessness. Only Karin and Maria have managed to break away, if only to find themselves in new and repressive relations, breeding children that are likely to carry the disease of idealism into the twentieth century.

Karin's life is one of cold rationality and self-denial. She avoids closeness, while yearning for a real human touch. At one point in the film she is undressed of all her Victorian clothing, garment after garment by Anna. The long scene becomes an illustration of cultural radical journalist Else Kleen's 1910 book *Kvinnor och kläder* ("Women and Clothes"), in which the stifling Victorian dresses are metaphors for "the intellectual corset" women had to wear (Skoglund 1993, p. 115).

Then, in a desperate act to cut through the "tangle of lies" of her loveless travesty of a marriage, she mutilates her vagina with a shard of glass and exposes the wound to her spouse. Smearing her face with the blood is an act of mocking the repression that has denied her a life of intellectual and sensual pleasures, including sexual pleasure. Maria's strategy is the opposite: non-committal and casual sex much like the men of her time. When David confronts her with accusations of narcissism and indifference, she counters that he is just talking about himself.

In this context, Karin and Maria's disgust with Agnes might be a sound, if desperate, response to the idealism she represents. In the sad and disheartening ending, the sisters leave the mansion to go back to their respective marriages. Status quo seems to get the final word, though we sense that the sisters' struggle against repression will continue.

The coda to the film is a memory or fantasy by Agnes, a variation of Isak Borg's reconciliation with his parents and his past in the closing shot of *Wild Strawberries*. We can choose to see the depiction of Agnes's moment of happiness either as a cruel joke on her or as the celebration of her ability to transcend the dismal lives of her sisters. It is a prelude to the modern living in a lie of Anna in *The Lie*, Marianne in *Scenes from a Marriage* and Jenny in *Face to Face*. Bergman uses it as a shorthand reference to Ibsen's *The Wild Duck*, staged by him in 1972, and its famous debate about whether living a lie is helpful, perhaps even essential, to our existence or the very opposite – dangerous and ultimately lethal.

In *The Lie*, Anna is on the verge of breaking out of the 'sanctuary' of her doll's house, and in *Scenes from a Marriage*, Marianne has done it, only to be stuck in another one. Now that we in *Cries and Whispers* have glimpsed the nightmare haunting them both, we must ask ourselves: is there a way out of idealist hell? I suggest that the search for a possible answer to this question was the reason behind Ingmar Bergman's project *Face to Face*.

PART FIVE

FACE TO FACE

TO THE ORGASM AND BEYOND: INGMAR BERGMAN AND THE SEXUAL REVOLUTION

> It would have been a sacrosanct cinematographic piece of poetry. To me, this is not a continuation of the line from *Cries and Whispers*. It goes far beyond *Cries and Whispers*. Here, finally, all forms of storytelling are dissolved.
>
> – Ingmar Bergman on the *Face to Face* he wished that he had made, 1995, p. 73

The sexual revolution was a key element of cultural radicalism from the start. British physician George Drysdale's bestseller *The Elements of Social Science; Or, Physical, Sexual, and Natural Religion* (1854) provided the initial ammunition.* Republished in numerous revised and enlarged editions and translated into most European languages – the first Swedish edition was released in 1878 – it stipulated that all organs, including the sex organs, "must engage in a sufficient measure of activity" or they would degenerate (Lennerhed 1994, p. 22).

Feminists all over the continent made use of Drysdale's arguments, and in Sweden the cultural radical student Knut Wicksell armed himself with the book to embark on controversial lecture tours on sex and contraceptives in the 1880s (Gårdlund 1956). Many well-known authors, especially those connected with the labour movement, wrote extensively about these issues before World War II, often calling for the rights of young men and women to choose their own partners, engage in sex before marriage and educate themselves in sexual health and pleasure.

During Bergman's formative years in the 1930s, Sigmund Freud became the sexual revolution's point of reference and Karl Marx the ideological replacement

---

* The book was in many editions published anonymously. The Swedish edition simply stated: "by a Doctor of Medicine"; see Anon. 1878.

of John Stuart Mill. Cultural radicalism was marching left from sex liberalism to sex socialism (Skoglund 1993, pp. 120–121; Lennerhed 1994, pp. 32–33). The physiological consequences of celibacy were no longer the main argument.

Instead, cultural radicals stressed the psychological consequences such as mental problems and neuroses (Lennerhed 1994, p. 37). The Freud-Marx combination would in the 1960s become the inspiration for analysing sexual repression as a vital part of social and political repression, for instance in films like Sjöman's *I Am Curious – Yellow* and Pier Paolo Pasolini's *Salò, or the 120 Days of Sodom* (*Salò o le 120 giornate di Sodoma*, 1975). Sexology studies, such as the Kinsey reports on men (1948) and women (1953), gave a further scientific boost to the continuation of liberal sex reforms, but as the censorship debate in 1963 on *The Silence* and a year later on Sjöman's banned *491* (1964) showed, there was still much to do.

A powerful reactionary opposition to sex education, contraceptives, 'perversion' (= homosexuality), abortion, sexual freedom and 'moral decay' (= youth culture) was still influential in the public debate. It became organised in a Swedish section of MRA (Moral Re-Armament, 1952) and later in the KDS (Kristen Demokratisk Samling, the Christian Democratic Party, 1964). In response, cultural radicalism marched to the battle fronts again.

In 1962 debaters in the liberal student organisation Sveriges Liberala Studentförbund called for a new wave of cultural radicalism. To provoke, they organised meetings about sex and pornography at which they also showed pornographic films and magazines. Like the sex socialists in the 1930s, the sex liberals of the 1960s saw free sex as fundamental to democracy. An authoritarian and moralising culture could never be considered normal in a democratic society of free individuals.

Numerous scholars, authors and journalists came to their support. They wrote debate books and novels, discussed sex on TV and pushed for liberal sex reforms. The social democratic government was sympathetic to the demands, if not to the sometimes controversial forms of protest. It had invalidated the censorship authority's decision to ban *491* and allowed the film to be screened for an adult audience (fifteen years old and above) with some minor cuts (Donner and Nordin 1977c, p. 173), and after several years of liberalisation, pornography was finally legalised in 1971. By then, the contraceptive pill had also been introduced, and abortion was about to be legalised in several steps, which finally led to an abortion law with few restrictions in 1975. Contraceptives and access to legal abortions were crucial instruments in the sexual revolution for women.

Curiously though, pornography was ignored by the feminists in the 1960s. One of the few who criticised pornography from the left was the editor of the prestigious cultural journal *Ord & Bild*, Lars Bjurman, who argued that the pornography restrictions should be abolished but that pornography in general implied conservative and misogynist values (Lennerhed 1994, p. 196). This was also the attitude of the feminists who in the mid-1970s finally engaged in the pornography debate by founding a national organisation against pornography and prostitution: Riksaktionen mot pornografi och prostitution ("National Action Against Pornography and Prostitution"). Their arguments were in the same vein as those of the American radical feminists at the time – that is, that pornography enhances the patriarchal hegemony and instigates abuse, including rape.*

Ingmar Bergman was clearly of another opinion, as can be witnessed in Charles Marowitz's 1973 interview for the *New York Times*, in which he engages in a long discussion on the merits of pornography from various countries. Swedish porn is "very disappointing", while German and Danish is far better and Japanese pornography with its long historical tradition is deemed "fantastic". That he still hesitated to include more sexually explicit scenes in his own films is perhaps not so puzzling considering the cliché-ridden reputation of Swedish film in the 1950s, 1960s and 1970s in the US. His early films had been distributed and marketed under misleading and suggestive titles. *Summer Interlude* became *Illicit Interlude* and *Summer with Monika* was turned into *Monika: The Story of a Bad Girl*.

After Bergman, as one newspaper put it, "broke the sex barrier" (Donner and Nordin 1977b, p. 153) with *The Silence*, his films never came close to the sexual imagery of Vilgot Sjöman and Jörn Donner, or for that matter their colleagues in new wave art cinema, like Dusan Makavejev and Bernardo Bertolucci. He was, however, still committed to cultural radicalism and its credo of sexual liberation. It is at the core of *The Rite*, *Scenes from a Marriage* and, as we shall see, the project that eventually became *Face to Face*. In comparison, though, to what in the more unrestricted times of the early 1970s was accepted in both art and Hollywood mainstream cinema, Bergman's films were very modest when it came to graphic sexual representation.

They seemed even more modest when pornography became mainstream entertainment with the worldwide success of films such as *Deep Throat* (1972) and *The Devil in Miss Jones* (1973). Pornographic films were reviewed in prominent

---

* Radical feminist ideas informed the Commission on Prostitution (S 1977:01), which worked on a new legislation, see the report *Prostitutionen i Sverige, del II* ("Prostitution in Sweden, Part II").

daily papers of the world as well as in prestigious film journals such as the British *Monthly Film Bulletin* and the Swedish *Chaplin*. There were even rumours that Hollywood took an interest in what was then called porno chic. Recognised auteurs such as Stanley Kubrick planned to make films that crossed the line between the Hollywood mainstream and pornography (LoBrutto 1997, pp. 329–330). Bergman took notice, as his workbooks and planners reveal, and renewed his interest in pornography by watching titles such as *Exposed* (*Exponerad*, 1971), *Flossie* (1975) and the international hit film *Emmanuelle* (1974) while preparing for the shooting of *Face to Face* in the spring of 1975.

His starting point for *Face to Face* was a sexually graphic scene of an orgy. That he did not follow through during shooting was by no means a concession to the awakening feminist anti-pornography activism. Sex and sexual repression continued to be central to most of his 1970s productions, including *The Serpent's Egg* (1977) and *From the Life of the Marionettes*. But besides his own hesitations, there were other considerations, principally that the American market had become increasingly important for his films, and he was negotiating the American rights for *Face to Face* with Dino De Laurentiis.

US rating was certainly a crucial issue, considering the market's importance for Bergman. Although Bertolucci's *Last Tango in Paris* (1972) had been cut before its premiere, it was still slammed with an X rating. However, the film had performed well at the box office, earning over twelve million dollars, to a large extent because it could boast of having Marlon Brando in the lead, fresh from success with *The Godfather* (Lewis 2000, pp. 224–225). But with an X rating that could turn out to be a marketing asset, Bergman would perhaps face success for the very same wrong reasons that in his view had made *The Silence* into a box-office hit. After all, graphic sex was still considered sensational, hence it took the focus off the artistic qualities and subtler meanings of a film.

Also of importance was that in the pornographic films of the time, as well as in mainstream cinema with soft-core scenes, the orgasm and the money shot and other representations of sexual pleasure were essentially just new variations of the happy ending formula. It was part of the idealist melodrama tradition that Bergman had played with only to undercut in *Scenes from a Marriage*. He had to go beyond the fantasy of 'pornotopia' to find a way to represent the ongoing struggle against the repressive forces of the mind.*

---

* For a definition of 'pornotopia', see Williams 1999, pp. 153–183 ("Hard-Core Utopias: Problems and Solutions").

In 1974, he found inspiration in psychotherapist Arthur Janov's international bestseller *The Primal Scream* (1970), which had been recently published in Swedish translation. Here, Janov claimed to have found the ultimate solution not only to the symptoms of neurosis, such as a dysfunctional sexuality, but to neurosis itself. This was an offer Bergman could not refuse: the promise of delivering a final blow to the reign of idealism and the terror of his own demons.

ARTHUR JANOV CONQUERS SWEDEN - AND BERGMAN

According to his engagement planner, Bergman read the recently translated Swedish edition of Janov's *The Primal Scream* in July–August 1974 while editing *The Magic Flute* and outlining ideas for a screenplay eventually called "The Psychiatrist" ("Psykiatern"). Possibly, someone in his circle of friends recommended the book. That someone could have been Christina 'Kerstin' Olin, who at the time was married to Max von Sydow and had been in primal therapy.* Continuing to work on his screenplay during the autumn, Bergman also read Doris Lessing's novel *Briefing for a Descent into Hell* (1971) and Sylvia Plath's *The Bell Jar* (1963), both published in 1974 in Swedish translations.

Lessing's novel is ostensibly a story of amnesia and mental illness that describes a journey into another universe. While it has psychological implications for the main character – Charles Watkins, professor of classical languages – the story could also be read as an allegorical representation of the real world. Like in her novel *The Four-Gated City* (1969), Lessing criticises psychiatry and its techniques while giving credibility to insanity and/or dream as a reflection of an absurd existence most of her contemporaries would call normal. Bergman took an interest in the novel not only because it criticised psychiatry and its concept of normality but because it was a modern dream depicting a post-war nuclear age in its parallel, 'insane' world.

Plath's famous book – her only novel, originally published under a pseudonym shortly after her suicide – is a semi-autobiographical portrait. Though ending on a note of optimism, the story of Esther Greenwood's institutionalisation after a

---

* Author's interview with Tomas Videgård, 29 June 2015.

suicide attempt is harrowing, and the novel portrays psychiatrists and their treatments with both harshness and ridicule. The strong resemblance between Plath's Greenwood character and Marianne Höök's background could not have been lost on Bergman: limited career opportunities, the repression of being female in a patriarchal society and the hellish loneliness that followed the bouts of clinical depression.

In an early scene in *Face to Face*, the protagonist has two books at her bedside that Bergman had possibly read or, at least, was well familiar with, although this is not noted anywhere in his planners: psychiatrist Harry Stack Sullivan's *The Psychiatric Interview* (1970) and lawyer-activist Bruce J. Ennis's *Prisoners of Psychiatry: Mental Patients, Psychiatrists and the Law* (1972).

Sullivan was an influential lecturer, who stressed social, cultural and interpersonal relationships as causes behind mental illnesses. He regarded loneliness as the most painful human experience, and he rejected the term "mental illness", preferring "problems in living" (Sullivan 1996, p. 137). In psychiatry professor Thomas Szasz's book *The Myth of Mental Illness* (2010, p. 220), "problems in living" was made into a key term that challenged the historical concept of mental illness.

The book made Szasz into a central figure in the 1960s so-called anti-psychiatry movement that also included names such as Jacques Lacan, R. D. Laing and later Michel Foucault.* To the 'anti-psychiatrists', the history of psychiatry, its institutions and its treatments was one of social control, acting as repressive instruments for the ruling class. They argued for a change in society's definition of mental problems and for a non-coercive psychiatric treatment (Ennis 1972, pp. 251–253).

Ennis's book, which includes an introduction by Szasz, is a collection of riveting but horrific case histories from his practice as a lawyer for patients in mental institutions. They serve to exemplify the gratuitous circumstances behind the institutionalisation of people, many of whom often were locked away for decades while suffering humiliating and dangerous treatments that harmed them for life. Ennis's oral history of life in psychiatric hospitals corresponded with Frederick Wiseman's controversial and widely debated documentary *Titicut Follies* (1967), about the everyday bullying, degradation and neglect of patients in a Massachusetts psychiatric hospital.

---

* 'Anti-psychiatry' was a term coined by South African psychiatrist David Cooper. Although many of the individuals he included in this movement rejected the term itself, their basic points of criticism were quite similar.

Other well-known points of reference in the psychiatric debate were Ken Kesey's bestselling novel *One Flew Over the Cuckoo's Nest* (1962; in Swedish translation 1973) and Foucault's *Madness and Civilisation* (*Histoire de la folie à l'âge classique*, 1972; in Swedish translation 1973). In 1975, Kesey's novel was the basis of a critically praised and Academy Award-winning film that became a box-office hit in Sweden in 1976–77.* The popular impact went far beyond the public interest about the maltreatments of patients in mental institutions since the mental institution could also be interpreted as a metaphor for modern society.

The open controversies of psychiatry led to a public interest in new and alternative therapies. The *Handbook of Innovative Psychotherapies* (1981) has texts on sixty-six of the most well-known and includes a list of about a hundred and forty others practised in the 1970s (Corsini 1981, pp. xv–xviii). Psychiatrist Arthur Janov's primal therapy, promoted by a string of international bestselling books, had by far the biggest impact of them all.

Then as now, primal therapy was largely ignored by the standard works on psychiatry and psychotherapy,† and in major magazines like *Psychology Today* it was summarily dismissed and even ridiculed (Torrey 1976). The aggressive criticism and derision of primal therapy by the psychiatry establishment was, however, not necessarily to Janov's disadvantage at the time. On the contrary, it probably helped to put him on the map for those seeking the exact opposite of what established psychiatry had to offer.

When primal therapy was introduced in the early 1970s, it got a warm reception by both readers and the media, and Janov's bestsellers were quickly translated into many languages. A year before the Swedish translation of *The Primal Scream*, in 1973, Janov's theories were discussed in the Swedish press, and several Swedes travelled to Los Angeles to become paying clients at the Primal Institute.‡ At the pinnacle of Janov's fame in the mid-1970s, Svenska Primalföreningen ("Swedish

---

* Milos Forman's *One Flew Over the Cuckoo's Nest* premiered in Sweden on 26 February 1976, but Bergman was most likely aware of the success of the book, the stage adaptation and the plans for a film version way ahead of the premiere. The early to mid-1970s was a period when Bergman was in close contact with Hollywood, and he made several business trips to the US. Besides selling his Swedish productions, there were also advanced plans for him writing and directing two Hollywood productions: the musical *The Merry Widow* with Barbara Streisand in the leading role and a film about Jesus (Nordmark 1974)
† See for example Cushman 1995; Norcross, Vandenbos and Freedheim 2011; Smith 2013.
‡ Videgård (1973) and Wrangsjö (1974) are the earliest examples of articles and reviews of Janov's theories and books that ignited the Swedish interest in primal therapy. That many Swedes came to Janov's Primal Institute to engage in primal therapy was confirmed by my interview with

Primal Society") was founded in Stockholm to promote Janov's radical new ideas. The organisation was active mainly in the capital, but it had subdivisions in several other cities between 1975 and 1979.

Poet-author Göran Palm and film director Kay Pollak were among Janov's outspoken supporters. In an interview for women's magazine *Femina*, Palm claimed that Janov was as important for the liberation of humankind as Mao Zedong (Tirén 1976). His statement was not only praise for primal therapy but also indicative of the crisis for the New Left, when many turned to psychoanalysis and psychotherapy to connect personal liberation with the call for a political revolution (see Josefsson and Zetterberg 1976).

The interest in Janov's theories soon spread far beyond the New Left and the cultural circles of Stockholm as Janov's books flew off the shelves in the Swedish bookstores. In major newspapers, his ideas were scrutinised and sometimes attacked for lacking a social perspective by critics of the New Left (Fornäs 1977). Primal therapy's road to fame in Sweden had been paved by the popular interest in other challengers to the psychiatry establishment such as R. D. Laing and German-American psychoanalyst and feminist Karen Horney. Many of their books were translated, published in paperback editions and discussed shortly before Janov became a household name.

Bergman had read some of Horney's work in Swedish translation (Timm 2008, p. 395), and he certainly became aware of Laing when Ken Loach's Laing-inspired film *Family Life* (1971) was widely debated.* Like Horney and Laing, Janov criticised contemporary social structures and conventions, although he mainly focused on the nuclear family as a dysfunctional institution. Psychology PhD and therapist Tomas Videgård, author behind the only scientific study of primal therapy, argues that the main reason behind its appeal in Sweden was the emphasis on emotions and especially pain. That was of no great concern to Freudian psychoanalysis at the time.†

Reading Janov, one is also struck by his engaging prose and emotional appeal. Many readers probably felt that he was talking to them personally about their

---

psychotherapist Tomas Videgård (29 June 2015), who was there in the mid-1970s to study Janov's method. This resulted in a doctoral dissertation (published as Videgård 1983).

* *Family Life* was a revised version of Ken Loach's TV play for *The Wednesday Play*, *In Two Minds* (1967). Both were Laing-inspired studies of schizophrenia written by David Mercer; see Monaco 1980. The film got much attention in Sweden, and it was soon a staple screening at many schools. I saw it in high school (in a gymnasium) in the mid-1970s.

† Author's interview with Videgård, 29 June 2015. See also Videgård 1983, p. 3.

feelings. Moreover, he claimed to be backed up by scientific evidence when he cured his patients not only of mental disorders but also of various physiological conditions and diseases from homosexuality and drug addiction to epilepsy, ulcers, frigidity and cancer. One might assume that some of his most outrageous claims would cause concern. For instance, he argued that primal therapy could cause physical changes such as female patients growing larger breasts or near-sighted persons suddenly having twenty/twenty vision (Janov 1970, pp. 124–130, 135 and 164–165). But at least in the Swedish debate, that was largely overlooked.

When holding meetings in Stockholm, Janov was greeted as a guru and a rock star. To many, primal therapy was rock and roll, not least since two of Janov's star patients had been the famous couple John Lennon and Yoko Ono (Davies 2012, p. 176). For their album *John Lennon/Plastic Ono Band* (1970), sometimes called *The Primal Scream Album*, Lennon had written the song "Mother", based on Janov's therapeutic method of having the patient calling out for their mother and father until the original trauma of childhood was supposedly released in a so-called primal scream.

Like the therapy sessions Janov wrote about in his first and most successful book, the song begins quietly but ends in loud cries: "Mama don't go/ Daddy come home.'" In turn, Janov wrote about a post-primal opera fan throwing away "those operatic agonies", turning to rock and roll since it was "gutsier" and felt like "a celebration of life" (1970, p. 168). The Janov-Lennon connection appealed to Bergman on many levels. The Beatles were one of his favourite popular bands (Simon 1971, p. 74), and Janov's ability to release Lennon's innermost feelings into a seemingly liberating and healing musical scream must have seemed remarkable to him.

The popularity of both Janov and Lennon with the younger generation also meant that they perhaps held the key to an audience Bergman had still to reach. Most important to Bergman's inspiration when writing "The Psychiatrist" was that primal therapy, like music, seemed to speak directly to the emotions. Moreover, Janov and Bergman agreed on the origins of childhood trauma, locating its causes with the truly disturbed ones in the family: the parents.

---

* Compare with Janov 1970, p. 88, on a therapy session.

WORKBOOK NO. 29, PART I: EVERYTHING IS A DREAM

In *Images*, Bergman quotes extensively from his Workbook no. 29 on "The Psychiatrist", later renamed *Face to Face*. The quotes provide a Rosetta stone to his crabbed handwriting, but it soon becomes clear that he had edited them. Words were changed, sentences were left out.

At first, it appears that the changes were simply corrections. When looking at some passages in his workbooks on *Cries and Whispers* and *Face to Face*, one gets the impression of automatic writing. Sometimes words are missing or they change places or Bergman mixes the tenses. Considering Bergman's constant revisions of his memories over the years, however, one can presume the changes are conscious.

Furthermore, his selection of passages does no justice to his work process, which is alternating notes for the screenplay with diary entries and self-reflective comments about film art. Perhaps in recognition of his tendency to doctor his past, he cautions the reader about his previous and categorical dismissal of *Face to Face* in the years following its making:

> In *The Magic Lantern*, I dismiss it briefly and lightly. Earlier on I simply dismissed it or declared it an idiot. That is, in itself, slightly suspicious. Now I see it like this: from the beginning and up to the main character's attempted suicide, *Face to Face* is perfectly acceptable. The story is clearly told, though rather compressed. There are no real weaknesses in the material itself. If the second part had maintained the same level as the first, the film itself would have been saved. (Bergman 1995, p. 66)

The second, weaker, part he refers to is where the protagonist, psychiatrist Jenny, was supposed to enter a condition in which she slips in and out of dreams with no clear distinction from reality. This idea for a film of blurred borders between the two ontological states was already sketched in his Workbook no. 26 (Sunday, 2 May 1971) on *Cries and Whispers*: "One must put in dreams without having to explain that they are dreams. Nothing like this: 'I dreamt about walking in a forest.' Only: 'I walked in a forest' [...] That is how simple it should be."

Seamlessly intermixing reality with memories, dreams, fantasies and insanity is an old idea in film history, as can be seen in German expressionist films (*The Cabinet of Dr. Caligari/Das Cabinet des Dr. Caligari*, 1920), classics of surrealism (*The Andalusian Dog/Un chien andalou*, 1929) or American film noir (*The Woman in the Window*, 1944). In post-war art cinema, Alain Resnais made his name as a director with a string of titles – perhaps most famously *Last Year at Marienbad* (*L'Année dernière à Marienbad*, 1961) – where he left the audience with no clues as to what was real and what was only in the mind's eye of the protagonist.

Bergman was clearly under the influence of Resnais when making *The Silence*. Then he pushed the envelope with *Persona* and by making his very own *A Dream Play* in *Cries and Whispers*. What could possibly be the next step? Let us go down the long and winding road of his workbook and see how he got from "The Psychiatrist" to *Face to Face*. (Note: since the protagonist's grandparents have no names, they will henceforth be referred to as Grandmother and Grandfather.)

EASTER EVE, 13 APRIL 1974

Bergman begins his workbook on "The Psychiatrist" by dismissing his 1972–74 work on two Hollywood projects: *The Merry Widow* (for Barbara Streisand), to which he completed a screenplay, and an untitled film about Jesus that never left the drawing board. Now he wants "to walk along my own path", because "at the theatre I always follow others' paths; when it comes to films, I want to be my own".

His resolve to "force my way into the secrets behind the walls of reality" is renewed. So is his commitment to formal austerity: "To find a maximum of expression with a minimum of outer gestures." Still, he is hesitant to "continue on the old routes" since he considers *Cries and Whispers* to be "the outer limit for that technique". However, he holds on to the intuitive strategy that brought him the success of *Cries and Whispers*: trust in the images that haunts him you.

At the start of the workbook he feels good. He notes from time to time while writing that he is a lucky man: pleased with his marriage, content with working with a small and loyal crew and confident that the recently completed shooting of *The Magic Flute* will turn into a great film: "I cannot picture a happier man than me, and no one ought to be more suitable to convey the holiness of humankind." Occasionally during his work on the screenplay, he broods over his inability to write comedy or light entertainment films:

> Why does it become so gloomy even though I have it so good, and why does it come out so sad when I have this much fun? I do not understand it. I love it when the audience laugh and have fun. I love it when it is warm and generous and overflowing on the stage or at the cinema. What the hell is in the way, stopping me from doing all that? (Bergman's Workbook no. 29, Monday, 2 September 1974)

This reflection is perhaps a relapse to the days when he competed for fame with fellow director Hasse Ekman. In the 1940s and 1950s, Ekman had been at the centre of Stockholm nightlife, both as a *bon vivant* and as a successful director of sophisticated urban comedies. Bergman had been neither, and even now when he was living in bliss he could not emulate his rival's artistic forte. He counters these self-defeating thoughts with words of comfort; inspiration will come to him if he only is patient enough: "I feel that I am nowhere near the spring from which I can draw fresh water and much water. Nothing at all shows up yet. But eventually it will surely come. So far, I can just sit and wait" (Bergman's Workbook no. 29, Monday, 9 September 1974).

The initial sketches for the project, written in April, are set in Stockholm during summertime. A young unnamed woman moves into her paternal grandparents' huge and mysterious apartment at Strandvägen in Stockholm.* Her husband and kids are away for the summer, and the family's house is under repair. Alone for the first time in her life, she is pleased to spend time working on "some kind of doctoral dissertation" at the National Library (Kungliga biblioteket).

In the apartment, she enjoys the silent company of Grandfather, who is ill, but there is no sign of Grandmother. In this museum celebrating yesterday's ideals and social customs, just like the one Bergman's father kept his family in, she will face an inner crisis. Her initial harmony cracks under pain and fear about not being loved; she is feeling humiliated and degraded by unanswered love. Three months later, on 13 July, Bergman adds a brother who is the woman's opposite: closed off, forced in his composure and artificial. Consequently, he is at a loss when confronted with his sister's crisis.

---

* In *Images* (1995, p. 68), Bergman's quote from this early sketch has altered "paternal grandparents" ("farföräldrarna") to "parents" ("föräldrarna").

The apartment is another one of Bergman's bourgeois 'sanctuaries', the missing link between the 'doll's houses' of the previous television productions set in modern-day Djursholm, *The Lie* and *Scenes from a Marriage*, and the rural manor of old aristocracy in *Cries and Whispers*. Most important, Strandvägen is the grand façade of Östermalm, the upper-class district where Bergman grew up and where he had an apartment of his own for many years. In other words, this is not a setting close to home, it *is* home, and it is haunted by demons from the past.

WEDNESDAY, 7 AUGUST

Having finished the editing of *The Magic Flute*, he decides to turn the perspective 180 degrees so that "the dreams are real and everyday reality is the unreal – you enter it with pain and insecurity". He pictures the film's ambience as a silent Sunday at Karlaplan – the square where his own apartment was located. The streets are empty and the only sound comes from "the desolate church bell ringing", most likely from Hedvig Eleonora Church around the corner, where Ingmar's father Erik was a priest.

For most of Ingmar's youth, the Bergmans lived across the street from the church:

> the ringing of the church bells haunted Ingmar Bergman all through his schooldays and in many of his films. During the night, the lighted clock face in the tower stared through the windows like an all-seeing eye, just as one can see it in *Woman Without a Face* and *Prison*. (Höök 1962, p. 29)

In the "slightly feverish" twilight hours, filled with "yearnings", the old apartment takes on an unreal, dream-like quality. There is "a carcass", a "mother's look" and a lover who turns away from the protagonist, but the images are not described in more words than this.

THURSDAY, 8 AUGUST

He plans to write "Seven dreams with small islands of reality in between". But he has no idea what the dreams should be about, which he finds curious: "By the way, is it not strange that when I read about dreams in books, I always skip over them because I find [them] so uninteresting?" He only gets as far as writing headings for the dreams:

The humiliation dream.
The erotic dream.
The boredom dream.
The horror dream.
The amusing dream.
The annihilation dream – the death dream.
The dream about the mother.
(9 August)

SUNDAY, 11 AUGUST

Bergman finds a personal dream interesting enough to write down. It is "strange and long" and touches only slightly on what he is looking for in the project. In the dream, he arrives at a huge city apartment to get therapy. Left in a bed, he starts crying over "the futility of life" in front of some people. His cry is one of both despair and pleasure. When relieved of his overwhelming feelings, he converses with a woman with short hair, a green dress and brownish skin. After this notation, he is away from the workbook for almost a month.

MONDAY, 2 SEPTEMBER

Bergman is in high spirits: "Fantastic days. Fantastic weather. Calm. Harmony." He outlines a dream-like masquerade scene with people coming in and out of a consciousness, presumably the protagonist's. It includes "sexual humiliations and other inventions", and there is a mother watching. The protagonist listens to some people discussing what should be done to her sexually. Out of the seven separate dreams he proposed to write, he has now combined at least three of them into one dream: the humiliation dream, the erotic dream and the dream about the mother.

The masquerade with the erotic element suggests an influence from Arthur Schnitzler's *Dream Story* (*Traumnovelle*, 1926; aka *Rhapsody: A Dream Novel*). It was not translated into Swedish until 1999, but Bergman was fluent in German and probably familiar with the original text.[*] Not only does the novel feature an erotic masquerade, it also has an enigmatic narrative in which dream and reality intermix without distinction. Furthermore, it takes place in the era – just after the turn of the century in 1900 – when his protagonist's grandparents where young

---

[*] The novel – or, rather, novella – also features an inspection of a young woman's naked dead body – a scene of sex and death, fascination and revulsion, that could have been the model for similar scenes in *The Hour of the Wolf* and *The Serpent's Egg*.

and moved into the apartment that now has turned into a monument of the past. He would return to this time again in *Fanny and Alexander*.

Before elaborating on the dream narrative, he cautions himself: "It is hard to write dreams. One could so easily end up in banal capriciousness and nonsense. I have to think carefully about my previous successes and mistakes in this field." After another lament about his incapability of writing films that make people laugh, he dismisses his latest success: "I am so tired of *Cries and Whispers* that I cannot bear to see it." This is indicative of his temperamental and often revisionist relationship with his previous works, and it forebodes Bergman's problems in handling the reality/dream narrative when working on *Face to Face*.

MONDAY, 9 SEPTEMBER

In his next entry, he seems more confident about the dream masquerade, which he plans to make into the project's recurring theme. He also considers letting the irrational qualities of the dream make for a surreal film from the first to the last image: "It begins suddenly and without explanations. That would be yummy. And then it continues without explanations. That would be no less yummy. And then end it all without explanations. That would be the yummiest of all."

The inclination to do away with a conventional narrative is a project that grew out of Bergman's experiences as a director:

> At first I was simply entranced by the movement of the figures, and by being allowed to make films at all. Afterwards, I've become more and more aware of the theatre's, film's and TV's limited capacity for communicating fiction. Today, when I see how badly the novel has gone off the rails and how less and less able we are to experience and accept a fictitious course of events in an elemental way, the more reluctant I have become to tell stories with a beginning and an end – and the more dubious I've become. (Björkman et al. 1973, p. 210)

There are notes on "different costumes, different masks", big old rooms with secret entries and exits, an old theatre with a big window looking out into the night and over a yard. But something is lacking: "I thirst for images. Images and images and images of situations." Dipping into a book on surrealist painter Leonor Fini,* he is struck by her "exceptional world", and he lists short descriptions of images that flash in his mind:

---

* In the workbook, he erroneously writes her name as "Eleonore Fini".

The black tower.
The women in the half-full basin.
The tower with the footsteps.
They go into the tower.
The closed eyes.
The ceremonies.
The unnecessary dress.

As he has done before with other people's lives and other artists' work, Bergman absorbs Leonor Fini, letting her paintings fertilise his imagination. One image in particular strikes a chord with him. Two weeks later he writes a scene in which his female protagonist is seated naked in a dark room lit by candelabras, supporting her breasts on a shiny black table, surrounded by a masquerade party in which the dead dance with the living. The inspiration most certainly came from Fini's dystopian painting *The End of the World* (*Le Bout du monde*, 1948).

It shows a young woman up to her breasts in a black sea with a shiny surface, reflecting her image. She is surrounded by floating withered leaves, a dead plant

Fig. 12: Leonor Fini, *The End of the World* (*Le Bout du monde*), 1948.

and skulls of animals, both dead and living. In the background a red sun is setting behind black hills. The eroticism of the naked, alluring woman is combined with an apocalyptic landscape.

From her breasts – universal symbols of life and fertility – the black sea of death seems to flow. Both Fini's painting and the imagery produced by Bergman's mind might be modern in form, but in their motif, they are classical: a nightmarish horror scene combining sex and death. Later, Bergman would refer to the scene inspired by the painting as "the film *as it ought to have been*" (Bergman 1995, p. 70; original italics).

In his daughter Linn Ullmann's autobiographical book *De oroliga* ("The Anxious", 2016, p. 144), Bergman is quoted talking about a favourite title he would have liked to use for one of his films: *The Fuck of Death in Eldorado Valley* (*Dödsknullet i Eldoradodalen*). Perhaps this project was the missed opportunity he thought of.

WEDNESDAY, 25 SEPTEMBER

Below is the original, unedited version of the dream sequence, following a heading in capital letters announcing that

EVERYTHING IS A DREAM

She is sitting on the floor in her maternal grandmother's apartment and the statue is moving in the sun. On the stairs, she meets a large dog that growls and bares its teeth. Then her husband arrives. He is suddenly dressed as a woman. She then looks for a psychiatrist. She is a psychiatrist herself and says that "this dream she cannot understand although she has understood everything that has happened to her in the last thirty years." Then the old lady raises herself from her large dirty bed and looks at her with her bad eye.

But Grandmother and Grandfather are hugging each other, and Grandmother is gently stroking him on his cheeks, whispering tender words to him even though he cannot utter more than a few syllables. But behind all this, behind the drapes, there is a conversation about what would be the proper thing to do to her sexually, perhaps widening her anal opening. And immediately she appears, the other, who takes such matters lightly and who now caresses her in all sorts of ways, and it is unexpectedly pleasant.

But now somebody arrives, asking her for help (really asking her!), one who is in a desperate situation. But she bursts into a fit of rage and then an anxiety attack because the tension does not abate. [In the margin: "THE MURDER OF MARIA"] It is therefore a relief to plan and execute the murder of Maria that she has been thinking about for so long. But then it is even more hard to find someone who cares about me and who tells me not to be afraid. But if I change my clothes completely and go to a party, then everyone is bound to understand that no one is innocent and cast their suspicions on someone else.

[Undecipherable sentence.] But everyone wears a mask and suddenly they dance a dance she does not know, a pavane, in the dark room with candelabras, and somebody says that many of the dead have come to honour the party with their presence.

The top of the big dinner table is black and shiny, and she supports her breasts on the table top, sinking slowly as someone licks her all over her body, especially between her legs. This does not agonise her; on the contrary it is most pleasurable. She laughs and a big dark-haired girl with big red hands lies down on top of her.

Beautiful music from an out-of-tune piano or cembalo, it does not matter. At this moment, the door opens – the big old-fashioned double door – and her husband enters together with some policemen. They accuse her of the murder of Maria. She then speaks passionately in defence of herself, sitting naked on the floor in the old-fashioned room. The one-eyed woman raises her hand and puts her finger to her lips in a commanding gesture of silence. And she falls silent.

TRAUM AND TRAUMA

This scenario raises many questions, but that was in line with Bergman's "yummy" thoughts of making a dream narrative without any explanations from beginning to end. However, some light can be shed by going back in time in the workbook.

TUESDAY, 10 SEPTEMBER
Bergman decides that "The Psychiatrist" is to be the title of the project. The protagonist will be one who is unable to save her patients, and they "more and more seem to be the wise ones". The film is to be an interplay of reality and dreams, with the latter becoming more like reality and vice versa. Insanity is to be portrayed as more sane than conventional sanity as defined by society's institutions.

Insanity as sanity in an insane society was, as noted above, a topical issue at the time. The spring premieres of *One Flew Over the Cuckoo's Nest* and *Face to Face* were followed in November by Marianne Ahrne's feature film debut *Far Away and Close* (*Långt borta och nära*), which received the Guldbagge Award for best Swedish film in 1976. Ahrne had been the only student at the 1960s film school who wanted Bergman for a tutor, and it is no coincidence that she is on his list of "our most gifted filmmakers" in *The Magic Lantern* (Bergman 1988, p. 230; Timm 2008, p. 366).

Most likely they had stayed in touch afterwards, and Bergman might even have influenced Donner's decision to produce her film for the Swedish Film Institute. *Far Away and Close* is about Mania (Lilga Kovanko), a young psychiatric hospital nurse falling in love with non-speaking male patient Arild (Robert Farrant). He is portrayed as a warm, authentic and sane human in contrast to most other people in Mania's life and specifically to the cold, unfeeling and deranged psychiatrist Jan D. Jaeger (Helge Skoog) treating Arild as a lab rat in an experiment.

SUNDAY, 22 SEPTEMBER

Another apprentice's work on Bergman's mind while working on *Face to Face* was Kjell Grede's TV adaptation of Strindberg's autobiographical novel *The Defence of a Fool* (*En dåres försvarstal*, 1893).* The project had been initiated by Bergman. He produced it at Cinematograph and supervised Grede during the writing and directing of the series. The novel is a feverish love story of jealousy, betrayal and revenge told by a male protagonist who feels humiliated and degraded by his mercurial mistress, later to become his wife. Her name is Maria.

Considering Bergman's close affinity with Strindberg, the novel most likely influenced him as a young playwright and screenwriter. When he made use of his recollections of the stormy affair with Karin Lannby to write screenplays, he remodelled her into the sexually alluring and dangerous Maria/Marie/Mari characters of his early plays and films. After a few years in hibernation, she was revived in *Cries and Whispers*, and for "The Psychiatrist" Bergman planned to make his protagonist a fool ("en dåre") – "a fool for everything that I am a fool" – in the company of a Maria of her own.

The Maria of *Face to Face* makes her first appearance in the workbook on 22 September. She is the protagonist's patient, who "in some strange way becomes her companion in the dreams". There, the patient will "go through a series of humiliations and horrors that the psychiatrist cannot help her out of. She is some kind of unexplainable, vicarious sufferer." A few days later, in the dream sequence quoted above, she is to be the victim of the protagonist's murder scheme. This might be the embryo of Maria's later function as the manifestation of the protagonist's repressed fears and desires.

What Bergman took from Schnitzler's *Dream Story*, besides the erotic masquerade, was the ambivalent character of the dream as both wishful fantasy and nightmare, *traum* and trauma.† This is even more prominently featured in the elaborate scenario on 25 September. We hear the masqueraders talk about what to do sexually with the protagonist. *Traum* or trauma?

As we learn later, our still unnamed protagonist is an anal-retentive character in the Freudian sense. She leads a strict, frugal and orderly life of all work and no play. She is controlled and controlling to the point of being rigid. The

---

* The novel has also been published in English translations under the titles of *A Madman's Defence*, *A Fool's Apology* and *A Madman's Manifesto*.

† See *Eyes Wide Shut* screenwriter Frederic Raphael's introduction to the 1999 English edition of Schnitzler's *Dream Story*, pp. v–vi.

masqueraders' talk of "widening the anal opening" could in this context be a metaphor for her liberation from the imprisonment of inhibition. Since the erotic masquerade suggests a sexual penetration, the "widening" could also be interpreted as a widening of the protagonist's sexual horizons, perhaps to the polymorphous perversity idealised by the Marquis de Sade (Hallam 2012, p. 113).

Considering Bergman's religious background, however, anal sex has negative connotations. It is a taboo, designated as sodomy from the Bible's story of how God destroyed the libertine city of Sodom. Symbolically, it is associated with death, a negative to procreative vaginal sex (Hallam 2012, p. 11). It is no coincidence that Bergman stages the anal sex ritual as a masquerade party in which the living and the dead mingle. This symbolism is very much present in 1970s cinema, and not only in the fascist death cult of Pasolini's *Salò, or the 120 Days of Sodom*.

In *Last Tango in Paris*, Paul's (Marlon Brando) anal rape of Jeanne (Maria Schneider) is associated with his sexual rage against the dead wife. The rape is an act of necrophilia by proxy. Bergman would elaborate on this symbolic triangle of anal sex necrophilia in *From the Life of the Marionettes*. Correspondingly, the above dream scene's anal sex symbolism could be the first clue to the psychological condition of the protagonist in *Face to Face*.

Another traumatic marker is the one-eyed old woman dressed in dark clothes who at first stares at the protagonist and then silences her with a commanding gesture, a continuation of the stern and forbidding "mother's look" mentioned earlier. She is the symbol of death we are well acquainted with from previous Bergman films, beginning with Mrs Calwagen in *Summer Interlude*. Over the years these old women are used as symbols of "the women's inner sabotage of themselves, the secret aggressions expressed in sexual aversion, the ambition to live up to a role created by their mothers". Her dirty bed in the outline for "The Psychiatrist" signifies the dirtiness of sex.

Why is the husband dressed as a woman? In the Bergman context, we know this 'cross-gender' appearance from many previous films, last time in *The Lie*'s portrait of Albert, the cross-dressing author-prophet locked up in a psychiatric hospital. This time, however, he seems to be Bergman's convoluted reference to Strindberg's mask-swapping between men and women. Leading the vice raid on the masquerade and his wife's sexual transgression suggests that he is a patriarchal agent disguised as a woman, perhaps the mother's double.

This ideological subtext is further emphasised by the scenario's new setting: in the maternal, not paternal, grandparents' apartment, where the protagonist now sleeps in her mother's childhood room. Grandfather is suffering from the effects of a stroke and does not talk, but Grandmother is very much alive and darting about like mad in the apartment "full of anger and love", acting as both patriarch and matriarch. Later, Grandmother will be described as the source of the protagonist's inner rage against her repressive upbringing.

The opening scene of the protagonist sitting on the drawing room floor and watching the statue move in the sunlight we recognise from *Fanny and Alexander*. It is inspired by the childhood memory of a magic Sunday moment when objects, figures and statues in his maternal grandmother's huge bourgeois apartment came to life in the sunlight from the windows. In the original story, it was not the statue that moved but the small figurine of a golden girl triggered by the clock striking twelve to dance to a boy's flute (see Bergman 1988, pp. 20–21).

After the elaborate dream scene was written on 25 September, there are but a few scattered and often crossed-out sketches for dreams in the workbook. While yearning for, searching for, images, Bergman realised that he had to have an artistic method in the madness: "We cannot ignore the need for a method. Fuck knows how that will look. Courage. It is all about having courage. And not feeling like an idiot. Although it is fun. Idiot" (9 September).

Given that he had made the protagonist "a fool for everything that I am a fool", he was afraid to be too personal, to narrow the perspective into navel-gazing by telling the story from an "auto-angle", thereby losing "universalisability" ("universialitet").[*] A related term he had used before is "objectify" ("objektivera"), by which he means to be clear and understandable to others (Sjöman 1963, p. 21). Both terms stress the importance of shaping deeply personal material into something valid for – and accessible to – the general audience, and this is possibly why his vision of a film built out of a series of unexplained dreams gives way to another and more realistic narrative.

On 10 September, he urges himself "not to be chary of material for the real world", and immediately starts sketching a story about a very real psychiatrist having real problems in the real world. Twelve days later he reflects, "I want this story to be open, accessible and intimate." He therefore splits his narrative into two: one set in the real world, one in the protagonist's dreams.

---

[*] "Universalisability" is originally a concept from Immanuel Kant's categorical imperative (Kant 2002, p. 167ff), stating that the only morally acceptable maxims of our actions are those that could rationally be willed to be universal law.

WORKBOOK NO. 29, PART II: JENNY THE PSYCHIATRIST

THURSDAY, 26 SEPTEMBER 1974

Bergman begins to sketch out the realistic storyline we recognise from the final screenplay, TV series and film. His working speed and frequency of writing increases. The still unnamed protagonist, simply called "she", "comes to stay with her maternal grandparents during the summer months while her kids are in the country, her husband is on a trip abroad and the house is under repair". In the evening, "Grandmother makes coffee while Grandfather sits and reads (or is looking in a photo album) and the clock is ticking".

The apartment is untouched by 1970s consumer society, furnished with old furniture (no TV!) and arranged to uphold a traditional bourgeois lifestyle. Grandmother has made pastries and darns socks when they all sit together. The living room turns into a women's space since Grandfather is no more than a remnant of his patriarchal glory. He is speechless – possibly the result of a stroke – and close to death.

The two women spend the evening "talking about the hospital and the patients". Only now and then does Grandfather make a sound, but they are only minor interruptions because "he has escaped into a world of his own. The past." At the end of the evening, the protagonist is taken, not to her mother's childhood room (as in earlier notes) but to "her childhood room that is much like it has always been". They say goodnight to each other, and there is "great friendship and tenderness".

This scene appears to be one of harmony, bliss even: "Everything is security, order, calmness and waiting." Grandmother is the archetypal motherly guardian of home and hearth, radiating "much tenderness and warmth". But like the opening scene of *Scenes from a Marriage* – and the opening scenes in many of Ibsen's plays – we sense that this warm moment is illusory, theatrical, deceptive.

The apartment might seem like a homely sanctuary preserved in time, but it is also a mausoleum over a Victorian past associated with old class and gender structures and with sexual repression. When the protagonist is taken to her room, we learn that it has been her childhood room. Like the rest of the apartment, it is frozen in a time long past.

These interiors are another example of Bergman's doll's houses waiting to crumble as a result of forces from within. When describing the apartment, Bergman blends his memories from his maternal grandmother's home with Marianne Höök's childhood residence at her maternal grandparents' house . The clock is ticking, and although we might be in a place out of time, as in *Cries and Whispers*, there is a countdown to death and therefore to standing face to face with oneself both for the grandparents and, ultimately, for the female protagonist.

Consequently, something stirs underneath the calm of the status quo. An existential time-bomb is waiting to explode so that the protagonist can confront her traumas of the past to either collapse under their pressure, like Höök, or break free from them, like Janov's primal man.

Bergman further complicates matters by introducing the protagonist's parents, who in a following scene are alive and well and taking care of her children for the summer at their countryside home. Was her childhood room at the grandparents' apartment only for temporary visits or was she taken in by them for some reason? Bergman never ponders the question. He only sends his protagonist on a weekend visit to the parents, and she comes to a house packed with visiting relatives: aunts, cousins and uncles.

At first glance it looks like a modern update of his previous paradisiacal vision of the sentimental and slightly crazy turn-of-the-century family gatherings around the big dinner table from *Wild Strawberries*, later to be revived in *Fanny and Alexander*. Zooming in, though, we note the vitriol in Bergman's description: "Everything is about eating, money, that it should be nice, that no one is to speak about unpleasant things, that the world is unchangeable."

The revised family scene is a variation of the idyllic opening shot – soon to reveal its cracks – in *Scenes from a Marriage*. It is influenced by Ulla Isaksson's novel *Paradise Place* from 1973, an Ibsenian tale about an extended family coming together at a monumental bourgeois summer residence called Paradise or, more precisely, Paradise Square.* Idyllic at first, the repressed conflicts and lies soon erupt, and the novel ends in a tragedy, in which one of the teenagers kills himself for much the same reason as Hedvig does in *The Wild Duck*.

Bergman's cynical portrait of the family clan is close to the one in Isaksson's novel. When writing about Jenny's parents, he elaborates on the unflattering details: "Mother is a great actress in her private life and phenomenally dominating. Father is sarcastic, lovable, successful and nasty. I must figure out who he resembles. He dedicates himself to politics rather intensely, but mostly to fill the unwelcome empty gaps." The best answer to the interjected rhetorical question is that the father, although not named Vergérus, is another Harry Schein incarnation.

By the end of the day he reconsiders: "This is the wrong path. There is something essential to the desolation in the town. In the abandonment and the socialising with the old ones." He crosses out the scene at the parents' house, but the influence of Isaksson's novel would linger in the final version of *Face to Face*.

FRIDAY, 27 SEPTEMBER

Bergman introduces a new character – an agent of sexual anarchy – in the life of the orderly and rather uptight protagonist: "Could it be that she by coincidence meets a man, whom she without batting an eyelid jumps into bed with and who makes life strange. That she the decent, the proper! Yes, there is something about this." The details of the affair and the man himself are up in the air: "Possibly she knows him from before, possibly they were in contact with each other through work. I don't know." He goes on to suggest and discard various alternative details of the lover and scenarios of how the protagonist will meet him. Is he to be recently divorced and living alone? Perhaps not, Bergman objects to himself. Does he have a girlfriend or someone else in his life? Bergman cannot tell. More agreeable is the proposal that he should be an old and close friend who is also alone in the city during summertime and who invites her for dinner.

Do they, perhaps, meet at the cinema? At a concert? Or does he call her, asking her to come over for beer and sandwiches? The last suggestion has a familiar ring to it. In an interview about *Scenes from a Marriage*, that was how Bergman pictured people unceremoniously solving their marital problems: over a glass of beer and a sandwich.

---

* The original title of the novel is more accurately translated as "Paradise Square". The novel includes a dialogue about the wonderful idea of having a summer residence which is to be a democratic *forum* – referring to ancient Greek and Roman forums open to people of all classes (Isaksson 1973, p. 32).

Could this unsentimental, down-to-earth mood be what Bergman wants for his realistic scenario? Possibly, since he – literally – stresses the importance of the lover being "nice" and "sane" and "goddamn genuine". He must inspire confidence, and "under no circumstances should he appear to be a fool". Suddenly, Bergman is unable to continue: "And then everything becomes so strange that I cannot write about it." He clearly fumbles for ideas and images. Nothing gels. Still, he finishes the day on an optimistic note. Or are the following words of concern meant for the protagonist?

> Secure warm days. Dusk. Solitude. Being with oneself. Feeling that something is growing.

SATURDAY, 28 SEPTEMBER

Bergman decides to pin down some details of importance. The grandparents' apartment is to be situated more precisely in the "distinguished blocks between Narvavägen and Strandvägen-Djurgården". His protagonist's first name is Jenny, which we recognise from Bergman's early career. In both his directorial debut *Crisis* (1946) and his screenplay draft "The Comedy About Jenny", later revised into the play *The Day Ends Early* (*Dagen slutar tidigt*, 1946), there is a vain, middle-aged woman called Jenny having a sadomasochistic affair with a reckless young lover (Koskinen 2002, pp. 138–143).

The Jenny in his "Psychiatrist" project is to be married to the blandly named Stefan, while her grandparents are blessed with the biblical names of Adam and Eve. Could her lover be the serpent in the Garden of Paradise? In the opening idyllic scene at the grandparents' apartment, Jenny is now served tea, not coffee.

Sometime in the early hours of dawn – possibly the hour of the wolf – she wakes up. Grandmother is also up, pottering about. Jenny is in a state of anxiety, feeling that she cannot meet the big demands made on her: to help others, to care for them, to love: "Has she reduced it all to words?" There is an impenetrable barrier between herself and others: "People are calling for help, but she has no resources to help. She is ready but nevertheless incapable."

Then Bergman gets a new idea, another sexual assault on the bourgeois 'sanctuary' Jenny is living in:

> RAPE: This also happens to her one evening when she is assaulted and suddenly feels sorry for the men who attacks her. She feels an immense compassion. And

yet she cannot handle the situation. She reports them to the police for assault, battery and rape. This is possibly the third real episode I am looking for.

Bergman hesitates. In the middle of this realistic scene, he considers Jenny to be remarkably calm and clear-headed up until the moment when she is nearly beaten to death. After having reported the four boys, "she feels that something is wrong, yet she cannot change what has happened".

SUNDAY, 29 SEPTEMBER
Short notes. Bergman considers Jenny's vague physical discomfort to be important. "The wild one", meaning Maria the patient, calls her and wants her to come by in the evening.

MONDAY, 30 SEPTEMBER
More short notes. It is the first day of writing the screenplay. Jenny moves in with her grandparents. Feeling under the weather, she will go to a doctor called Joakim for some blood tests. The name Joakim goes back to Bergman's literary ambitions in the late 1940s. In three play drafts, the character was known as Joakim Naked, a pioneer filmmaker driven to suicide by inner demons much like Johan Borg in *The Hour of the Wolf* (and so is Jenny in "The Psychiatrist"/*Face to Face*, as we shall see below). The name was revived in *Cries and Whispers* for Maria's weak and infantile husband, who also tries to kill himself, although for reasons of the heart: Maria's infidelities. Here, he is portrayed as a soulless but charming libertine.

TUESDAY, 1 OCTOBER
Two sketches for Jenny's night-time conversations in the grandparents' kitchen. The first is one with Grandfather. It is crossed out. The second is with Grandmother, who talks about her own life as the happiest and the best. She proceeds to talk about her daughter's death, and now Jenny's background comes even closer to that of Marianne Höök.

Furthermore, Grandmother talks about the benefits of her life, taking care of someone, only to change the subject to what she will do if and when she becomes single. She also tells Jenny about the time when she fell in love with Grandfather. The romantic image of him soon faded, "but there is this thing called love". Bergman stresses the importance of this conversation. It is to portray a sense of equilibrium and stability in Jenny's increasingly chaotic mental state.

Jenny's world now becomes more and more disrupted. She is disturbed in her sleep by the one-eyed old woman and wakes up screaming. It is raining outside. She feels alone and "denied as a woman" – a euphemism for her sense of being starved emotionally and sexually. In Joakim's consulting room, she is advised to overcome her inhibitions and to break free of her marital bonds: "It is so easy. Just run riot."

From the following notes on Joakim we learn that he is exactly the opposite of Jenny, a man of impulsive sexual pleasures that he has turned into a life style, indeed into his Sadean philosophy of life. This is a stark contrast to her previous opposite, the ultra-rigid conformist brother, who is now out of the picture. Note how Bergman in the following quotation goes in and out of the character when writing about him:

> Joakim is a person who has decided to really enjoy the desolate state that is his real life. When his cock is aching after several days of good fucking, then I feel that I am a true person and that life has meaning. He is a gynaecologist and has his profession as a hobby. He is overwhelmingly desolate but funny. I think one should like him.

WEDNESDAY, 2 OCTOBER

Bergman elaborates on Jenny's hour-of-the-wolf experiences. Sitting in Grandfather's chair in the drawing room, Jenny watches a scene of her grandparents' loving everyday relationship. When the muddled grandfather wanders in, Grandmother comes after him and guides him back into the bedroom. Jenny wonders: "My God, what is it with her? What is it with me?" In the following scene, Jenny meets with Maria and gets a wake-up call, the real world suddenly erupting in her life:

> This time the lid must blow off reality. [The scene] must be one of a goddamn row between the two. Maria hits her hard on her cheek or in the face. [...] Jenny considers sending her away to someone who can better understand what is going on. In any case, there is some kind of betrayal that [Jenny] must take responsibility for. At the meeting, there is probably another psychiatrist who is happy to treat Maria. But then Jenny decides to take Maria herself. Later, she renounces her promise. That is worth considering.

The scene is a bit odd, since Jenny is to betray Maria by handing her over to a colleague. But there is yet to be a scene establishing trust between the doctor and her patient. In the final screenplay, it is implied that Maria has been a patient of Jenny's for some time. But like the nightmarish one-eyed woman, the fight between Jenny and her patient is primarily instrumental in triggering Jenny's need for change.

Bergman plans to follow Jenny's row with Maria with a scene at Joakim's apartment, where Jenny is to spend an evening of zipless sex. At night, though, she gets another attack of insomnia and anxiety and leaves his apartment. Back at her grandparents' place, she meets with Grandmother and there is to be a scene of "tacit understanding" between them. Going to sleep in her own bed, she is again subjected to her demons: "the dream comes to her with a fearsome palpability and provocative power. She cannot hold it off any more."

In his final notes for the day, Bergman wants the husband to have more presence in the drama. He is to come back from America for a short visit after Jenny has been raped. She has pity for one of the rapists: he who has a fixation on her breasts, making him into a substitute child for the protagonist. It also makes for another version of the *pietà* scene, albeit with a meaning quite different from the one in *Cries and Whispers*.

FRIDAY, 4 OCTOBER

Short note: "MARIA has now become a VERY STRONG main opponent to Jenny. She escapes from the hospital and looks her up in her own world and reality." Here is the embryo of the scene in the final screenplay where Jenny finds Maria at her empty house.

MONDAY, 7 OCTOBER

The only entry for the day is a crossed-out diary note about a phone call that brings Bergman "a lot of concerns", though he does not go into details. He is primarily upset by the call because it disturbs his writing, but he resolves to continue on the path of intuitive search for narratives and images:

> What is real is to reach the sources, the blood, to what is living. I will undoubtedly damn damn damn well solve this. That I shall do because I know that somewhere inside the material is lurking about, and it knows how it should be done.

The interrupting phone call will, as we shall see below, be included in the screenplay.

WEDNESDAY, 9 OCTOBER

Suddenly overcome by a tidal wave of ideas, Bergman revises the entire outline into a new story that echoes Ulla Isaksson's novel *The Blessed Ones*. However, unlike her story, "The Psychiatrist" is not about two lovers heading for a double suicide. Or is it? The sketches for the screenplay could certainly head for a love story – a *folie à deux* – to be consummated by Jenny going insane like Maria.

In the revised outline, Jenny leaves her family apartment after having a scary dream. Her sleep has been interrupted by a phone call from her husband, who pulls her back into reality.* She goes to pick him up at the airport. "That is the beginning. Then she goes more and more crazy, and the interaction with Maria is to become more and more violent – and stranger."

The name of Jenny's lover is changed to Tomas, which in the Bergman universe refers to the doubting priest in *Winter Light*, who in turn is ironically named after the doubting apostle. In this context, however, it is perhaps more important to remember Karin Bergman's lover Thomas, who threw her well-ordered married life into much turmoil. Tomas, Jenny's lover, is no longer described as a libertine, and Bergman is now unsure about the nature of Jenny's relationship with him.

He only has a vision of her losing control at Tomas's place, laughing like mad: "That is to be the first sign." Then Maria is to escape from the hospital so that Jenny must go looking for her. A telephone call from a man informs her of the address where she can find Maria. It is in some suburb: "a nameless misery, where [Maria and her company] have been for a week".

When she arrives there, Jenny is "more or less raped", a phrase that suggests that the rape is perhaps to be depicted as a dream or a fantasy or at least as an ambiguous situation. A new addition to the list of characters, Dr Wankel, is the one who takes care of Jenny afterwards, and his treatment "sends her into a world of horror". After a week in treatment, she is scheduled for some sort of operation. The introduction of a mad psychiatrist suggests that Bergman has resolved to introduce a sterner anti-psychiatry motif into the story.

His biggest concern is, however, dramaturgical – the lack of "a turning point where everything changes and imperceptibly crosses into madness for Jenny". The audience is not to notice, but Bergman thinks it is important that he as the writer-director knows when that point is. The first half of the drama he sees Jenny as

---

* The inspiration for the interrupting phone call is probably not only from the disturbing call on Monday, 7 October 1974. It connects with the Bergman-lookalike boy who in *Persona* wakes up at the morgue – from death – when hearing a phone ringing.

passive, to the point of being "madly non-existent". In the second half, "all hell should break loose".

THURSDAY, 10 OCTOBER

Bergman has another bout of doubt and discomfort concerning "The Psychiatrist". He thinks his condition is worse than on any of his previous works, but then he doubts that too: "perhaps one forgets from one time to another". His search for Jenny goes in and out of character, and in at least some aspects she is to express his innermost feelings.

> What does she do? She goes to someone to complain. What is happening to me? Am I going insane? Or doesn't she? Does she fight it? Feelings of darkness and isolation and desperation. Perhaps her husband calls. NOTE: now I can perhaps connect with the sorrow that I have inside. But where does it come from? What is it about? Does anyone have it as good as me?

He gets a new idea: a suicide scene. Jenny tries to call her husband only to hear "a feedback signal". This triggers her to drive to Lill-Jan's Forest or to Drottningholm outside Stockholm to "sleep herself to death", meaning: take an overdose of sleeping pills. However, Bergman is frustrated with the scene because there is something missing, namely a reason and an emotional depth to her act: "It must be well founded. The rest of the film is dreams and confrontations and blood and screams and misery and the progress of the [mental] illness."

He finishes for the day by listing some of the characters. The daughter is to be named Helen, a first in the Bergman universe. Tomas's new surname, Jacobi, is familiar, though. In *The Shame*, there is a Mayor Jacobi (Gunnar Björnstrand) who uses his money and position to get sexual favours from the female protagonist Eva (Liv Ullmann). Of more importance is the Mrs Jacobi in *Scenes from a Marriage* who tries to break out of a long and loveless marriage. Like her, Jenny is afflicted by "petrification", and in adding a suicide Bergman moves the story another notch closer to Marianne Höök's life.

While some of Mrs Jacobi's features have been passed on to Jenny, the Jacobi character of "The Psychiatrist" is about to transform into something new: the helper. He now becomes the therapeutic listener to the female protagonist's troubles, and in *From the Life of the Marionettes* he returns as Tim Mandelbaum (Walter Schmidinger). Bergman will eventually write the role for Erland Josephson, who bears the name again in *Fanny and Alexander*, then a Jewish merchant and a friendly helper to the Ekman family.

FRIDAY, 11 OCTOBER

Bergman revises and restructures the story yet again. He writes in short sentences, some consisting only of a word, which makes it difficult sometimes to fully understand his intentions.

Jenny calls her husband but gets a feedback signal. She drives alone to search for the escaped Maria at a location whose address she was given earlier. There, three men attack Jenny: "she is not raped; they try but the guy cannot get it up". Jenny takes Maria to the hospital and calls Dr Wankel, who takes over the treatment of the patient. Again, Bergman stresses that Maria sees this as an act of betrayal. Bergman underscores this in a note for a shot of "Maria's gaze", that is an image of Maria looking at Jenny in a way that conveys her sense of betrayal.

Later, Jenny meets with Tomas Jacobi, but now she is to be silent while he does all the talking. There is to be a "fiasco", meaning an emotional fiasco rather than a sexual one since he writes about Jenny's "emotional coldness and the petrification which is eating its way into her flesh and mind". She has "a strange laugh after they have fucked", then she goes home. Back at her own apartment, which is "empty and unreal", she finds a note about Grandfather being taken ill and that Grandmother is with him at the hospital. Alone with her pain for a long time, Jenny decides to kill herself by taking sleeping pills: "I think she goes out into the woods. It is a quiet summer morning. And everything is suddenly very pleasant. Then she wakes up to a new life, and then she becomes seriously insane. Really insane."

At this point, Bergman has writer's block. He cannot find the words to express Jenny's insanity and her dreams, only that there is to be "a monologue and confrontations swinging between dreams and waking reality all the way to the end". As a second dramatic turning point he introduces "a real fucking scream, all the way from the guts – body and soul", but the result is not mentioned. He just notes that some people appear in and/or out of her dreams: the returning husband, her daughter Helen, Grandmother ("who understands and wants to take her home"), Jacobi ("who I still cannot get a good grasp of"), Maria ("her victim") and Dr Wankel ("last but not least!").

For a moment, Bergman contemplates ending the narrative with the dream he wrote two weeks earlier: "when the woman was hushing [Jenny] with the awful sound and everything whitens to ice and she gets her electroshock treatments". He decides that it is a good idea to let her stay in the hospital to "shut her in between four walls that open up to various dreams".

So far, Bergman has considered his work to be a screenplay for a film, but now – perhaps because of the success of *Scenes from a Marriage* and/or the possibility of elaborating on the more and more complicated plot – he decides to transform "The Psychiatrist" into a six-part TV series:

> Episode 1: "Grandmother and Grandfather"
> Episode 2: "The Puzzling Day (Maria-Jacobi-The Party)"
> Episode 3: "Searching for Maria. The Rape. The Betrayal."
> Episode 4: "The Suicide"
> Episode 5: "The Madness"
> Episode 6: "The Madness and 'Recovery'"

Episodes 1 to 4 have been roughly outlined, but the last two remain blank. In them, Bergman plans to go in and out of Jenny's dreams and fits of madness. So far, he has sketched only one dream, although it is unclear where it will fit in the narrative. Then there is the primal scream, the dramatic climax and second turning point, followed by 'recovery' (Bergman's quotation marks). A recovery to what? Primal man?* That would mean an upbeat, utopian ending, which is rare in Bergman's oeuvre.

---

* I have decided to keep Arthur Janov's key concept 'primal man' even though it seems odd concerning Jenny.

WORKBOOK NO. 29, PART III: THE PRIMAL SCREAM

SUNDAY, 13 OCTOBER

Bergman has another fit of dispiritedness – "GREAT DEJECTION" – but these negative impulses eventually pass into "some sort of determination". He derides his work on "The Psychiatrist" as "slave-writing without joy". However, at the end of the day and after much drudgery, he hopes to find "the real film". Cursing his lack of patience, he tries to comfort himself with the thought that "if I am hauling and pulling and bluffing myself forwards, maybe I can pull [the production] out of the darkness and then it will be worth the trouble".

His only note for the day on the screenplay is that Maria is to be dead when Jenny finds her. Later, in Jenny's isolation at the psychiatric hospital, Maria comes back to haunt her in dreams and hallucinations. He decides to finish the first part about Jenny the psychiatrist in the real world, then work on the final mixing of *The Magic Flute* and "then we will see". Finally, he adds a suggestion for music to the film/TV series, two works by Mozart during what biographer Robert W. Gutman (2001, p. 637) calls the composer's "annus mirabilis" – 1784 – and published together in 1785: Piano Sonata no. 14 in C minor, K. 457, and Fantasia in C minor, K. 475. Bergman eventually chose to use only the latter.

THURSDAY, 17 OCTOBER

Bergman struggles to elaborate on the dreams and to find out how they can fit in the narrative structure. It is apparently very difficult since he goes through three rough outlines in quick succession.

OUTLINE 1

It begins at the point in the story when Jenny is about to call her husband. She doesn't receive an answer. Grabbing her sleeping pills, she drives away to a forest to kill herself: "And it is all very sad." Here, the first part ends, and the next begins with the dream about Jenny sitting naked by a black table: "It is real and unreal." Dr Wankel appears in women's clothing, but he is still Jenny's psychiatrist. She tells him that she has had a dream that is reality and that she does not understand it.

OUTLINE 2

Grandmother wakes Jenny telling her that she has been sleeping like the dead and that the hospital has called. It is Saturday morning. The grandparents are about to go off for the weekend to some friends in the countryside. Jenny will be alone. Tomas is in town, but Jenny falls asleep again only to wake up when the church bells are ringing on Sunday morning. Walking in the empty apartment, Jenny meets the one-eyed woman, "screams like mad", calms herself and then takes the sleeping pills. Bergman makes a note to himself that "it is of importance that she has lost her orientation in time".

OUTLINE 3

Jenny comes home and sets the alarm clock. It seems to ring instantly. Unable to get up, Jenny tells Grandmother to call the hospital and tell them she won't be coming due to illness. She wakes up again to find Grandmother by her bed, telling her that she and Grandfather are to go away for the weekend but that she is afraid to leave Jenny alone. Jenny assures them that everything will be fine, and they leave. Cut to the first dream, in which she consults Dr Wankel, dressed in women's clothing.

She wakes up on Sunday morning, tries in vain to call her husband and "Reality slips away through her fingers." A new dream, in which she meets the one-eyed woman, screams in all the rooms and wakes up to take "all the sleeping pills that she can get hold of". Before she "sinks down into the bosom of death" she calls her husband. No answer.

SUNDAY, 20 OCTOBER

Some short notes, continuing previous reflections on the masquerade dream:

> To be forced to be somebody else in order to be loved. To cry out for understanding and love. To be humiliated on all levels. The anxiety of total isolation. The sexual

humiliation. When I begin to write the second part of this strange film or whatever it is, I must make careful considerations.

FRIDAY, 25 OCTOBER

Bergman comes home after a few days in Stockholm, completing the sound mix of *The Magic Flute*. He notes that he is "both tense and stimulated before the start of part II" of "The Psychiatrist", but the workbook notes made during the following weeks reveal that he is grasping for images, insecure about what to make of the ones he gets and how to make them connect with the overall narrative.

He comes up with an idea for a letter "that in some way is also a testament". Jenny dictates it in the company of Dr Wankel, but it is not clear if this is to happen in the real world or in a dream. Bergman is also unsure about the function of the doctor: "He is a funny person but so far, I do not know what to do with him." A few lines later, Tomas is the one assigned to be Jenny's trusty companion "in her pain".

The masquerade and the suicide are somehow connected, and the latter is to be an act of aggression. What follows is silence: "NOBODY SAYS ANYTHING. At times, it looks like someone is trying to communicate with her, but no sound is produced, nothing is heard." Bergman reiterates his previous statements about insanity being sane in an insane society, perhaps to keep this subtext in mind when writing the dream sequences.

SATURDAY, 26 OCTOBER

Jenny dictates her letter on a tape recorder, stating her motives ("or will she?"): "She feels that suddenly everything is clear to her, giving her a justification for the suicide. It is not hysteria or aggression or something emotional, it is a wise insight." This is a complete changeover from yesterday's notes, stressing Bergman's search for a satisfactory insight into his protagonist's motives, perhaps also his own true feelings on the subject. The husband and daughter have new names: Erik, like Ingmar's father, and Anna, like several of his key female characters from *The Silence* to *Cries and Whispers*. Erik is to be at a congress in Chicago. Anna is to be at a riding camp.

SUNDAY, 27 OCTOBER

Another revision of Jenny's motivation for killing herself: she no longer has any fear of dying. At this point, Bergman feels lost. Like an actor of the Stanislavsky school – and there are many similarities in his attempts to create the characters in the screenplay draft – he questions the emotional truth of this idea: "Well, what have I got out of this? Will I be able to get close to the point where my own despair is hiding, where my own suicide lies in wait for a good opportunity? I don't know."*

In a crossed-out section, he half-heartedly goes on to make notes on the scenery and Jenny's parents. There is to be snow in the dream sequence, and Jenny will shiver with cold while the others are rather unaffected. Her parents are now both dead, and Jenny meets them in one of her dreams, only to see them turn away from her. For some reason, she feels guilty, although she was quite young when they both died in a car crash.

MONDAY, 28 OCTOBER

Jenny wakes up from death to a new life, a rebirth "that is misery, screams and vomiting and a strong yearning to go back". Bergman tries to picture her primal scream, using words and metaphors of his own and some from Janov's *The Primal Scream*:

> This is the true birth! The scream: Hold me. Help me, be kind to me, hold me tight. Why is there no one to care for me, why is no one holding my head? It is far too big. Please, I am so awfully cold. I cannot live like this. Kill me again. I do not want to live. It cannot be true. Look how long arms I have got, and it is just empty everywhere. There is empty land around me. Pick me up. Carry me. Speak.†

The Bergmanian metaphor about Jenny's long arms seems rather cryptic until we go back to the final scene in *Scenes from a Marriage* and Marianne's nightmare about her arms being cut off and therefore being unable to reach Johan and her children. It is a metaphor for her fear of not being able to communicate with them, embrace them – touch them. Jenny has the exact opposite problem: her ability to touch is enormous, as she is about to become primal man. Her problem is that she is alone in an empty universe with no one to touch.

THURSDAY, 31 OCTOBER

Bergman specifies why Tomas can be Jenny's helper: "I think it would be correct that Tomas is a homosexual and thereby able to come close to Jenny's tragedy."

---

* Note: this quote is incorrectly dated 20 October in Bergman 1995, p. 75.

† Note: this quote is incorrectly dated 20 October in Bergman 1995, p. 75, and it is both incorrectly translated and edited. This is the full version.

There is a history of prejudice behind this view, one in which homosexuals long after the decriminalisation of homosexuality in 1944 were considered to be tragic, self-hating and mentally unstable persons. According to the press and also in literature and films, homosexuals were supposedly on the fast track to suicide, alcoholism or the psychiatric hospital.

Before the 1970s one could read in Swedish papers about people being "accused of homosexuality", and it was not until 1979 that the National Board of Health and Welfare threw out their classification of homosexuality as a form of mental illness. Curiously, for all his pretensions to be revolutionary and modern, Arthur Janov aligns himself with this conservative view in *The Primal Scream*. Like Christian fundamentalists, he defines homosexuality as some kind of neurosis that can be cured by connecting with supposedly authentic feelings: "It is based on a denial of sexuality and the acting out symbolically through sex of a need for love. A truly sexual person is heterosexual" (1970, p. 324).

But then we have noted above how Bergman has portrayed many of his artists as representing the Other within the patriarchy regardless of their sex. In being homosexual, Tomas and later Tim in *From the Life of the Marionettes* are outsiders to society's norms in much the same way. Bergman now begins to write about Tomas and Jenny's relationship as a kind of love affair, but one transcending physical, sexual, attraction: "some sort of passion for humans and humanity".

He stops to think that it might seem odd that Tomas is a gynaecologist, "but then why not?" For some reason, he finds it reassuring that Tomas is a homosexual, because "he can bring her back into life, get her to accept". What Jenny is supposed to accept is unclear, but in practice Tomas becomes her primal therapist – an ironical twist considering Janov's view on homosexuality.

Moreover, he now has two doctors pitched against one another over Jenny: Tomas the helper versus Dr Wankel the opponent. Dr Wankel represents medicine and patriarchy as an institution, while Tomas has defected from both. Thus, Tomas has rejected the male gaze and is therefore suited to being the midwife in Jenny's rebirth as primal man.

Turning to elaborate on the husband, Bergman decides that Jenny does not want to see him and when she finally does, she scolds him. The husband is to be castigated without mercy. After that, Jenny slides back into her dreams. Dr Wankel is there to accuse her of causing Maria's death, presenting it in a way that sounds like murder.

To underscore the humiliating nature of the procedure, Bergman plans to stage the accusation as a public hearing at a medical conference. Jenny is to sit up front to answer to the accusations: "Nurse Edit is there to present all the facts." Then he reflects: "*Wild Strawberries*, is it not?" Consequently, Bergman would rewrite the scene in the final screenplay.

FRIDAY, 1 NOVEMBER

Bergman has completed his first draft of the screenplay. He is unsure of the result but he hopes to adjust in the rewrites that will follow. One thing he is certain he wants to do, though, and he stresses his resolve with capital letters: "To write about the KNIFE-WIELDING SLASHERS OF PSYCHIATRY AND HACK SURGEONS AND VETERINARIANS." No wonder we find Bruce J. Ennis's and Harry Stack Sullivan's angry books on psychiatry at Jenny's bedside.

WEDNESDAY, 13 NOVEMBER

Almost two weeks has passed since the last entry in the workbook. Bergman rewrites his screenplay. He wants to "correct and try to understand what I have done. It is not as easy as one might think." Of primary concern are the dream scenes. One depicts Jenny lying in a coffin, hearing the people outside while in horror realising that they are about to fasten the lid on the coffin. "What do I get out of this scene?" He fears that it will turn into a gruesome farce and cautions himself: "One has to be fucking clear about these dreams so one does not make a fool out of oneself."

He sketches a monologue in which the shot is to be a long take of Jenny while she talks about her experiences leading up to the breakdown. She speaks about her fearsome self-discipline and self-control. Bergman pictures her inner turmoil as a dialectical struggle. Her narcissism is contrasted to her calls for someone to "BREAK THE SHELL. AFFECT ME. LET ME BE REAL! IF I AM REAL, THEN DEATH HAS NO POWER. AS LONG AS I AM UNREAL, I WILL COUNT THE GRAINS OF SAND THAT RUSH THROUGH THE HOURGLASS IN FEAR."

This inner struggle is modelled on Janov's discussion of real and unreal selves (1970, pp. 35–36). In Janov's terms, Jenny has up until now lived a "depersonalised" life. She has been one who goes through the motions of life but is cut off from her feelings, other people and even life itself. She is, essentially, a living dead since her "unreal self is a superimposed system". By going through the pains of the primal scream, Jenny regains her true authentic self, hence overcoming the most Bergmanian of fears: the fear of death.

SUNDAY, 24 NOVEMBER

Bergman contemplates how Jenny would describe herself, and he applies a traditional Freudian concept of her psychological make-up: "DADDY'S GIRL. TROUBLES WITH MOTHER. HELPLESS PSYCHIATRIST. HESITATES ABOUT THE TREATMENT. CONSTANTLY TORMENTED BY VAGUE DISCOMFORTS. LOCKED OUT OF LOVE."

TUESDAY, 26 NOVEMBER

Jenny's breakdown and primal scream is far too weak in Bergman's mind. He wants a much tougher confrontation with Jenny's inner defence mechanisms. Grandmother is chosen as the target for her rage. The old woman whom we met as a warm and nice old lady is to grow into a monster, personifying Jenny's repressive mechanisms of fear and guilt. Yet when meeting Grandmother again in real life, both Jenny and we are to see her as a small and tired person longing for tenderness.

Like Marianne's visit to her sexually repressed mother in the final episode of *Scenes from a Marriage*, Jenny's healing becomes complete in her reconciliation with the past. In Bergman's career, these forgiving scenes represented something new and would be more pronounced in subsequent works referring to his parents, specifically *The Best Intentions*, *Sunday's Children* (*Söndagsbarn*, 1992) and *Private Confessions* (*Enskilda samtal*, 1996).

His own reconciliation is specifically with his grandmother, Anna Åkerblom, born Calwagen. In *Summer Interlude*, she was represented by Mrs Calwagen and in *Wild Strawberries* by old Mrs Borg. Both are unforgiving portraits of cold and heartless women. Her reappearance as Jenny's grandmother in *Face to Face* represents a decisive change, to be completed in the loving portrait of old Mrs Helena Ekdahl (Gunn Wållgren) in *Fanny and Alexander*.

TUESDAY, 3 DECEMBER

A new dream, in which Jenny, dressed in red, is meeting with several patients. Even though they are all crowded in her small consulting room, she feels the vast distance between them and herself. She speaks to them, but they do not seem to respond. Instead they begin to act and look like a non-threatening version of the bourgeois chamber of horrors in *The Hour of the Wolf*.

A man takes off his mask to reveal a hideous face. Another one can only say numbers, and a third one is lobotomised. Then there is Grandfather, who is afraid to die. Under pressure, Jenny tries to escape and wakes up "with all the difficult questions". Finally, Bergman decides to cross out his entire day's work.

SATURDAY, 7 DECEMBER*

Off to Stockholm to prepare for his staging of Shakespeare's *Twelfth Night* at Dramaten, Bergman is depressed. When looking back at his work on "The Psychiatrist" – now renamed *Face to Face* – he feels that he has been tired and indifferent throughout the work process. While simultaneously working on the postproduction of *The Magic Flute* and the *Face to Face* screenplay, he also initiated the two Cinematograph productions *Summer Paradise* and *The Defence of a Fool*, and the latter would turn into a complicated and costly TV series, much to Bergman's dismay.

Fearing that this psychological state has affected the quality of the writing, Bergman is determined to get a second opinion from Erland Josephson: "I hope he will be frank. If he thinks so, then I will cancel the whole project." He is also fearful of staging *Twelfth Night*, and he wonders if this might be the result of too much work in the last year. Some notes reflect his state of mind:

> Everything is in flux. Everything is vague. I am all discomfort and weariness. At the same time, I know that the weariness is caused by the difficulties in getting started. Fear of people. Fear of ending up with nothing at all. Fear of living, to even move. That is how bad it can be. Fear of dying.

---

* In his engagement planner, Bergman notes that he completes the final version of the screenplay on 7 December 1974 and his published screenplay confirms this (see Bergman 1976a, p. 106). In any case, Bergman does not travel to Stockholm on 24 November, as stated in *Images* (1995, p. 75), but at a later date.

THE SCREENPLAY

When Bergman published the screenplay to *Persona* in 1966, he included the text to a speech – "The Snakeskin" – that he had given in Amsterdam the year before, when he was awarded the Erasmus Prize together with Charles Chaplin. After that, he continued to include introductions in some, though not all, of his screenplays. They might originally have been intended as informal memos to his cast and crew, but by sharing them in the printed edition they become official statements about the work.

In the screenplay to *The Lie*, he lets the two protagonists, Anna and Andreas Fromm, introduce themselves in two monologues that are also included in the TV version. The *Scenes from a Marriage* screenplay has a formal introduction, in which Bergman presents the six episodes much like the framing comments to the filmed episodes. And in writing *Cries and Whispers*, he abandoned both the introduction and the formal structure of the screenplay itself. It was essentially an edited version of his workbook, a loose dream-like structure of a narrative with comments that he envisioned crystallising into a film.*

INTRODUCTION

Face to Face goes back to a more traditional screenplay format. There are occasional notes on visual details and a few indications of the narrative style, but overall it is sparse, much like Bergman's stylistic palette. As a text, it reads more like a play

---

* *Scenes from a Marriage*: see Bergman 1973b; *The Lie* and *Cries and Whispers*: see Bergman 1973a.

for the stage or radio than a film. His introduction was originally a letter to the crew and cast (Bergman 1976a, pp. 5–8). It begins with the greeting "Dear Fellow Workers!" followed by a kind of trade description of "a film which, in a way, is about a failed suicide", though "actually it deals ('as usual' I was about to say!) with Life, Love and Death" (1976a, p. 5).

Reflecting on the motivation for doing the production, he cannot give "a clear-cut answer"; instead, he refers to "an anxiety which has no tangible cause" that has bothered his for some time, "like having a toothache". To his aid came "another person's vicissitudes" (ibid.), read: Marianne Höök's personal history and suicide.

In an interview about the TV series, he again stresses the importance of this influence from "a woman I regarded as a sister" (Harrysson 1976, p. 9). He feels that she shared his experiences, although her state was "much clearer and much more painful, more pronounced". Therefore, he regards the working process as therapeutic, which is an ironic comment considering the embarrassment of Alma in *Persona* when she thinks of art as beneficial "for people who have a rough time" (Bergman 1966, p. 25). But Bergman seems to have considered this himself: "Thus, we [the artists] shall exist to mirror human complications, behaviour and happenings and serve as some sort of support to other people or some kind of enlightenment or self-examination or what have you" (Sundgren 1968, quoted in Steene 2005, p. 43).

A peculiar comment in the letter/introduction – and Bergman himself finds it "bizarre" (1976a, p. 7) – is his expressed reservations about staging dreams. Anyone familiar with his films would say that it sounds like he is disowning himself and his most acclaimed films, such as *Sawdust and Tinsel*, *Persona* and *Cries and Whispers*. His solution to the contradiction is to eliminate the distinctions between dream and reality, which is what he had already set out to do when writing his workbook notes for *Cries and Whispers*.

But he does not stop there. Now he considers the staged dreams to be "an extension of reality … a series of *real* events, which strike the leading character during an important moment of her life" (1976a, p. 7; italics in original). Here, he might have been influenced by Doris Lessing's *Briefing for a Descent into Hell*, in which the dreams were perhaps a truer representation of the real world than what the protagonist could access wide awake with his senses.

Before her mental crisis, Jenny is to Bergman not only a psychiatrist but an example of a person without any outer signs of a mental crisis. In the introduction, she is pictured as "a well-adjusted, capable and disciplined person, a highly qualified professional woman with a career, comfortably married to a gifted colleague and surrounded by what are called 'the good things in life'" (1976a, p. 5). She and her colleagues are "mentally illiterate" (1976a, p. 7) to Bergman. They are unable to grasp a reality beyond what they can see with their naked eyes.

The consequences of Jenny's breakdown and recovery are, however, left open. As an art cinema auteur, he could just leave it at that: an open ending of maximum ambiguity (Bordwell 2008, p. 156). Still, he cannot resist the temptation of speculating about Jenny as primal man: her life after the healing primal scream. He gives us three alternatives to which we shall return when discussing the epilogue.

Based on his experience of *Scenes from a Marriage*, Bergman originally planned to make the screenplay for *Face to Face* into a six-part TV series of 40–50 minutes per episode for the domestic market (see above for the episode titles). He would then re-edit the material to a feature film version for US and world cinema distribution. However, there are no indications of a six- or even a four-part structure in the screenplay. It is written as one piece with no subheadings. The reason might be that he wanted to leave the structure open for experimentation. At the back of his engagement planner for 1975 he has written the tentative titles for the four episodes – or "acts" as Bergman prefers to call them – that eventually were produced:

"Uppbrottet" ("The Breakup")
"Nedstigandet" ("The Descent"), later revised to "Gränsen" ("The Border")
"Skymningslandet" ("The Twilight Land")
"Återkomsten" ("The Return")

To make it easier for the reader to compare passages in the screenplay with the TV series, the screenplay is here broken down into the four acts that came to be. An epilogue section is also added that discusses the final scenes following the dramatic climax of Jenny's final breakdown and primal scream.

ACT ONE: THE BREAKUP

The part corresponding with the first act is made up of four scenes: a confrontation between Jenny and her patient Maria at the hospital; Jenny moves in with her maternal grandparents; Jenny and her colleague Helmuth Wankel discuss Maria and the limits of psychiatry; Jenny meets Tomas at a party held by Wankel's wife Elisabeth.

A notable addition to the symbolism of the protagonist, Jenny now has a surname: Isaksson. It suggests a connection between Jenny and the leading character in *Wild Strawberries*, Isak Borg, whose name connotes an icy fortress shutting out the people and the world around him. But it is also identical to the name of Bergman's former collaborator Ulla Isaksson, which is a departure from his usual references to actual persons by masking them under different names and professions: Stig Ahlgren/Mr Alman in *Wild Strawberries* and Harry Schein/Dr Vergérus in *The Magician*, for example. Bergman's use of Isaksson's name implies that his protagonist is at least in some regards based on her. But it also signals that there are close ties between *Facme to Face* and her work.

The *Face to Face* screenplay opens in Jenny's consulting room at the Psychiatric Clinic of the General Hospital, a description so vague that it could be just about anywhere in the world. Later in the screenplay we note that Bergman has stripped it of all geographic references, making the specific settings of Djursholm and Östermalm in the workbook drafts into a generalised upper-class milieu. He has thereby loosened the connection between the fictional world and real world, implying that the narrative is set in an abstract Western world and that the protagonist already lives in a mental state disconnected from reality.

It is a Friday afternoon in June, which sets the stage for a contrast between the warm and lush exteriors and the cold and sterile interiors of the hospital. Jenny has received her last patient before the weekend: Maria, a beautiful young woman with emotional and sexual issues. Maria has been crying and they have been sitting in silence for half an hour. When they finally talk, we become aware of a continuing power struggle with sexual undertones between them.

From their dialogue, we learn that Maria is an agent of chaos that challenges the orderly Jenny by insisting that she, the psychiatrist, is the one in real need of psychiatry. Maria suggests that they should "share the responsibilities", meaning that the treatment ought to be a mutual task, but Jenny dismisses it as "practically impossible" because "Such experiments have been done. With limited success" (1976a, p. 12). What Jenny is referring to is most likely R. D. Laing's world-famous and controversial experiment with a psychiatric community of patients and doctors at Kingsley Hall in London's East End from 1965 to 1970 (Laing 1994, pp. 101–149).

Maria laughs away Jenny's objection and mocks her controlled exterior by imitating it as a deceptive mask covering deep anxieties. Moreover, she counters the institution and hegemony of the psychiatry Jenny represents by making her own diagnosis of the doctor. Maria's verdict is that Jenny is unable to love and that she is rather bad at sex as well. To her, Jenny is almost unreal, signifying a theatrical barrier against real life.

Trying to break the armour of what she sees as emotional illiteracy, Maria makes frank sexual invitations, both in words and by touching Jenny's thighs and trying to steal a kiss. Jenny keeps her composure. Maria laughs out loud at her efforts and then leaves a trembling Jenny in the empty room with a crack in her mask.

Knowing Bergman's history, the scene is another of his many variations of Strindberg's play *The Strongest*. But there are also similarities to Ulla Isaksson's novels *The Blessed Ones* and *Paradise Place*. In the sexual allure of Maria, there are hints of the *folie à deux* portrayed in *The Blessed Ones*, as mentioned above. At first, Jenny does not seem to respond to the invitations, but her trembling afterwards confirms that they have shaken her. She is perhaps not only responding to the sexual allure, but also to a desire to lose control and give in to chaos.

In *Paradise Place*, there are portraits of two close friendships of women that strongly suggest love stories. One is between middle-aged physician Katha, stoically resigned to the world and its injustices, and social worker Emma, who is fierily engaged in fighting the modern world's incitement to comfortable numbness. Inspired by a 1965 socio-psychological study of young criminals,[*] Emma – the novel's voice of concern – makes a dystopian prophecy of the coming of the Aniara children. Born to consumerist parents, they promise to be a new generation of cold-hearted, ruthless and egotistical individualists.[†]

Isaksson's novel holds up the amoral young delinquent Alex De Large in Stanley Kubrick's 1971 film version of *A Clockwork Orange* and the cinema audi-

---

[*] Humble and Settergren-Carlsson 1974.

[†] *Aniara* (1956) is the name of Nobel Prize laureate Harry Martinson's science fiction poem, picturing a doomed space expedition in which the crew and passengers gradually lose all their moral inhibitions, knowing that they are bound for death. The concept of a new generation of 'Aniara children' was also used in Per Gunnar Evander's novel *Uppkomlingarna: En personundersökning* ("The Upstarts: A Personal Case Study", 1969), on which Göran du Rées in 1995 based his film *Tag ditt liv* ("Take Your Life"). Evander's young hoodlums have in du Rées's film become young Nazi skinhead brutes, who in the 1990s are the logical heirs to the 1960s/1970s 'me' generation. The Aniara children prophecy has much in common with historian Christopher Lasch's cultural analysis of the 'me' generation in his popular study *The Culture of Narcissism: American Life in an Age of Diminishing Expectations* (1979).

ence that enthusiastically responds to his ultra-violence as prime examples of the Aniara generation. As we shall see, Bergman also has a string of portraits of Aniara children in *Face to Face*. Maria is only the first one to be presented to us. We can imagine them all being born out of the proverbial Bergmanian cold womb.

The other and more pronounced love story between women in *Paradise Place* is the one of Katha's prudent daughter Sassa and the anarchic Ingrid. The intense, chaotic and jealousy-ridden on/off relationship between Isaksson's socially and temperamentally mismatched couple has rubbed off on this scene in *Face to Face*. However, since Bergman failed to follow through on the attraction between Jenny and Maria, for instance with his originally planned orgiastic dream scene, in which we easily could picture Maria taking the sexual initiative, this overture to a risky love story becomes reduced to a mere curious detail in the final screenplay.

The scene at the hospital is followed by Jenny moving in with her maternal grandparents. It is dusk. Thunderclouds are in the air when she enters their building, standing in the shadow of a church. Its staircase has preserved its luxurious late-nineteenth-century origins, making it a dark and haunting sight barely lit by small sconces. Just as Jenny enters, the creaking lift reaches the bottom floor and a huge old woman dressed in black steps out. When Jenny gets a closer look, she notes that one of the woman's eyes is missing, and she is looking at a black hole. Returning the gaze, the old woman flashes a faint smile, but the text has nothing to say about Jenny's reaction, although this meeting foreshadows her breakdown and suicide attempt.

Up in her grandparents' apartment, Jenny enters "a world lost in World War I", the bourgeois sanctuary cluttered with draperies, vases, framed photos, statuettes ad infinitum (1976a, p. 15). This is a contrast to Jenny's sparse environment at the clinic. When Jenny sits down for a cup of tea, Bergman uses the first part of her dialogue with Grandmother to explain the premise: the renovation of Jenny's house, Anna's summer holiday at a riding camp, Jenny's husband Erik's participation at a conference in Chicago and that Jenny is working all summer at the hospital as a deputy chief psychiatrist.

When Grandmother becomes suspicious of Jenny's assurances that she is happy, we get a premonition of the crisis to come. Again, Bergman makes nothing significant of the situation. Instead, he lets everyone go to bed, only to have Jenny and Grandmother meet in the middle of the night to continue the dialogue in the kitchen. They talk about Grandmother's lifelong marriage, a lesson of love quite different from the one in *Scenes from a Marriage*. Instead of picturing marital life as loveless, repressive and built on idealist lies, Bergman has Grandmother celebrate it as something nurtured by everyday tenderness and a practical reconciliation with life.

Jenny gets her own room, but now it is only an unspecified room, neither her own childhood room nor her mother's old room.* In bed, she has the first in a series of nightmares. The one-eyed woman dressed in black comes to haunt her. She wakes up as she is unable to scream and goes to sit in the living room. While the clocks strike four in the morning – the hour of the wolf – Jenny is in confusion about her condition.

The third scene is set in Jenny's hospital workroom. She confers with her colleague Helmuth Wankel about the day's work, the case of Maria and the shortcomings of psychiatry. Dr Wankel is a heavy smoker and a cynical advocate for psychiatry as a cold and mechanical process in which the patients are mere machines to be serviced, and he urges Jenny to leave Maria to him, so she can be processed economically and with more efficiency. He is clearly the personification of everything Bergman hates about clinical psychiatry, and his incessant smoking brings out his industrial quality.

Late in the afternoon Jenny goes to the party at Elisabeth Wankel's apartment. From Elisabeth's husband, Dr Wankel, she has learned that Elisabeth has a new lover, the young actor Mikael Strömberg, who we are to understand is gay but keen to enter into the relationship for the money. The Wankels are, like the Egermans in *Scenes from a Marriage*, a possible mirror of what the protagonist and her spouse might become: Dr Wankel has retreated into cold cynicism, while his wife has bought herself the illusion of happiness and love for money – keeping up appearances with theatrical mannerisms. In the filmed version, Elisabeth is wearing a red dress that is mirrored by Jenny's dress in the dream scenes, suggesting a deeper connection between the two and their love lives.

The party, which is almost over by the time Jenny gets there, is a showroom for intimate relationships in capitalist consumer society: sex as a commodity. Love without lovers – to quote the title of another 1970s Bergman project – is the theme. Present are two young women who have opened a boutique with sexy clothes, a gynaecologist, Tomas, who teaches about contraceptives in Third World

---

* The screenplay references a "Karin", who might have lived in the apartment and even in the room Jenny moves into, but we never learn who she might be. Possibly, she is Jenny's mother, although her mother does not have a name when she appears later in a dream. There is also a mention of a "Karl", both in the screenplay and in the filmed material, which might possibly be Jenny's uncle.

countries, and, finally, a young revolutionary, who has scolded all the others – presumably for their consumerist lifestyle – only to fall asleep soon afterwards. Unlike Emma of *Paradise Place*, the activist has tired of his social engagement, as had his generation by 1976.

The only one of interest to Jenny is Tomas, whom she on the spur of the moment and out of an impulsive sexual interest decides to have dinner with. The pretext is to discuss his half-sister and her patient: Maria. Before leaving the party, she phones her lover Martin to cancel their rendezvous. Hanging up, she is shocked by her daring behaviour. The reader of the screenplay, I think it is safe to say, is probably more shocked by the fact that she even had a lover – "she the decent, the proper!" as Bergman himself puts it in the workbook.

On her way down the stairs, Jenny encounters Strömberg, who wants to talk about his fear of death. Bergman puts his words from the workbook in the mouth of this young man, who is described as beautiful, full of life, self-confident, talented and gifted with the ability to climb the social ladder. Strömberg introduces a classical vanity/vanitas motif of the transience of life, the futility of pleasure and the certainty of death. However, Jenny does not seem to be personally affected by Strömberg's confessions, not even when she admits that she, like most of us, is in denial of death.

ACT TWO: THE BORDER

Elisabeth and Strömberg have delivered their warnings about Tomas being "crazy about women" and "an Alice in Wonderland, only more boring" respectively (1976a, pp. 31 and 35). Jenny therefore hesitates outside the restaurant. But it is too late. Tomas has spotted her, and she agrees to have dinner with him, feeling both attracted and repelled. Tomas talks about Maria, and not favourably. In his opinion, she was highly strung and prone to dramatic love affairs as well as dramatic breakdowns.

When her mother took her own life, Maria got worse. Tomas describes her condition in convoluted, sarcastic phrases about "love as elephantiasis", "kindness as cruelty" and "self-sacrifice as selfishness" (1976a, p. 37). He rounds off with a sadistic story from his childhood. It is about the killing of a dog, which was shot several times and finally finished by being burned alive. In this context, the story comes out as an allegory of Maria.

But what does it mean? That Maria is treated like the dog by Jenny and her psychiatrist colleagues? That she *ought* to be treated like the dog since she apparently is such a needy drama queen or, worse, an emotional vampire who drains the life out of everyone around her? We will never know. Tomas has just been described as a humanist by Elisabeth and her lover, but now he stands out as a cold and sarcastic cynic close to Josephson's Elis Vergérus characters of *A Passion* and *The Lie*. Strangely, Jenny never comments on his story as they leave for Tomas's place.

On the road, he describes his house as an old and decayed villa, somewhat reflecting himself. We assume from the dramatic build-up that they are about to have sex. Instead, they engage in a conversation about Tomas's successful divorce, about Jenny's longing for her husband and about her lover Martin being a bore. When Tomas asks her about how she handles her anxieties while pointing to his heart and genitals, she replies that her family is about to move into a new house in the autumn.

They apparently talk at cross-purposes, as Jenny responds like a devoted consumer, sublimating love and sex into the pleasures of consumption, and there is a confused silence. Tomas makes a clumsy pass at Jenny by asking her if she has gorgeous breasts, but the hedonistic atmosphere in the workbook sketches has not made it into the screenplay. Instead, the sexual pleasures with playboy lover Joakim have turned into a boring affair with Martin, and now Tomas, supposedly a suave ladies' man, is portrayed as a cheap pickup artist.

Jenny gets angry at his question and insists on going home promptly while spewing her contempt for the prospect of having sex with him and its supposedly ridiculous details of undressing, intercourse and what to do afterwards. This is to be the part when Jenny's "secret aggressions expressed in sexual aversion" come to the surface, but her reaction is utterly surprising given the premise of the scene. After our initial astonishment at learning that Jenny has a lover, we are now doubly astonished by watching her turn into an angry prude, portraying lovemaking as a contemptible theatrical act. Her intention of going to bed with Tomas was, after all, rather obvious from the outset.

What Bergman wants to do is to portray a woman torn between the legacy of sexual repression and the new era of sexual liberation. The instant psychological shifts are also consistent with the art cinema strategy of maximum ambiguity. Jenny's puzzling behaviour opens up numerous narrative possibilities as well as interpretations intended to keep the audience in suspense about who she really is.

But it also jeopardises the psychological credibility, especially since Jenny, yet again and for no apparent reason, changes her attitude completely a few moments later. At Tomas's doorstep, on her way to the waiting taxi after refusing to let Tomas drive her home, she suddenly warms to him and suggests that they should meet again, perhaps go to a movie. She even promises to call him. Unsurprisingly, Tomas is surprised, and so is the reader/audience.

Back at her grandparents' apartment, Jenny slumps into Grandfather's armchair before silently witnessing a tender scene that illustrates Grandmother's idea about love. Grandfather wanders about in confusion and mourns his aging, only to be cared for by his wife. Moments after Grandmother has carefully led him to her bedroom and into her bed, the phone rings. Jenny picks it up and "a man's voice says something to her" (1976a, p. 45), after which she drives off in the early summer morning to the family's empty house.

In her bedroom on the top floor, Jenny finds Maria lying on the floor in a condition "far beyond any reason" (ibid.). She goes to phone the hospital when she discovers the presence of two males, a fifty-year-old man and a teenager. After claiming that they only assisted Maria in finding Jenny, the man holds her to the floor while the teenager tries to rape her. The boy is the second Aniara child in the story – dirty and unkempt, acting out of a desperate need to be mothered.

His sexual aggression seems to have an ulterior motive: that of becoming her infant, perhaps even her foetus. Sucking hungrily on her breast, he tries to penetrate her, perhaps to find a way back to the womb. Since there is neither nourishment nor shelter for him to find, he soon gives up, saying that she is "constricted". The man takes some money from Jenny's purse, telling her: "Some women have to pay for a fuck. You did not know that, now did you?"

By staging the scene on the top floor in her house during the hour of the wolf, Bergman suggests that we are witnessing an attack from the id on the controlling superego. Jenny is haunted by demons, just like *The Hour of the Wolf*'s artist Johan Borg (Max von Sydow) and Isak Borg of *Wild Strawberries*. In *The Hour of the Wolf*, Johan kills a boy-demon, who besides repressed homosexuality also represents the child he has denied his wife in order to be her one and only child himself.

However, the scene in *Face to Face* connects more with *Persona* and Elisabet's rejection of her needy young son. Here, the boy is older and acts as an agent of Maria, who lies like a foetus on the floor as he rapes Jenny. The rape becomes a staging of Maria's sexual desire to penetrate and break down Jenny's repressive defence mechanisms.

In the opening scene, Maria represented Jenny's aborted emotional and sexual desires. Now, she represents the return of Jenny's aborted child, cast out of the cold womb. Later, in the narrative strand we take as reality, she will come back as Jenny's estranged daughter Anna. The money collected by the man in the rape scene could then be a representation of Jenny's consumerist compensations for her lack of love. As we have learned in the dialogue with Grandmother, Jenny lavishes money on horse-riding camps and travels to keep the daughter away from home and out of the way of her career, thereby contributing to her becoming alienated, possibly turning into an Aniara child.

Having sent Maria to the hospital in an ambulance, Jenny calls Tomas to inform him about what has happened to his half-sister. They decide to meet at a concert in the evening. It is held in a nineteenth-century mansion, connecting it with the grandparents' apartment, the mansion in *Cries and Whispers* and the bourgeois sanctuary motif of Bergman's Djursholm trilogy.

When Tomas and Jenny arrive, they are late. All seats are taken, and they are reduced to sitting on the stairs overlooking the crowded room. As mentioned in the workbook section, Bergman hesitated between two Mozart compositions for piano. In the screenplay, he has decided on Fantasia in C minor, K. 475, perhaps under the advice of Käbi Laretei. Despite the beautiful summer evening outside, the luxurious interiors of the concert room and the soothing piano music, several listeners are unable to relax. There is an air of anxiety in the mansion, and Jenny is tuned in to it. What is about to happen to her seems to be an indication of a general phenomenon.

Back in Tomas's house, we note that Jenny and he have entered into a new relationship of platonic friendship. From now on, Tomas is assigned the role of the quiet, supportive and understanding listener, that is, the primal therapist. Later, we learn that he is gay or perhaps bisexual.

Jenny does not want to talk. She just wants to survive the night. Therefore, she orders sleeping pills and a place beside Tomas in his bed. Her rational creed for normality is: "If you force everything to be as usual, then everything is as usual" (1976a, p. 53). Of course, she is now about to begin her descent into the land of demons.

It starts by Jenny telling Tomas about the rape and her impulse of wanting the teenager to penetrate her: "Suddenly she starts to laugh. It forces its way out like she for a long time has tried to control it, a dead laughter. She is shaking with laughter, tries to control it, and for some moments is successful, then it breaks out again" (1976a, p. 54).

This is a classical portrayal of what used to be called hysteria, a condition that in Bergman's childhood was regarded as emanating from the *hystera*, the womb.[*] Since Tomas is a gynaecologist Jenny refuses psychiatric help: "Here is all the relevant expertise" (1976, p. 55). In contrast to the scene in the concert hall, where Jenny's anxieties represented the human condition, Bergman now defines her solely as a representative of a specific female condition.

But what follows is hardly classical hysteria but a portrayal of clinical depression. When Jenny returns to the grandparents' apartment, she sleeps for two days and nights. She only wakes up for a short moment on Saturday, after being asleep for more than a day, to hear Grandmother inform her that she and Grandfather are going away for the weekend. Waking up again, alone, on Sunday morning, Jenny hears church bells calling to mass. Perhaps it is for her the bells are tolling, the sound of repression calling her back to the impossible life she leads. She again tries to insist on reality, now by going through her morning routines.

In an effort to be cheerful, she decides to call Tomas and make him take her to the cinema in the evening. After a few words on the phone, she stops in her tracks when the old, black-clothed and one-eyed woman appears, standing in a ray of sunshine in the living room. Jenny hangs up and starts to wander about in the apartment, taking note of the ordinary life going on outside: joyful music from a radio and two girls playing hopscotch.

She sits down and starts her pocket tape recorder to make a spoken suicide note to her husband. It begins with a declaration that she is about to take her own life, acknowledging that it is a decision that has been lying dormant within her for some years. Echoing Mrs Jacobi in *Scenes from a Marriage*, she talks about her isolation and alienation, going through the motions of everyday family life while feeling nothing.

At this moment in life, Jenny considers herself to be no more than "a marionette" – a choice of word that connects her self-diagnosis with Peter Egermann's existential condition in *From the Life of the Marionettes*. Facing death, she feels "no fear, no grief or loneliness". Rather, she is "contented, almost elated, like when I was young and about to go on a trip", and she considers her suicide to be "a recovery from a lifelong illness".

The monologue closes with a cryptic statement: "I promise, word of honour." Bergman adds to the mystery: "What she would have promised on her word of honour, Jenny cannot figure out" (1976a, pp. 61–62). Perhaps it is intended as an

---

[*] See, for instance, Leahey 2013, pp. 273–275.

enigma, like the "No" at the end of *The Lie*, but it seems more like a demonstration of Jenny's alienation from the world and its representation in language – a parallel to the breakdown of Alma's language in *Persona*.

ACT THREE: THE TWILIGHT LAND

Jenny takes fifty Nembutal tablets and falls into "a dark maelstrom of visions and dreams" (1976a, p. 62).[*] In her first dream, she hurries down a long dark corridor with high walls, broken windows and a rubbish-littered floor of planks. It is cold and there is snow and frost all over the interior, but Jenny is sweating. When she catches a glimpse of herself in a mirror, she sees herself in a beautiful long dark red dress with flounces and lace, as if she was going to a party. On her head, there is a red hood with decorations.

The air is stale and cold. Dirty snow and frost are everywhere. Eventually, she reaches a decayed drawing room, recognising it as the remnants of her grandparents' apartment. An elderly man in an old and ill-fitting tailcoat sits on a broken chair in the middle of the room. At his feet stands a little girl in a red dress. On a table beside them, a candle light flickers. That frightens the man and the girl.

The scene has echoes of an Edgar Allan Poe story and/or elements of Marianne Höök's personal history. Like *The Fall of the House of Usher*, this is the downfall of the Ibsenian doll's house, its class and idealist values. There is also Poe's suggestion of incestuous rot, connecting the scene with Höök's traumatic memories of the love story – consummated or not – with her grandfather (Kullenberg 2008, pp. 314–316).

Jenny's dress connotes female sexuality, while her hood connotes childhood. Both suggest a connection to the old tale of Red Riding Hood that will be more prominent in the filmed version.[†] The little girl at the man's feet is, of course, Jenny herself as a child, when she was close or, rather, too close to Grandfather. Now he is about to share the fate of his dying world as soon as the candle light goes out.

---

[*] Nembutal is a barbiturate that has pentobarbital as its active component. In high doses, it causes respiratory arrest. It has therefore been used in euthanasia and to carry out death penalties by lethal injection.

[†] Jacques Berlioz (2007) dates the Red Riding Hood tale back to the tenth century, and there have also been suggestions of close similarities to ancient folk tales from North Africa (Goodman 2005, p. 62).

Next, we are about to witness the asexual remains of the masquerade sex orgy scene sketched in the workbook. Jenny notices that there are other people in the drawing room, all dressed in old and worn party clothes – men in tailcoats, women in ball gowns. They are the living dead bourgeoisie, and one of them is Jenny's resigned colleague Dr Helmuth Wankel. Jenny is sickened by the stench from their necrosis, and she tries to take control of the situation by telling Wankel (and herself) that she can wake up by sheer will.

Nevertheless, the dream continues as a scarred clown dressed in a Napoleon hat and with one of his eyes gouged out steps out from a doorway to scare Grandfather and little Jenny. He is another aspect of death, just like the one-eyed old woman. We will meet him again in the TV production of *In the Presence of a Clown* (*Larmar och gör sig till*, 1997). As the lights go out, the clown reaches out to take Grandfather with him. This is apparently not hell, only a limbo between life and death.

Despite Dr Wankel's warning, Jenny flees the scene through a door, and now she is back in the grandparents' apartment as it was when she took the pills. The only difference is the soft light without a shadow – "like the light on a rainy autumn day" (1976a, p. 68). And like the light in many Bergman films of the 1960s, one could add.

In vain, Jenny calls out for Grandmother while searching the rooms. Then comes a new twist to the Leonor Fini-inspired scene in the workbook: "Finally, she drops down at the big black dining room table. Her yellow skin and deep red dress are faintly reflected by the table top, as in a deep and still water" (ibid.).

Jenny is freezing, but the one-eyed woman appears out of nowhere to lend her a cardigan and to comfort her with a motherly embrace. When Jenny leans against the woman's breast, the moment invokes the *pietà* scene from *Cries and Whispers*. The original nightmarish sex-and-death symbolism of the original scene has now been replaced by a reconciliation – even a spiritual atonement – with death.

While this reflects Bergman's own struggle with the subject, noted in the workbook, the change completely undermines both the imagery of the scene and the symbolic continuity of the narrative. What in acts one and two was clearly hinted at as Jenny's emotional and sexual neuroses has suddenly turned into an easily resolved anxiety.

Moreover, there have been no indications of incest or incestuous feelings between Jenny and Grandfather in the previous scenes, neither will there be in the subsequent scenes. This symbolism is therefore also detached from the characterisation of the protagonist. Consequently, the Ibsenian theme of living a lie that was essential to the previous titles in the Djursholm trilogy is lost. What we are left with is Mikael Strömberg's existential neurosis by proxy, his inability to live because of an overwhelming fear of death.

Jenny wakes up at the moment of embracing death. She is in a hospital. Tomas is by her side to explain how she survived the suicide attempt. But Jenny (and Bergman) has a restless urge to get on with the story. In an instant of meta-narrative interruption, Tomas's story of how he got to the apartment and called the ambulance is cut short by Jenny yawning: "God, how boring. Now I'm going to sleep" (1976a, p. 70).

The second dream is about Jenny meeting her dead parents in the grandparents' apartment. Father is tall and round-shouldered. He has clear blue eyes and thin grey hair. Mother is described as very beautiful, with regular features and big dark eyes. They are both nervous, looking every which way as if lost. To connect with them and calm their fears, Jenny opens her monologue with a declaration of love.

She continues by telling them how she as a nine-year-old girl saw them at the morgue after the road accident. Her memories of her parents are both good and bad, but there are no details, no stories, only vague notions of closed doors, secrecy, guilt and a bad conscience. Ashamed, the parents whisper to each other, after which they adjust their coats and hats as if they are about to leave the apartment. Jenny starts to hit them while she also tries to embrace them, ripping through their brittle clothes with her hands until she stumbles on her red dress and wakes up once more.

The scene in the screenplay is a summary of Bergman's key notion of 'being guilty of guilt',* since the verbal confrontation is articulated in generalised terms only. We find nothing of personal details or intimate memories in the dialogue, hence nothing that engages or disturbs. Furthermore, there is no clear connection between the dream and the premise of the narrative. So far, the only reference to Jenny's parents is a brief look at a photo of young Jenny with her father in Grandfather's album and the following lines:

Grandmother: "You were always Daddy's little girl."
Jenny: "Oh, there were probably reasons for that."
(1976a, p. 18)

---

* See protagonist Isak Borg's nightmare of failing his examination in *Wild Strawberries*.

If the photo and the "Daddy's little girl" comment had been about Jenny and Grandfather, there would at least be some small sign of the incest motif introduced and then swiftly abandoned in the first dream. Instead, we only learn that Jenny's parents died when she was nine and that she harbours some mixed feelings of love, guilt and anger towards them. Later, there are more details about the family situation, although the new revelations raise more questions than they clarify.

"Jenny!" Tomas shouts, and Jenny wakes up in the hospital room. She is overcome by her appearance, unwashed and sweaty, but before she can make a move, her husband Erik walks in. Holding her audio suicide letter in his hand, he smiles oddly and starts the conversation with the ironic and insensitive line: "You certainly know how to come up with surprises." Jenny replies with sarcasm: "Don't you think?" (1976a, p. 73). We immediately gather that this is a couple which Bergman would characterise as emotional illiterates.

Erik is pictured as a neatly dressed, weak and immature man, who cannot face what his wife has done – death even less. After a short and nervous conversation about guilt and what to say to the relatives, he hastily withdraws. We sense that his promise to "tell the truth" (1976a, p. 75) to Grandmother will never be fulfilled, and probably there will be no more discussion of the suicide attempt.

Jenny returns to her land of dreams. This time she ends up in a revised version of the humiliating public hearing sketched in the workbook. The setting is a dirty and decayed hospital room with windows overlooking a winter landscape. Jenny has a doctor's coat over her red dress and looks at Maria, who lies dead in a gynaecologist's chair. Dr Wankel and some other doctors are there to observe and make notes while Jenny speaks in a monologue.

She defends her distanced relationship with Maria as a controlled disgust with the patient's body, wondering if she has broken any scientific or ethical rules. None of the other doctors seem to respond. Continuing, Jenny assures that she believes in something called love and that she has tried, but failed, to live like other people. Dr Wankel closes what he calls the interrogation by telling Jenny that her case will be submitted to the disciplinary board.

When Jenny asks what will happen next, his answer is "Nothing" (1976a, p. 78). The scene ends as Jenny echoes Elisabet's final words in *Persona*: "Nothing... nothing... nothing..." Individual repression in *Persona* has in *Face to Face* become an institutional practice.

When Jenny wakes up at the hospital, Tomas is there. It is two o'clock in the morning, perhaps a sign of a new dawn in Jenny's life as the summer sun soon will rise over the horizon. After some small talk, Tomas discloses his love affair with Mikael Strömberg and his grief that it ended the year before. He talks about "our cruel market", in which "faithlessness is total and competition is terrible" (1976a, p. 81).

The Tomas we previously knew as the 'ladies' man' now turns into a bitter and cynical homosexual man modelled on Bergman's long-time assistant Lenn Hjortzberg, who died in 1975. In *The Magic Lantern* (Bergman 1988, pp. 195–196) Hjortzberg is called Tim, and in *From the Life of the Marionettes* the Tim character is a continuation of Tomas. Robin Wood's (2000b, pp. 15–16) essay on *From the Life of the Marionettes* offers an excellent analysis of the Tim character and his self-contempt that could also include Tomas. However, Wood forgets that Bergman was not only influenced by his close friend and assistant, but also by the zeitgeist revealed in the depictions of gay men in contemporary films such as Rainer Werner Fassbinder's *Fox and His Friends* (*Faustrecht der Freiheit*, 1975).

Fassbinder's portrait of love as a capitalist transaction of money and services in a modern consumer society closely corresponds with Tomas's and Tim's portrayal of gay love as a heartless meat market. It also corresponds with other films about gay life in the late 1960s and early 1970s: homosexual men and women marked by social stigma, low self-esteem and even self-disgust. Bergman's aborted 1978 project "Love Without Lovers" – a title suitable for just about any of Fassbinder's films – would later elaborate on the subject and eventually produce *From the Life of the Marionettes* from its cold womb.*

Just like Tim in *From the Life of the Marionettes*, Tomas is, however, more than just a caricature of the poor deplorable gay man. He is also an early example of what Wood analyses as the asexual and supportive gay friend to the female protagonist in late twentieth century romantic film comedy (2000a, pp. 39–41).† Moreover, he is the primal therapist that will eventually release Jenny from her repressions.

When Tomas's confessional story comes to an end, Jenny goes back to sleep. In her dream, she is at the hospital, checking patients. A man rips the skin off his face, revealing a face covered in pus-filled blisters and bleeding wounds. A

---

* "Love Without Lovers" was written in 1978 but refused by several producers. The screenplay was published in the 2000 book *Föreställningar* ("Performances"). For a detailed history of gay people on film, see Vito Russo's book *The Celluloid Closet* from 1981 and the documentary film by the same name from 1995.
† Wood uses as examples titles such as *My Best Friend's Wedding* (1997), *The Object of My Affection* (1998) and *Blast from the Past* (1999).

woman communicates by a strip of paper coming out of her mouth, announcing that her anxiety has been surgically removed but that the doctors forgot her daily terror.

Grandfather appears to talk about his fear of death. This revised version of *The Hour of the Wolf* is now in the service of portraying the true face of psychiatric treatment: deformed minds in deformed bodies, appearances and behaviours. Jenny is disgusted, at a loss for words, and she masks her inability to help with pills and clichéd advice. The scene illustrates Dr Wankel's industrial view of the psychiatric profession not as a treatment but as a system to manage those who do not fit the hegemony of 'normality'.

Trying to embrace her daughter Anna, who appears only to shy away from her, Jenny is confronted by Tomas. He scolds her, but not because she is unable to find the *right* words. Instead, he advises her to talk with the patients in *their* words, connect with *their* feelings, not apply her own words and feelings. Jenny is devastated and concludes that she is no longer suitable to be a psychiatrist. Tomas continues by telling her a story about a mighty prince who first tortured his subjects, only to comfort them with presents and endearments. It is, of course, a metaphor for the 'insane' institution of psychiatry that Jenny is a product of.

ACT FOUR: THE RETURN

When Jenny wakes up, Tomas tells her that she has only slept for two minutes. She starts to speak about children being frightened, beaten and killed and the fact that no one cares for them. It might seem to be out of context, but she is referring to her own childhood as well as the prospect of the Aniara generation to come – the one we have glimpsed in Maria, the rapist teenager and perhaps also in Jenny's daughter Anna.

Tomas rejects her sentiments as vain pity and refers to adults as overgrown children dying from emotional starvation. The metaphor goes back to *The Lie*, in which Andreas talks about modern-day children as materially well fed but emotionally undernourished. Making a speech on how biology has determined humankind to be chaotic and destructive, he attempts to rationalise the human condition as impossible to change. Although life has its beautiful moments, Tomas acknowledges, he essentially thinks of it as "a shithole" (1976a, p. 87). Suddenly, his cynical armour cracks and he starts to cry.

Like all dialogues between Jenny and Tomas, this is a good example of what Marianne Höök meant by Bergman's work being a monologue for many voices. The two are, of course, voicing his own dark thoughts, being fools "for everything that I am a fool". But I consider his ambitions to go beyond a mere introvert act of navel-gazing, as the contemporary audience not only recognise the existential issues but also how these were reflected in the ongoing debate in psychiatry and sociobiology. Bergman's next step is to go deeper into Jenny's trauma, but first he has decided on a final *traum*, marking the end of Jenny as we have known her.

When Tomas leaves the room, Jenny goes to sleep. She dreams of seeing herself again dressed in red but now lying in a white coffin in the grandparents' drawing room. While the priest delivers his lecture, Jenny's parents put on the heavy lid and the priest proceeds to cut off the parts of her dress that pour out from the closed coffin. Jenny in the coffin pounds on the lid and shouts from inside. But the Jenny who watches does not help. Instead, she sets the coffin on fire and watches while her alter ego turns to ashes.

The dream is a precursor to the primal scream through which the new Jenny will arise like a phoenix from the ashes of her former self, and when she wakes up she is ready to begin her therapeutic journey back to her childhood traumas. It begins with a story of how she had to attend an open-casket funeral in which her beloved cousin's dead body was displayed before it was buried, although Jenny was convinced he was still alive. She also talks about her frigidity and her display of contempt for a poem connecting love and death, which is what Bergman has celebrated in the intimate moments between Jenny's grandparents.

Now Jenny can finally see the social construction of her adult self as a woman with no connections between her rational thinking and her emotions, and how her display of self-confidence was only a mask covering an inner turmoil of self-doubts, inhibitions and vulnerability. She analyses it as "playing the game" and "learning the lines" (1976a, p. 91), thereby highlighting the Ibsenian subtext of the story, essentially how love is destroyed by theatricality and scepticism. The story continues backwards in time to her childhood and how her mother and grandmother (i.e. the Grandmother of the film's narrative) despised her alcoholic father's tender love for his daughter. So deeply was she imprinted by this contempt that she became disgusted and angry with her own infant daughter's heart-breaking cry.

Bergman suddenly stops Jenny in her tracks to address his critics. He has Jenny voice the leftist criticism directed against his films: that private suffering is the privilege of the wealthy and does not count for much when compared to the material suffering in the world. Tomas cuts in as Bergman's advocate to counter these objections by pointing to the fact that her suicide attempt suggests otherwise and that "the world begins and ends with yourself" (1976a, p. 93).

He encourages Jenny to go on, and she begins to speak in a variety of voices, both her own and that of her mother and grandmother. This is Bergman's most expressive staging of a mental breakdown, and it is intended to show the terrible legacy of idealism: "the women's inner sabotage of themselves, the secret aggressions expressed in sexual aversion, the ambition to live up to a role created by their mothers". Interestingly, it is staged like the monologues with many voices that Bergman writes in his workbook, where he sometimes interjects a voice of self-criticism.

The traumas are familiar acquaintances from the Bergman filmography: guilt, bad conscience, dread of authoritarian discipline and finally the horror of being locked in a dark closet. Hence, the primal scream is Bergman's own, to which he adds a message: a secular, anti-idealist version of the final plea in Victor Sjöström's *The Phantom Carriage*: "Lord, please let my soul come to maturity before it is reaped." In *Face to Face*, Bergman chooses a primal therapy alternative, in which Tomas calls out for authenticity, wishing to fully feel all emotions, joy as well as pain, without any rational checkpoints.

EPILOGUE

The final ten pages of the screenplay is essentially an epilogue to the drama. Tomas bids Jenny farewell as he plans to go to Jamaica and live a depraved life, which we take as a vision of having lots of free-spirited gay sex. Again, we are puzzled about the twists and turns of the psychology as Tomas transforms from a heterosexual ladies' man to a brooding homosexual man and finally to a hedonist that for unclear reasons approves of the cynical meat market he criticised before.*

Jenny meets with her daughter Anna, hoping that what has happened will bring them closer. But the rift between them has grown too wide, and we sense that Anna is on her way to becoming another Aniara child, or alternatively another Jenny. Back in her grandparents' apartment, Jenny realises that Erik had said nothing of her suicide, neither has Tomas Jacobi. She therefore plays along with

---

* Robin Wood (2000b, p. 16) mistakenly indicates that this scene is from *Scenes from a Marriage*.

Grandmother's belief that she was hospitalised because of overwork and that is that. However, the final scenes in the apartment are also used to show Jenny's reconciliation with her past.

Looking at Grandmother now, Jenny is no longer confronted with the cruel tormentor of her childhood but with an old, fragile and tender woman worrying that her husband is about to die. Watching the silent but strong connection between the two, Jenny realises the true meaning of how love and death are connected. She has become a different person than the Jenny who poured ironic commentaries over the poem addressing the very same issues.

The final scene depicts another reconciliation, that of Jenny and her fear of death. Going for a walk, she again encounters the huge one-eyed woman in black. Now they are outside on a sunny Sunday afternoon. The town is busy, and Jenny's demons have been exorcised, and the one-eyed old woman is just an old woman, no more. Recognising this, Jenny takes the woman by the hand and helps her to cross the street. There are people all around, but no one takes any notice.

THE END.

As mentioned above, when discussing the introduction to the screenplay, Bergman gives us three alternatives regarding what might happen to Jenny after her primal scream and the insight "that she is a conglomerate of other people and the whole world":

1. Jenny goes back to her old life as if nothing has happened; that is, she reverts to being "a stifling, static combination of charted qualities and patterns of behaviour".
2. Jenny becomes primal man and will "be drawn farther and farther towards the centre of her universe, guided by the searchlight of intuition, a voyage of discovery that will also make her open up to other people in an endless design".
3. Jenny tires of her endless horizons and "puts out the light, in the respectable certainty that if you put out the light it will be dark at any rate – and quiet". (1976, pp. 7–8)

The first alternative is clear, but the other two are rather vague. A hint of what alternative two means to Bergman is in Tomas's longing to be authentic – to experience life without alienation – a message right out of Janov's *The Primal*

Scream. His third and last alternative seems to imply death by suicide. As we shall see, Bergman would make numerous changes to the screenplay during the production and postproduction of *Face to Face*, thereby changing the implications of Jenny's psychological crisis and its aftermath.

THE PRODUCTION

To learn what happened during the four months that followed Bergman's completion of the screenplay on 7 December 1974, we need to go to the engagement planners for 1974–75. On 8 December, he delivered the screenplay to Cinematograph in Stockholm, and on 7 January 1975 he held a press conference in Stockholm about the production. Towards the end of that month, 25–26 January, Bergman met with his staff at the company's office to initiate the preproduction. He rehearsed *Twelfth Night* in January–February, and in the first days of March he flew to the US to negotiate the world rights for *Face to Face* before commencing the production.

TUESDAY, 4 MARCH
Bergman has lunch with Dino De Laurentiis. In the planner, Bergman comments on the skyscraper swaying, which suggests that they are in a top-floor restaurant, perhaps Windows of the World in the north tower of the World Trade Center. He sells the world rights to De Laurentiis, who has a distribution deal with Paramount.

THURSDAY, 6 MARCH
Bergman meets and dines with some other people in the film business. One of them is Kenneth Hagrann, with whom he has talks about making a pornographic film. In the evening, he goes out with his agent Paul Kohner and with Liv Ullmann. Afterwards, he watches the soft-porn hit *Emmanuelle* in one of the downtown cinemas.

FRIDAY, 7 MARCH

On the opening night of *Twelfth Night*, he flies back to Sweden. A month later, at Fårö, he screens Swedish porn films *Flossie* and *Exposed*. In his Workbook no. 30, there are some scattered notes for a pornographic project under the title of "Porrfilmen" ("The Porn Film"), but the project never amounted to anything.

MONDAY 10 MARCH

Back at Fårö, Bergman is in high spirits over the successful premiere of *Twelfth Night*: "the critics' response were good, even great". Although he claims to have been somewhat unhealthy for most of the time, everything went well and he notes that he has had a good time with the actors. Again, Bergman plunges into the production of *Face to Face*, and he makes some final notes in his Workbook no. 29 about this:

> I have very deliberately not worked on *Face to Face* for the whole time, except for the most urgent matters. Now I am about to rewrite the dreams in particular, perhaps also make a few adjustments to the structure. At the moment, I feel much happier and more eager to work than I did when travelling to Stockholm in December.

In the following dream scene that he writes or rewrites, we are back in the enormous apartment with "each room being stranger than the one before". There is snow and dirt and it is chilly. Wherever Jenny goes in her "nice red dress", she ends up in front of the very same door. Finally, she arrives at a big room with a small girl beside a single burning candle.

Everywhere there are people waiting, hesitating. Grandfather sits in a chair. The girl stands by his knee. A "monstrous figure" is leaning over the girl, caressing her. The light is fluttering and there is to be a dialogue with Dr Wankel, who might be the monster mentioned. Then the light goes out: "Strange noises are heard and a scream for help or something else."

MONDAY, 17 MARCH

Bergman contemplates how to best include fear of death in the narrative. Seneca, the Stoic philosopher, he feels has the best words on the subject. A quote from "On the Shortness of Life" about the necessity to live like we could never die while being fully aware that we can die at any moment is for Bergman the best answer to this recurring existential question in his films. But how to stage it? Perhaps Grandfather could articulate it in a manner "so real that it is shocking"? No, the beautiful actor Strömberg is to be the one confronting Jenny with it: "then everyone can construe it however they want".

MONDAY, 24 MARCH
Bergman revises his first dream: "It was a long time coming, but it has turned out much better." He would, however, continue to be dissatisfied with the dreams during and after the shooting.

FRIDAY, 18 APRIL
Bergman writes a letter to Liv Ullmann about Jenny:

> Dearest Liv,
> You will receive this letter from Katinka [Faragò, the production manager] if we do not find the time to meet and talk with each other before you meet with the girls for a make-up and costume test. To understand the course we have set, I will recapitulate what we talked about during our meeting in New York.
>
> Part One
> Jenny plays her part. She is altogether perfect, almost pedantic. Clothes are perfect, hair and make-up as well. There is not a crack in her armour. Her clothes are such that people who understand clothes notice that they are extremely refined and expensive. People who do not understand clothes think that she dresses discreetly and in good taste. We have therefore assumed that the dress is Jenny's favourite item of clothing. It gives the impression of coolness, openness but also of reserve, protection and standoffishness.
>
> Part Two
> Jenny has exploded. Nothing is what it has been any more. Her original personality peeps out, terrified, unkempt, very physical, smelly and new-born. When she, after having gone through her crisis, comes home to Grandmother, she is clean and fresh but only dressed in a sweater and a pair of old jeans. She is without make-up and without jewellery. For the first time in her life as a grown-up, she is unaware of her looks.

If you agree with my notions, that is very nice and we can then perhaps continue the course we have set. If you want it in any other way, we must arrange an express meeting on Tuesday evening. Katinka knows where I am and I will get in touch as fast as I can.

(I have a meeting with a couple of Italians the whole afternoon. A meeting that has been postponed three times, and so I cannot get out of it without convulsions.)

Hope that you feel well taken care of,
Big hug*

MONDAY, 21 APRIL

Bergman's last day at Fårö. The morning after he travels to Stockholm to make the last preparations before the shooting starts a week later. Looking forward to the production, he notes that the "awful depression after the script has completely subsided". He considers the trip to the USA to have been stimulating, "and it was also good for our finances".

MONDAY, 28 APRIL – MONDAY, 30 JUNE

Shooting the film alternately in Stockholm and in Cinematograph's Dämba studio at Fårö. Everything goes well, except for some minor illnesses and scratches on a few of the rushes. On 28 May he meets with Charles Champlin, senior film critic of the *Los Angeles Times*, for an interview. Wrapping up the production, Bergman notes that he is quite tired. In retrospect, he was also quite lucky since a strike broke out shortly afterwards that put a halt to all theatre and film production until September.

Liv Ullmann kept a diary of the production and published it in her book *Changing* (*Forandringen*, 1976; English edition 1977, pp. 212–241). To her, the production was of great importance, and she thinks it was too for Bergman. On the last day, she wonders if people are going to like the film. Bergman replies: "Regard it as a surgeon's scalpel. Not everyone will welcome it" (Ullmann 1976, p. 241).

TUESDAY, 1 JULY

Bergman arrives at Fårö after the shooting in Stockholm has been completed: "Time went awfully fast." He is unsure about the result but has the feeling that

---

* The text is from a copy with a Cinematograph letterhead in the Ingmar Bergman Archive.

"there probably are some things in this that will prove to be difficult and feel embarrassing".

WEDNESDAY, 16 JULY – FRIDAY, 29 AUGUST

Bergman makes the rough cut of the TV series while once again writing a screenplay about Jesus. He has mood swings, and at one point (30 July) he considers the material to be better suited to a unified whole – one film.

SATURDAY, 30 AUGUST – SUNDAY, 31 AUGUST

Bergman invites Erland Josephson and Liv Ullmann for dinner and a discussion while running a rough-cut screening of *Face to Face*. The day after he makes some complementary takes of scenes with Jenny and Maria, Jenny and Tomas and of the dream scene in the corridor.

TUESDAY, 2 SEPTEMBER – THURSDAY, 23 OCTOBER

Bergman takes another look at the material, including the new scenes, and has more talks with Liv Ullmann. He makes a final cut of the TV version on Sunday, 14 September. By then, he had also started working on the film version, finishing a rough cut on Friday, 19 September. After showing the TV version of *Face to Face* to Lars Löfgren, head of the TV theatre department at Swedish Radio, Bergman gets some suggestions for revising the first dream and decides to reshoot it. He rewrites the dream and shoots the new material on Saturday, 4 November.

SUNDAY, 26 OCTOBER – SATURDAY, 1 NOVEMBER

Bergman visits Los Angeles after getting "a telegram from that fucking Italian", which presumably refers to Dino De Laurentiis. At the time, he is busy digesting *The Primal Revolution* and *The Feeling Child*.

Finally meeting Arthur Janov in person, Bergman considers him to be a kindred spirit, and during a visit to the Primal Institute they agree on making a film together. At the time, Janov and his institute were in a crisis. He had just left his wife for another woman and a Swedish patient had died by suicide, but the bestselling psychiatrist captivated Bergman by showing films from his therapeutic sessions.*

At De Laurentiis's office there were talks about Bergman's next project, tentatively called "The Experiment", but "non-committal", according to Bergman's

---

* Author's interview with Videgård, 29 June 2015.

planner. Before going back to Stockholm Bergman also had discussions with Erica Jong about making a film based on her upcoming book, presumably *How to Save Your Own Life* (1977).

MONDAY, 17 NOVEMBER 1975 – SUNDAY, 25 JANUARY 1976

Having reshot the first dream, Bergman takes some time off from *Face to Face* to finish his screenplay of "The Experiment", which in January 1976 is renamed "The Serpent's Egg". He also finishes a screenplay called "The Prince", but there are no more notes on the Jesus film.

In the days before Christmas he mixes the sound and music for the TV version and makes the final cut of the film version. He shows the film version to a pleased Liv Ullmann in January. Both the TV and the film version are now ready for release, but unforeseen events would dominate the media at the expense of his new production, which is set to have its cinema and TV premiere in April.

TUESDAY, 30 JANUARY

The tax evasion affair begins when Bergman is apprehended by the police at Dramaten. After days of interrogation, he is hospitalised for six weeks due to a nervous breakdown.

THURSDAY, 22 APRIL

In an article published in the cultural pages in *Expressen*, Sweden's biggest newspaper at the time, Bergman declares his intention to work abroad for an unspecified time (Bergman 1976b). The statement causes a heated debate in the Swedish media and much speculation in the international press (Larsson 1976, Anon. 1976i).

THE TV SERIES

The TV series premiered on 28 April, more than three weeks after the film version opened in New York on 5 April. It ran during prime time – eight o'clock in the evening – for four consecutive Wednesdays on Swedish TV2.*

ACT ONE: THE BREAKUP

All the acts open with an image of streaming water accompanied by the sound of a spring not seen in the shot. The main title "ANSIKTE MOT ANSIKTE" in white capital letters of the font Bergman regularly used is shown against the background. It is followed by the word "Act" and the number – in words, not numerals – and then by the title of the respective act. The end credits are in black-on-white letters of the same font. Both the main title and the end credits are presented without music, and there is only music – both diegetic and non-diegetic – on a few occasions in the series.

Water is a potent, multi-faceted symbol that resonates in *Face to Face* on many levels. In most religions, including Christianity, water is a purifier; see for instance *The Virgin Spring*. Bergman wrote about the spring as the metaphor for creative inspiration in his Workbook no. 29, and in Scandinavian mythology it is the source of wisdom: Odin had to sacrifice one of his eyes to drink from the god of wisdom Mimir's spring.

---

* Bergman's previous TV series, *Scenes from a Marriage*, ran at 8pm on Thursdays in April–May 1973.

For Carl Jung (1934–54, p. 18), water represents the unconscious, and Bergman uses this symbolism in the opening of *Through a Glass Darkly*. The opening shot looks out over the sea, from which the film's four protagonists arise, as if they were born from the depths of the filmmaker's mind and the collective unconscious. That symbolism also applies to *Face to Face* as the image dissolves from the flowing water to a close-up of the protagonist Jenny, played by Liv Ullmann.

Jenny's eyes search in vain for something. She turns towards us and stops in her tracks for a moment, looking in silence directly into the camera – at us – with an unfeigned face. It looks much like the open face of the old wooden statue used by Bergman in his Cinematograph logotype, shown in a scene at the end of *Persona* and during the opening credits of *Scenes from a Marriage*. Watching a silent close-up of Liv Ullmann returning the gaze in a Bergman production also reminds us of her breakthrough role as Elisabet in *Persona*. In that film, as in this TV series, we become her mirror and she becomes ours:

> The mirror motif, this Bergman signature, appears continually. In front of the mirror, people see themselves. They stop to reflect on the gloominess of their life, experience the moment of truth. The mirror is an opening in the wall of reality. (Höök 1962, p. 61)

Jenny's searching eyes represent our collective search for something that haunts us, something that cannot be found in the outer world and that is only accessible by turning our gaze inwards.

She puts on her sunglasses and with it her mask: a smile and a theatrical performance. The glasses are a straightforward reference to Immanuel Kant's metaphor from *Critique of Pure Reason* of looking at the world through coloured glasses, that is, having a skewed perspective of reality (Kant 1922, p. 15ff). The theatricality she applies to hide her true self: the little lost girl trying to keep her bewilderment in check by acting mature and in control. Cut to a long shot of an empty room, save a potted plant and a grey telephone. Jenny enters the frame from the right, holding her handbag and a bigger bag.

In the previous close-up, we noted her tightly wound hair bun. Now, in the long shot, we register her strict and conformist beige skirt and white blouse, suggesting an innocence that is later echoed in the white doctor's coat. Jenny's wardrobe is like the outfits Marianne wore in *Scenes from a Marriage*, only a bit classier. When she picks up the phone to call "lilla mamma" ("little mummy"), talking with a

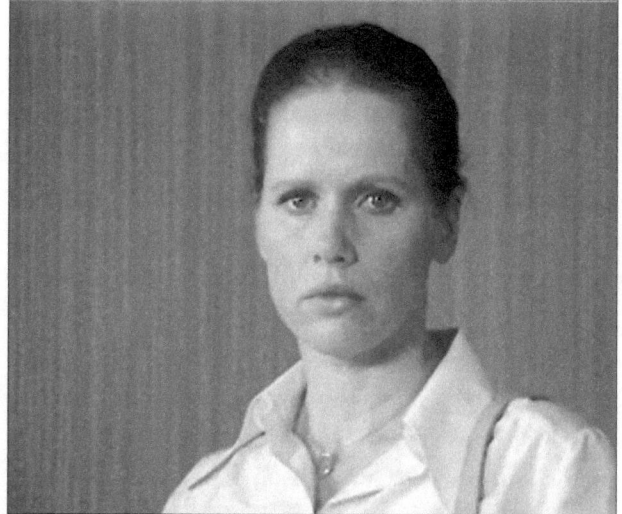

Figs. 13 & 14: Jenny Isaksson (Liv Ullmann) as the audience's mirror before and after putting on the persona. *Face to Face* (1976; TV version). (© Cinematograph AB)

girlish voice, the scene is virtually identical to the one in episode two of *Scenes from a Marriage*, in which Marianne calls her mother to cancel a dinner arrangement.

Cutting to a long shot from a hallway, we see Jenny leave the room. She is humming quietly. Cut to an extreme long shot as she steps outside the house. We note that it is a red villa with white corners that looks like a bigger and more expensive version of a Swedish countryside cottage, the archetypal symbol of Swedishness. There is no garden, only grass and trees, indicating that the people living there are too busy to do any gardening. When Jenny drives away, Bergman breaks with his static camera rules and has Sven Nykvist make a pan right to keep the car in frame as it drives up on the road and away from the house.

Dissolve to a close-up of Maria (Kari Sylwan). She is turned left and her face is partly covered by stringy hair. In the dissolve, she faces Jenny's house, foreboding the scene in which Jenny later finds Maria in the bedroom. But it is also the first of several split-screen and mirror images in the production. Here, the house represents Jenny's world, her mind, and it is reflected by Maria's face.* In the next scene Jenny and Maria come face to face with each other or, rather, Jenny faces a creature from within herself.

Cut to a medium shot of Jenny sitting by a desk in her doctor's coat, quietly doodling while waiting for Maria to speak. The scene corresponds with the screenplay's opening scene of the power game between psychiatrist and patient. Maria is placed left in the images throughout the scene, while Jenny is on the right. Hence Maria has taken the place of the house in the dissolve, and the power struggle that follows represents Jenny's inner turmoil.

This is the first sign of war between the id and the superego, chaotic reality and controlled theatricality, and, to the religiously schooled Bergman, perhaps also between 'evil' (left) and 'good' (right). However, we should keep in mind that, at this point in his life, Bergman was decidedly post-religious and anti-psychiatry, making his sympathies in the struggle more ambiguous, perhaps even sympathetic to the forces of chaos.

In the screenplay, the scene is intended as a first attack on Jenny and her complacent worldview. But some parts of the screenplay have been deleted in the shooting and editing: the reference to experimental psychiatry, Maria's attempt to kiss Jenny and the final image of Jenny trembling in her chair. Hence, Maria's challenge to Jenny is reduced. Moreover, we now see only Maria's obsession with Jenny, not vice versa.

Their stand-off comes to naught since Jenny never show any cracks. Maria, on the other hand, is all uncontrollable urges – pure sexual impulse – which diminishes her intellectually. Hence Jenny comes out as unaffected, and our impression of Maria makes Tomas's portrait of her as a drama queen seem less offensive.

---

* The house is a classical Freudian metaphor for the mind; see White 2008, p. 94. It can seem confusing to claim that Bergman used metaphors from both Freud and Jung in the same film. And there have been discussions about whether Bergman was a Freudian or a Jungian – see Björkman et al. 1973, p. 219. After reading and watching many interviews with Bergman, I have concluded that he simply uses whatever metaphors that inspire him.

Cut to a long shot of Jenny arriving by car outside her grandparents' block of apartments. In the screenplay, the scene is ominous: an upcoming thunderstorm is in the air of the summer evening. The filmed scene, however, is more idyllic. No clouds on the horizon. Birds are singing. The only foreboding of things to come is the sound of the repressive church bells tolling as Jenny walks up to the street door.

Entering the Art Nouveau building, Jenny sees an old lady in black and a mourning veil descend the stairs. The steps echo around the staircase. We share Jenny's point of view, but in contrast to the screenplay, the old woman neither is huge nor has a cane, and she walks vigorously down the stairs. The only threatening aspect about her is a strange mocking smile, mirroring Jenny's detached expression at the hospital. She is played by Tore Segelcke, a Norwegian actress famous in her home country but unknown for most of the TV audience in Sweden, which is probably why Bergman chose her: to be an enigma.[*]

We note that Jenny freezes at the sight, looking thoughtful when the woman passes her on the way to the street door. When Jenny continues up the stairs, the camera pans to a painted heraldic lion on the ceiling. Its significance is unclear, perhaps a social marker of the building as an upper-class residence, one of strength and force that does not recognise the 'weaknesses' of neurosis.

Cut to a shot of an Art Nouveau stylised stained-glass-window tulip, a spring flower perhaps inserted to suggest rebirth, thereby countering the connotations of autumn and death in the old woman. But in the context of Bergman's Ibsenian project, it is more likely a symbol of the nineteenth-century idealist woman, a fragile illusion soon to be "stained by emotional dirt", to paraphrase Peter Egerman in *Scenes from a Marriage*. Jenny enters the frame from the left. Her face in close-up symbolically replaces the window as the camera adjusts focus from the historical to the modern-day representation of idealism. The stained-glass tulip reappears in a dream in act three and in the final scene of act four. It is also the closing shot of the film version.

Jenny enters the apartment and is greeted by Grandmother (Aino Taube) and Grandfather (Gunnar Björnstrand). Taube was a veteran actress, who in her early career in the 1930s often played young aristocratic and upper-class women, an intertextual association suitable for the character in Bergman's production. Björnstrand was one of Bergman's regular actors, who now repeats his trademark arrogant intellectual, although with a twist. A stroke and the prospect of death have turned the Grandfather character vulnerable, tender and largely silent.

---

[*] A parallel to Bergman's use of then unknown Liv Ullmann in *Persona*.

What follows in the apartment keeps close to the screenplay with one notable exception: Jenny is to stay in her own childhood room. We can therefore deduce with certainty that her "little mummy" was Grandmother, who has restored her old room to its former glory with all the furniture and decorations. Like the sisters in *Cries and Whispers*, Jenny is about to regress to the doll's house of her childhood. The camera cuts to a close-up of Grandfather looking concerned. His expression is mirrored by Jenny when Grandmother leaves the room.

Outside a thunderstorm begins when Jenny goes to bed later in the evening, and the thunder continues to accompany her night-time conversation with Grandmother in the kitchen. When Jenny returns to bed to read Ennis's and Sullivan's anti-psychiatry books, another sound is added: a loud ticking from the alarm clock at her bedside table. We recognise Bergman's obsession with clocks and time from *Cries and Whispers*, but it goes back to a text Bergman wrote for the programme to his 1947 play *Unto My Fear* (*Mig till skräck*) called "In Grandmother's House" ("I mormors hus"). For him, it is a marker that the protagonist's days are numbered – death is drawing near – although it also marks the psychological time-bomb counting down inside Jenny (Koskinen 2002, pp. 192–193).

Jenny falls asleep. Slowly, the camera zooms in on the back of her head. When she sits up again, all sound is muted – a hint that we are now in the land of her dreams. She sees the old one-eyed lady rise from a chair in the room, but in contrast to the screenplay there is no anger in the woman's face, only fear and concern. It is as if she wants to warn Jenny about something. Jenny screams, but it is a silent scream, like the impotent scream of Frost the clown in *Sawdust and*

Fig. 15: Silent scream.
Face to Face (TV version).
(© Cinematograph AB)

Tinsel. Bergman zooms in fast on Ullmann's face to underscore the horror mirrored by her facial expression. She wakes up trembling and goes to sit in the drawing room, listening to the sombre, slow ticking of the ornamental clock.

What follows is a completely new scene, most likely added in the complementary shooting on 31 August 1975. The image of Jenny in the drawing room dissolves to a close-up of Maria in a state of psychosis at the hospital. Jenny comes to her room to try to get her to wash and get dressed. Maria ignores her and proceeds to masturbate.

Jenny tries to make Maria stop, claiming that she is only putting on an act.

Her words echo the doctor's diagnosis of Elisabet's decision to be mute in *Persona*. It is also what Maria implied that Jenny was doing by making the mocking imitation of her in their previous scene together. Now Jenny tries to throw Maria's accusations of being theatrical back in her face.

Maria stops to touch various parts of Jenny's face, saying their names: "forehead", "cheek", "eye", and so on, like teaching an infant basic facts about herself. Jenny stops her: "Not like that." Maria then repeats a gesture we just saw the one-eyed lady make in Jenny's bedroom: she puts her hand to her mouth as if in hesitation and looks worried, uttering words of concern repeated from their previous meeting: "Poor Jenny!" The scene was possibly added as an additional foreboding of Jenny's breakdown.

Cut to the scene with Jenny and Dr Helmuth Wankel at the hospital, then to the party at Mrs Wankel's apartment. Both scenes follow the screenplay almost verbatim. Played by Ulf Johanson, Dr Wankel is a continuation of his image on film as a slightly oddball character, often prone to cynical comments. See, for instance, *The Hour of the Wolf* and *The Shame*.

His wife is played by Sif Ruud, one of the most hard-working actresses in twentieth-century Swedish theatre, TV and film. At the time of *Face to Face*, she was close to sixty years old and had played lovable aging ladies for more than a decade. Her old woman in love with a man thirty-six years her junior reminded the contemporary audience of her celebrated role as the tragic Madame Flod in Bengt Lindkvist's popular 1966 TV production of Strindberg's *The People of Hemsö* (*Hemsöborna*), although Mrs Wankel is loud and whimsical and conspicuously dressed in red. Bergman probably wrote the role with her in mind.

To some critics in 1976 the party scene looked contrived and silly (Schildt 1976). Forty years later it still does. Born in the sanctuary of a nineteenth-century mentality, Bergman had never been comfortable with post-war youth culture. As noted above, he liked some of the music, but he never got the hang of contemporary subculture style, behaviour and lingo. In *Crisis*, the supposedly wild jazz party looks like a mild-mannered school dance, and in *Wild Strawberries* the trio of youngsters seem to have time travelled from a century before.

The party scene in *Face to Face* is supposed to show us life in the fast and decadent lane, according to Bergman. But instead of a coked-up sex orgy, we are introduced to a quiet afternoon tea party spiced with champagne, strawberries and slow dancing to Blue Swede's hit song 'Out of the Blue'. What Bergman aimed to do was probably to make a parody of sexual liberation as a crass market, although not so much about the commodification of carnal desires as the creation of another sanctuary to hold off reality with its promise of aging and death. Unfortunately, the wrong casting and failed staging diverts the attention, making us laugh at and not with Bergman's scene.

Among the guests, we note Rebecca Pawlo, daughter of actor Toiwo Pawlo (see *The Lie*), and then-unknown Lena Olin as the two chic boutique girls. They, at least, look the part and are of the right age. More damaging is the casting of the two disco-styled gay hunks. Fifty-year-old Bengt Eklund, known for his many proletarian roles, and thirty-eight-year-old comedian Gösta Ekman are simply too old, too stiff and too dressed-up to convince.* With his bleached-blond hair and armed with ridiculous jargon, the small and slight Ekman is an outright laughable representation of the screenplay's enchanting hunk, Mikael Strömberg.

Dr Tomas Jacobi in Erland Josephson's persona fares better, but then he seems to be at the party only to pick up Liv Ullmann's Jenny and leave. And the two do not mince matters. After a few lines of dialogue, they have agreed to go out on a date, effective immediately. Since we can assume that almost everyone in the audience was familiar with *Scenes from a Marriage*, expectations are high that Jenny and Tomas will end up in bed together at the beginning of act two. Even disregarding the fact that Tomas wears a blue jacket that tells us of the chill in his heart.

ACT TWO: THE BORDER

The whole act largely follows the screenplay with only minor deviations, mostly cutting a few lines here and there in the dialogue. Like the second half of act one,

---

* Bergman probably chose Ekman because they had worked together before, when Ekman was the assistant director on *The Seventh Seal* and *Wild Strawberries*.

acts two and three are mostly staged in medium shots and medium close-ups with the occasional long shot, for instance when Jenny leaves Tomas's house to take a taxi in act two. Bergman makes use of his signature close-ups only at the very end of act two, when Jenny wakes up after her long sleep to call Tomas and record her suicide note.

To break up the static setting of the screenplay's opening restaurant scene, Bergman moves the second half of the dialogue – the discussion of Maria – to Tomas's car. In the following awkward conversation in Tomas's house, Erland Josephson changes Tomas's persona by his acting (body language, facial expressions, tone of voice). Out of the cynic, who cruelly mocks his half-sister Maria's psychological history, another and more sensible character emerges. His subtle transformation helps the scene, although Jenny's abrupt mood swings from inviting to discouraging and back again still appear to be an unconvincing assemblage of contradictions.

When Jenny returns to the grandparents' apartment, she again looks confused and somewhat lost. Mirroring the opening shot of act one, her eyes search in vain for something. After observing her grandparents' tender interaction with a smile, she receives the telephone call that makes her drive to her family villa in the hour of the wolf. Rather than transporting Jenny and us directly to the scene of the crime, Bergman has her walking in and out of several rooms in the house, as if she is now acting out the searching look of the previous scene.

In a bedroom upstairs, she finally finds what she is looking for: Maria. Sven Nykvist's camera is placed in the hallway outside, peering not only into the

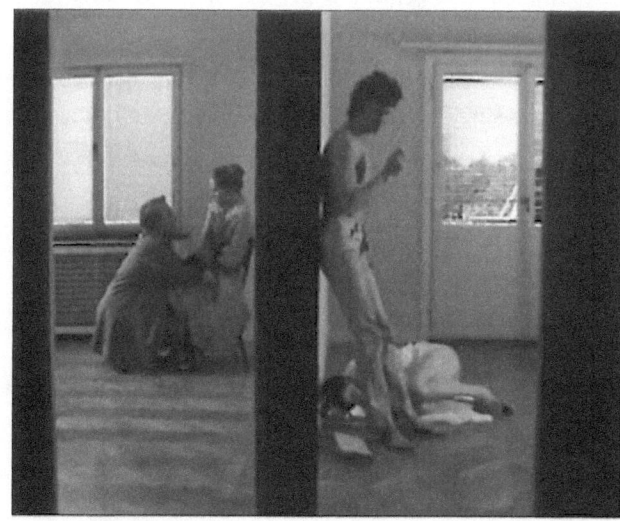

Fig. 16: Assault staged in split-screen. The aged rapist (Birger Malmsten), Jenny, the younger rapist (Göran Stangertz), Maria (Kari Sylwan). *Face to Face* (TV version).
(© Cinematograph AB)

bedroom where Maria lies in a foetal position on the floor, but also into the adjacent room on the left in which we see a chair and a telephone. The shot is a perfect split-screen of the two rooms; the doorframes becomes frames within the frame, making the rooms look like mirror images of each other.

Jenny quickly checks on Maria in the right room before going into the left one to call for an ambulance. She is stopped by a scruffy middle-aged man (Birger Malmsten), who proceeds to assist a likewise scruffy young man (Göran Stangertz) in an attempted rape of Jenny. The casting of Malmsten and Stangertz is notable. Malmsten was Bergman's young alter ego on film between 1946 and 1952, playing brooding outsiders in defiant opposition to mainstream society. Stangertz had just established his screen persona as a modern-day outsider in Jan Halldoff's acclaimed film *The Last Adventure* (*Det sista äventyret*, 1974), and he would go on to play another outsider in Halldoff's *Jack* (1977).

The scene attains a surreal, dream-like quality as the men seemingly come out of the woodwork to attack in Jenny's empty house. By staging the scene there, by arranging the rooms as mirrors and by switching Jenny's and Maria's respective places in the frame from act one, Bergman stresses that the power balance between the id and the superego has decidedly shifted in the protagonist's inner struggle. Although the attack does not fully succeed, it leaves Jenny trembling and vulnerable. The process of her breakdown begins.

A dramatic piano chord breaks the thundering silence as the rape scene comes to an end. It is a turning point in the drama, leading to Jenny's breakdown. Cut to the piano concert Jenny attends the very same evening in the company of Tomas. In the screenplay, the scene implied that Jenny's condition was indicative of a collective neurosis. Not so in Bergman's staging. Listening to Mozart's Fantasia in C minor, K. 475,[*] Jenny studies some children quietly taking in the music. In the context of the attempted rape, the scene now becomes a meditation on innocence and innocence lost.

Mozart's fantasia is a prelude to the dream world Jenny is about to enter, beginning with the first signs of a mental breakdown at Tomas's house after the concert. Jenny admits that she wanted the young rapist to succeed in penetrating her. Her post-traumatic response agrees with Maria's wish to have Jenny's barriers against the world shattered, and it becomes the initial step towards her primal scream. In a possible feminist interpretation, however, Bergman could be regarded as condoning or trivialising rape.

---

[*] In the end credits, it is referred to as Mozart's Fantasia in E minor, K. 475.

Bergman tones down the hysteria in the screenplay and puts more emphasis on Jenny's regression to an infantile state, as we see Tomas comforting her like a baby. It ends with her face engulfed in darkness, as a premonition of the lonely journey into the dark realm of her nightmares following the suicide attempt. Back in the grandparents' apartment, Jenny rests her head against the hallway mirror. She is literally standing face to face with herself. The image repeats the mirror motif of the opening, only this time, Jenny is about to turn her gaze inwards to come face to face with the truth about herself.

Maria is gone as a character – we never see her again in the series – since the repressed emotions she represents have finally surfaced from within Jenny herself. Like little Alice in Lewis Carroll's 1871 fantasy, she will go through the looking glass to find a world strikingly similar to the one she lives in, yet completely different. Her passageway is the two-day-long sleep, after which she wakes up to see another reflection of herself in the mirror: death in the form of the old one-eyed woman. Her suicide is therefore just an acknowledgement of her true state of being. As she declares in her letter to her husband Erik, she is already a living dead.

ACT THREE: THE TWILIGHT LAND

Jenny's suicide gets a more detailed treatment in the series than in the screenplay, as we follow her every preparation. After she swallows the pills and lies down on her bed, she moves her fingers across the wallpaper while humming a simple song and listening to the alarm clock's incessant ticking.

Here, Bergman references his *Through a Glass Darkly* – working title: "The Wallpaper" – in which the schizophrenic protagonist Karin envisions another world in the wallpaper. The motif appears for the first time in a 1948 play titled *Unto My Fear* and then again in the screenplay for *Prison*. During the shooting of *Prison*, Bergman found that he could not technically solve the wallpaper illusion as he wanted and switched to making a pulled-down blind come alive by the shadows from a fireplace.*

In *Face to Face*, the camera pans away from the wallpaper, across the room to search for another passageway into Jenny's mind. It rests on a pulled-down blind with a print of a fortress, yet another allusion to *Wild Strawberries*' Isak Borg. Like

---

* Höök 1962, p. 73; Koskinen 2002, pp. 279–280.

Figs. 17 & 18: The wallpaper and the fortress. *Face to Face* (TV version). (© Cinematograph AB)

Borg's road trip, this journey to the centre of the mind will shatter Jenny's defences against other people, against the world around her and, ultimately, against life itself.

To confront the repressed traumas, the dissolve figuratively breaks through her defences – the walls of the fortress. Entering the darkness inside, Jenny looks at yet another mirror reflection of herself by looking at the camera and us, reconfirming her status as our agent. Now she is dressed in a bright red dress and a red hood decorated with embroidery.

The brief dream is suddenly interrupted by Tomas, who wakes her up to explain how he found her and brought her to hospital. In the screenplay, this short exposition comes much later. Back in the dream, Bergman emphasises a fairy-tale motif more than in the screenplay. He connects *Face to Face* with his previous TV production *The Magic Flute* – the dreams correspond to Tamino and Pamina's trials – and Jenny becomes his combined Alice and Little Red Riding Hood.

Indeed, acts three and four of *Face to Face* seem almost customised to Bruno Bettelheim's psychoanalytical theories in his much-praised *The Uses of Enchantment*, although the book was not published until 1976, a year after the completion of *Face to Face*. But there is an abundance of earlier studies of the fairy tale as a rite of passage from prominent names in psychoanalysis such as Otto Rank, Ernest Jones, Géza Róheim and not least Julius E. Heuscher, whose 1963 book *A Psychiatric Study of Fairy Tales* Bettelheim, at least in parts, plagiarised (Dundes 1991). Any or all of them could have influenced Bergman.

In the filmed version's dream scenes, it is notable that Grandfather is almost out of the picture. Now it is Grandmother who looms large in Jenny's dreams and traumas. The Jekyll/Hyde portrait of her as both warm and loving but also cruel and fearsome corresponds with the symbolism of nurturance and cannibalism in the Red Riding Hood tale. Here, Grandmother and the wolf become one and the same.

Act three has significant deviations from the screenplay. At the start of Jenny's first dream, she no longer has an oedipal encounter with Grandfather. Instead, she meets with Grandmother, who reads a fairy tale of a girl locked in a castle by an old and mean couple. The fairy tale girl has been abandoned by her father, who is a knight out to war. Every day she searches through the corridors and rooms in her castle for someone to confide in, finding no one. All her fine clothes and precious toys are taken from her to be burned, and she is to be raised in sackcloth by the vile old couple.

The tale is never finished, but the allegory is obvious, though we have yet to see its correspondence to Jenny's life in the primal scream scene.* Judging by the scenes in the grandparents' apartment, we have, so far, only seen the opposite: a nice and tender old couple. But Jenny insists on the repressive and suffocating atmosphere coming from the bad smell of old people, including the grandparents. In the background, we see men dressed in turn-of-the-century clothes flashing by, and Grandmother reads under an old paraffin lamp. Bergman suggests the decay of the old Victorian society.

---

* Törnqvist 1995, p. 73, mentions Bergman's use of the fairy tale as another dangerous world of illusions that is imprinted from mother to daughter in his 1989 staging of *A Doll's House*.

Fig. 19: The only fragment left of Bergman's initial dream-vision. *Face to Face* (TV version). (© Cinematograph AB)

Jenny's disgust is met by repressive measures. An old woman's hand is placed on her shoulder. Jenny says that she is repulsed by Grandmother's touch. Nevertheless, she tries to kiss the hand. It suddenly takes a firm grip over her mouth, and another hand holds her forehead. Jenny is to be silenced and possibly choked to death. Grandmother's green dress flashes by the camera. We hear her voice spitting out the words: "You are to be quiet. You are to be quiet now!" Then we see the face of the one-eyed woman that haunts Jenny's nightmares. She wears Grandmother's green dress. Bergman underscores the significance of the scene by repeating the dramatic piano chord from act two.

The ambiguous symbolism of the scene could be a representation of a twofold repression: Grandmother's and that of Jenny's own internalised mechanisms. Grandmother's hand of repression is followed by the horrible face of death: the one-eyed woman who manifests Jenny's innermost fear. Mikael Strömberg's diagnosis of himself is all about Jenny: the fear of death has kept her from being fully alive. Like Marianne Höök, she has petrified until finally deciding that suicide is only a confirmation of her state as a living dead.

Trying to escape through a door, she is stopped by the voice of Tomas, who replaces Dr Helmuth Wankel in the dream scenes and speaks most of Wankel's dialogue from the screenplay. He informs her that the suicide attempt might have completed her transformation into a living dead. Possibly brain-damaged and in a coma, she could be kept alive for years by the medical staff at the hospital. In the context of her own practice as a psychiatrist, this is Bergman's poetic justice meted out to her for turning patients into medicated zombies – living dead just like herself.

Despite Tomas's warnings that "one should be thankful of the horrors one knows", Jenny opens the door and comes out through a closet to the grandparents' apartment.* She searches in vain through the rooms for someone to confide in, just like the girl in the fairy tale. Finally, she sits down at a black table with a shiny table top that reflects her image: the last remaining fragment of the orgy envisioned in the workbook.

She pleads with herself to wake up. The one-eyed woman – still wearing Grandmother's green dress – reappears to comfort her with a warming shawl and a motherly embrace. It is the Little Red Riding Hood symbolism in reverse: first cannibalism then nurturance. Now the symbolism of Jenny's fear of and then reconciliation with death is more clear and makes more sense than in the screenplay. Perhaps to keep focus on that, Bergman plays down the *pietà* pose to something looking more like a simple motherly embrace in an everyday setting.

At this moment, Jenny wakes up to an unscheduled visit by her husband, Erik. She is embarrassed because of her unwashed and smelly body, to which the dream context has added the smell of death. Erik is played by actor Sven Lindberg, whose image as a mild-mannered mother-in-law's dream is parodied in this portrait of an emotionally distanced and soft-spoken man who acts more like he is Jenny's adolescent son than her middle-aged husband. His weak and bland character is underscored by a jacket and a sweater in shades of beige.

In the screenplay, their meeting comes after Jenny's conflict-ridden dream reunion with her dead parents, stressing the parallels between the two dysfunctional families. Since that scene has now been moved to the very end of the act in the filmed version, two scenes away, the parallel is significantly weakened. The dream that follows is based on a scene that comes later in the screenplay.

Jenny goes back to sleep, crying desperately. Grandmother opens the apartment door to scold Jenny for being late for work. Her patients have been waiting for hours in her bedroom-turned-consulting-room. Jenny's red dress is now partly covered by her doctor's white coat as she hurries to work. The sound of Jenny's crying continues in her dream to mix with the sound of a naked female patient

---

* The closet could possibly be yet another fairy tale reference, this time to C. S. Lewis's *The Chronicles of Narnia* (1950–56), in which the closet is the portal between the real world and the fairy tale world.

moaning and wriggling on a bed. She could be Maria or Jenny, who in her hospital bed back in the real world has come to look quite like her patient. Hence, Jenny the vulnerable patient meets Jenny the insensitive psychiatrist.

Bergman adds some comic-book-cliché doctor lines – "Don't forget the pills", "Come back next month" – that turn the scene into satire. Anna (Helene Friberg, the face in the crowd watching *The Magic Flute*)* suddenly appears amid the patients, only to run away without a word. Jenny stays to check on the wailing patient, who tries to grab hold of her, triggering the other patients to do the same. She manages to escape out of a door, visibly shaken by the experience. Bergman underscores the emotional impact by repeating a few chords from the Mozart piano concert in act two.

When Jenny opens the door again, everyone is gone. She is ashamed. Tomas's supporting hand comes into the frame to rest on her shoulder. We note his green cardigan; he has also become a ghostly apparition, perhaps another representation within Jenny's mind more than a real person. His voice is heard, offering advice, and in a medium close-up of him in a separate frame he tells the story of the prince who tortured and then comforted his subjects. Anna reappears in the doorway, but runs away again when Jenny addresses her. Jenny follows, sobbing and crying for her to come back.

She wakes up in the middle of the night in the hospital to find Tomas sitting in a chair by her side. He tells a comical story from his childhood and then proceeds to confess about his broken heart after being abandoned by his lover Mikael Strömberg. The scene is followed by the dream in which Jenny confronts her parents, who look like wax dummies representing the 1940s.

They are played by two rather unknown veteran actors: Marianne Aminoff, who in her youth generally played fragile upper-class women on film and would return in *Fanny and Alexander* as the bishop's mother, and Jan-Erik Lindqvist, often seen in minor, quiet roles. Neither of them speak any lines. The mother is no longer the striking beauty she is described as in the screenplay, and, curiously, Lindqvist as the father bears a striking likeness to Bergman himself.

Both scenes closely follow the screenplay, save the ending of the dream, when Jenny rushes out of the grandparents' apartment after scolding her parents. As she bangs the back of her head against the wall on the staircase, we hear a dramatic

---

* Those who have seen Ingmar Bergman's *The Magic Flute* (1975) may remember her as the young girl with a radiant smile in the audience as Bergman frequently cuts to her during the performance.

chord from Mozart's piano piece. The image freezes on her anguished face and turns white.

ACT FOUR: THE RETURN

In contrast to the many revisions in the previous acts, especially act three, the final instalment stays close to the screenplay. To heighten the emotional impact of the dramatic climax in Jenny's final breakdown and primal scream, the scene is largely shot in close-ups, extreme close-ups and discreet zooms in and out of close-ups. Bergman even makes use of his signature framing from *Persona* in a dialogue between Jenny and Tomas by the hospital window: Liv Ullmann stands to the left in profile and close to the camera, while Erland Josephson is in the background centre of the frame with his face turned straight towards us.

The act begins by Jenny waking up crying at the hospital, lamenting the suffering of children – the Aniara generation. This is followed by Tomas's monologue on the emotional starvation of confused and child-like adults plus a short biological history of the human brain. The dialogue is slightly edited, but the scene largely follows the writing.

Jenny's last dream of burning her living dead self in a coffin has some minor alterations. The priest is gone. Jenny's parents are replaced by two undertakers, who nail the lid on the coffin. From the inside, we hear the living dead Jenny pounding and screaming for "Mum" and "Dad".

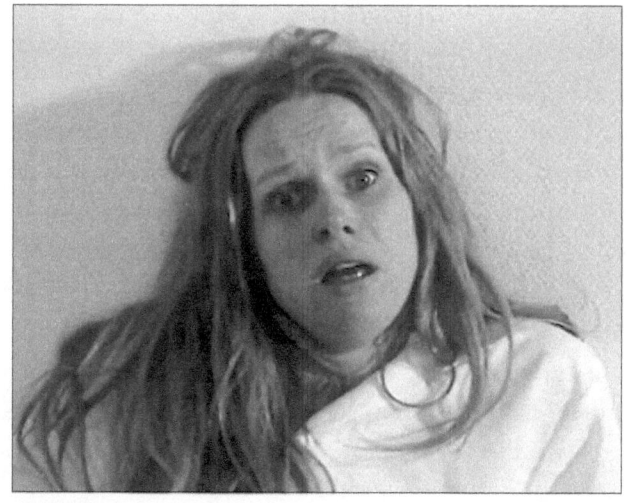

Fig. 20: Jenny's primal scream. *Face to Face* (TV version).
(© Cinematograph AB)

In the filmed version, Bergman puts more emphasis on the links between the fear of living and the fear of death. Thus, Jenny's monologue about the history of her fear of death, frigidity and contempt for emotional ties becomes subtext made text more clearly than in the screenplay. It still seems odd, though, that these insights precede the primal scream instead of coming afterwards, as a revelation of the inner repressive mechanisms.

The final breakdown and primal scream are bound to be problematic. How to stage a believable mental collapse and recovery in ten minutes? Liv Ullmann makes an exceptional effort to make Jenny's horrors come alive, but the scene still comes out theatrical, that is, exactly the opposite of Bergman's intentions – hence his sarcastic comments about it in *Images*.

In part this is because Jenny's wrestling with the inner demons becomes almost literal. Looking ravaged while speaking in the people's voices and thrashing about in the hospital room, she appears to be possessed rather than traumatised. Bergman cuts to a baffled Tomas, who might not apply a traditional male gaze to the scene but nevertheless seems to be watching a freak show. Compare the scene with the more subdued staging of Karin's self-mutilation in *Cries and Whispers*. The less-is-more representation is clearly more suitable to Bergman's sparse style and recurring theme about the silent, deadening repression of the bourgeois sanctuary.

On top of this, Jenny's recovery is instant. A few minutes after she has completed her primal scream, Tomas decides that she is well enough to be released from hospital. The remedy for his own existential problems is a one-way trip to Jamaica and a supposedly depraved life of gay sex. Judging by his resigned look, however, he does not seem to look forward to it. This discrepancy makes his authentic appearance look like an act, another case of phony theatricality. Also, the whole prospect of sexual liberation seems to be, at best, questionable.

The next scene, in which Jenny meets with her daughter Anna to talk about the suicide attempt, makes more sense both thematically and artistically. It is set in an impersonal visitors' room at the hospital, and it reflects the cold and distant mother/daughter relationship. Jenny tries to break the barrier between them, but to no avail.

Her daughter, possibly like Jenny has done *vis-à-vis* her mother and grandmother, has cut all the emotional ties and adopted an impenetrable smiling mask of detachment and rigid self-control. The choice of Helene Friberg in the part – the girl with the unfeigned face and radiant smile in the audience of *The*

Magic Flute – has now applied a theatrical mask of cynicism. Innocence destroyed; the legacy of the cold womb has come full circle.

EPILOGUE

Jenny leaves the hospital, Sophia-Hemmet. This is another autobiographical reference since it was the clinic in which Bergman himself was hospitalised several times and from which he drew his inspiration for the prologue to *Persona*, which *Face to Face* is closely connected with.

Her return to the grandparents' apartment is a repeat take of the scene in act one. She wears identical clothes, not the more informal ones stipulated in Bergman's letter to Ullmann above. The sun is shining and the repressive church bells are tolling while she walks towards the building. Has she reverted to her old self?

We note one difference, though: Jenny no longer keeps her hair in a tight bun but lets it all hang down. Is this a sign of her new free state of mind?[*] It should be, but what about her old formal clothing then?

When opening the street door, she spots the old woman in black again coming down the stairs. This time, she does not freeze but rushes up to help the old lady. In contrast to the screenplay, their encounter does not conclude the narrative but is only an intermediate moment that lasts for a few seconds.

Afterwards, Jenny hurries up to the apartment to reunite with Grandmother. The following scene stays close to the screenplay, save for Jenny's voice-over reading parts of Bergman's description of how she observes and takes in the old couple's closeness and solidarity even when death is about to come. Her earlier account of making ironic comments on a poem about how love embraces death is countered by this tender scene.

She phones the hospital to inform them that she will come back to work. The image freezes and fades to white. Piano chords from Mozart's Fantasia in C minor, K. 475, are heard, and a text announces, "When Jenny Isaksson completed her temporary work, she handed in her resignation, left her marriage and is now doing research in the USA."

End credits.

---

[*] We recognise it as an old movie cliché of 'letting it all hang out' that implies having an open mind for sex and adventures; see numerous Hollywood films from *Gilda* (1946) to *Marnie* (1964) to *The Mummy* (1999) and onwards.

THE FILM

*F*ace to Face was shot in the widescreen format of 1.66:1, then reframed to 1.33:1 for the TV version. When editing the film version, the material was again reframed to the widescreen ratio of 1.78:1, sometimes resulting in the upper frame cutting the top off the actors' heads but mostly cutting off space at the bottom of the picture. Now, medium close-ups turn into close-ups and many close-ups are on the verge of becoming extreme close-ups.

Ironically, considering that the close-up was the preferred type of shot for the intimacy of TV, the film version became the more intimate format. This reframing is most notable in the dramatic climax of Jenny's final breakdown and primal scream, where Nykvist's use of the zoom brings us closer to the actors' faces and thus becomes more effective – more so on the big cinema screen. Bergman preferred the film version possibly for this reason and for the "different rhythm" of the cutting (Löthwall 1976).

A few alternative takes are notable in the film version. One is at the very beginning of the film. Following the Paramount logo, main title and credits (now including the end credits of the TV series), there is a dissolve to a close-up of Jenny. She is looking straight into the camera, at us, from the very beginning. A moment later, she throws side glances left and right before putting on the glasses and donning a smile.

The material was cut by 42 minutes, from 177 minutes (TV series) to 135 minutes (film version). Scenes have been thrown out, trimmed or moved, such as the first scene with Jenny and Maria. Dissolves have been replaced by cuts, save for the initial dissolve from flowing water to the close-up of Jenny and the

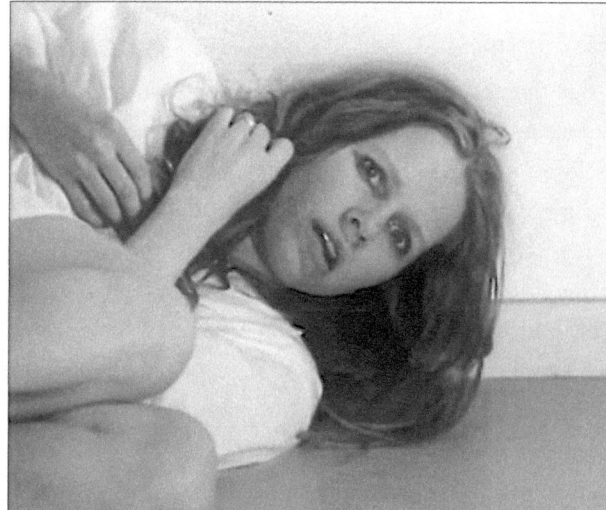

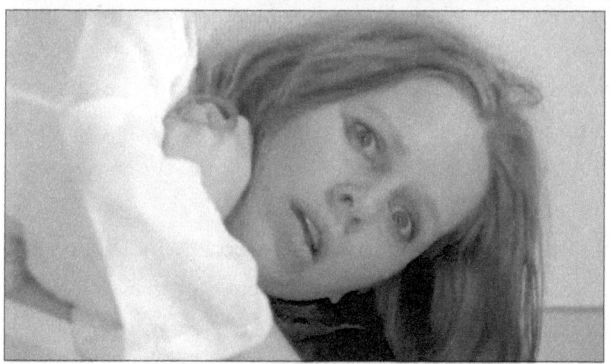

Figs. 21 & 22:
Reframing *Face to Face* for different aspect ratios: TV version (1.33:1) and film version (1.78:1).
(© Cinematograph AB and Paramount Pictures)

dissolve from a close-up of Jenny in a dream to her lying in a hospital bed. The opening scene in Jenny's house ends in the film version with her getting into the car. Bergman then makes a cut – not a dissolve – to her meeting with the masturbating and psychotic Maria. In the TV series, this scene was their second meeting.

At the grandparents' apartment, the night-time conversation between Jenny and Grandmother is missing, and the first nightmare ends with Jenny rushing out into the living room. Cut to the scene with Wankel, followed by the party minus Jenny's talk with Mikael Strömberg. She meets with Tomas outside the restaurant, but the film version has nothing of their conversation inside the place or later in Tomas's car. Instead, the film cuts directly to their arrival at Tomas's house.

Then come several successive scenes left intact or just slightly trimmed: the rape, the piano concert, the first breakdown in Tomas's house, the two-day sleep and the second dream rendezvous with the one-eyed lady that finally triggers Jenny's attempted suicide. At this point, Bergman makes perhaps the most significant change of all: he throws out the entire scene in which Jenny tape-records her suicide note to Erik. Scenes like this – intimate moments with characters who speak from their heart in close-up – are one of Bergman's stylistic strong points. Still, he decided to remove it, possibly because we get some of the information in the final breakdown.

The first post-suicide-attempt dream eliminates the long shot of Jenny looking at the camera as if it was a mirror, and the interrupting scene in which Tomas explains how he took her to the hospital comes after her reconciliation with the one-eyed woman. This is followed by her dream of the patient consultation in her bedroom at the grandparents' apartment, leaving out Tomas's story about the torturing/comforting prince and Anna's second appearance.

Only then comes the scene with Erik visiting, after which Jenny's crying continues into her dream reunion with her parents. By moving the two scenes together, although in reverse order from the screenplay, the legacy of the dysfunctional family becomes more obvious: in Erik, Jenny has found an oedipal substitute for her quiet father, in Anna a new double of herself to come. When we return to the grandparents' apartment, we note another weak father figure: Grandfather.

The last thirty-five minutes is act four minus a few details and with some significant changes at the end of the film. Jenny wakes up to listen to Tomas's amusing childhood story, but Bergman leaves out the quasi-scientific history of the human brain. The three following scenes are left largely intact: Jenny's dream about burning her living dead alter ego, Tomas's goodbye and the talk with Anna.

Bergman then cuts from the hospital room to the apartment, leaving out the exit from the hospital, the repeated walk up to the apartment building while the church bells are tolling and, most important, the second meeting with the old lady on the staircase. The scene in the apartment is complete, including the phone call to the hospital. However, Bergman adds a new final shot, in which Jenny goes out to the staircase.

Cut to a camera position outside the front door of the apartment. Jenny goes by the camera, and the camera zooms in on the stained-glass tulip. THE END. Paramount logo. No text about how Jenny quits the hospital job, divorces her husband and moves to the USA to do research. Instead, an added clip showing us that she leaves the apartment, perhaps a symbolic farewell to the bourgeois doll's house sanctuary and its idealist illusions.

OVERTURE TO THE RELEASE

During the spring of 1976, Cinematograph held several preview screenings for the press, TV managers and other people. A look in the log book of screenings shows who saw it and when.

THURSDAY, 22 JANUARY 1976

The first preview screening of *Face to Face* (TV version) is for a group from SR/TV2 assigned to make a TV trailer from the material. Cinematograph also made a cinema trailer for Paramount. In the Ingmar Bergman Archive, there are documents with Cinematograph letterheads that feature the voice-over text in both Swedish and English. Bergman probably oversaw the making of the trailers and approved the trailer text, perhaps even writing it himself. The trailer consists of a montage of short excerpts from the film – all randomly selected and not building a coherent narrative – accompanied by an excerpt of Mozart's Fantasia in C minor, K 475. No dialogue is heard, only the music and a speaker saying:

> This film brings you face to face with life,
> face to face with your longing, your dreams,
> your secret dread,
> face to face with life.
> Reality has created it.
> Ingmar Bergman has recounted this reality.
> Liv Ullmann has given it her face.
> We want you to see this film.
> It is important.

Fig. 23: US poster.
(© Paramount Pictures)

The cinema trailer was part of Paramount's US marketing campaign, which also featured a poster and advertisement picture. Both feature a graphic rendering of Liv Ullmann's head turned in profile and facing a mirror image of itself. The colour poster is toned in beige-brown over a big black inkblot that suggests a Rorschach test. The tag line is: "A woman's most intimate encounter with the one person she didn't know. Herself."

SUNDAY, 25 JANUARY
Bergman, his wife Ingrid, Liv Ullmann and Erland Josephson meet for a press screening of the film version. According to the engagement planner, Ullmann liked the result.

WEDNESDAY, 28 JANUARY
The TV version is shown to all the heads of the theatre departments of the Nordic public service broadcasting companies, except Iceland.

MONDAY, 22 MARCH – FRIDAY, 26 MARCH

Press screenings of the TV version for critics and reporters from major weekly, bimonthly and monthly publications. Interestingly, most of them were from women's magazines, indicating the new audience Bergman's productions got with the successes of *Scenes from a Marriage* and *The Magic Flute*. Notably, no critics from the film journals of the Nordic countries attended any of the screenings.

About the same time, Paramount held preview screenings for the US press in New York, handing out a lavish forty-page "Handbook of Production Information". Following the credits, the handbook features a short presentation of the cast, strangely omitting both Jan-Erik Lindqvist as Jenny's father and Helene Friberg as Jenny's daughter Anna. More extensive presentations of the major actors in the cast and distinguished members of the crew are featured at the end of the book. Bergman's letter to his cast and crew, which some critics quoted in their reviews, is also included.

The most extensive text in the handbook is called "Background Notes", in which Dino De Laurentiis recalls his meetings with Bergman through the years and his decision to buy the world rights for *Face to Face* to get a distribution deal with Paramount. He calls the film "a masterpiece", and to Bergman's outline of its contents – "the lack of love and a number of taboos like suicide and death" – De Laurentiis adds what he considered as more commercially appealing ingredients: "old age and rebellious youth; homosexuality and bisexuality; dreams and hallucinations; frigidity and rape; sleeping pills, tranquilizers and drug abuse; incest, unrequited love and extramarital sex."

A curious detail is the inclusion of the end title featured in the TV version, the one stating that Jenny quits her job, leaves her husband and goes to the US to do research. It is printed after the technical credits, but it is not included in the DVD transfer Paramount released in 2011. Presumably it was only included in the handbook and not in the prints of the film released in 1976, although this has not been verified.

TUESDAY, 30 MARCH – THURSDAY, 22 APRIL

Press screenings of the TV version for the Nordic daily press and for Bergman's editors at Norstedts, the publishing company that handled the publication of the screenplays to his most famous films and would later publish *The Magic Lantern* and *Images*.

RECEPTION

Compared to the wealth of advance publicity for Bergman's previous productions in the 1970s, *Face to Face* got little attention. The reason? The tax evasion affair, which during the spring of 1976 overshadowed everything else about Bergman. In the autumn and winter of 1975, it looked promising when the *New York Times* – Bergman's most fervent supporter outside Sweden – began to build the interest for the film.

On 24 September 1975, the paper published the letter Bergman sent to his cast and crew, the one he later published as an introduction to the screenplay. The headline was "A Briefing for a Film, By Ingmar Bergman". They followed in December with an extensive Bergman interview over sixteen pages in the *New York Times Magazine*. It is an interesting contrast to the feminist animosity to Bergman at the time of *Cries and Whispers* (Alvarez 1975).

In the interview, the director is presented as a champion of feminism. He talks about women's liberation as part of the Swedish society's aim for individual freedom, high divorce rates as a sign of mental health and social progress and day care for children as superior to his own family upbringing. Bergman the 'women's director' becomes 'the man who knows women' – a frontiersman of gender exploration.* His work is portrayed as something of a daring expedition to a terra incognita.

His feminist sympathies are further underscored by a full page of photos of Swedish women in various professions with the caption: "In Sweden it seems as if the goals of Women's Lib have been achieved. There are women in the

---

* I, of course, coined the phrase as a partly humorous analogy to 'the man who knows Indians' in the western genre.

government, the professions, and every kind of job, even the most manual" (Alvarez 1975, p. 90). As usual when interviewed by US journalists, he spends much time dismissing and countering clichéd notions of loneliness and anxiety as particularly Swedish afflictions or the result of some sinister workings of the social democratic government. The interview provides a context for the reception of Bergman's films at the time since it exposes key notions about how the director and his work were perceived at the time.

If Bergman before the tax evasion affair was a symptom of 'the Swedish condition',* which he as an artist supposedly had an intuitive understanding of, he is afterwards made into its foremost critic – whether he knows it or not. Most film critics, like Jay Cocks of *Time* (1976) or Tom Milne of the *Monthly Film Bulletin* (1976), only mention the affair incidentally, but in a follow-up on his original review, Vincent Canby of the *New York Times* (1976b) depicts Bergman like he is the Solzhenitsyn of Sweden.†

Under the heading "Bergman Explores the Terror of Blandness", he initially states that the film is not an "intentional metaphor for Sweden". Then he turns 180 degrees to confirm that it indeed is: "The bland efficiency of the society in which it is set dramatizes the magnitude of the emotional terrors that cause Jenny's breakdown." Sweden, in which "all social ills have been cured", leaves the inhabitants with "no excuses not to tend to the inner self". He considers Sweden's state of the nation as nothing less than devastating.

> It is as if mankind has achieved the two-day week and didn't know what to do with the other five days. In an earlier era one got on one's knees, going through the rituals of atonement, supplication and thanksgiving. But now that has been denied. The Volvo transports one to the country but not out of oneself.

Ergo: the material wealth and secularity of the welfare state kills you by making you want to kill yourself. In contrast, Philip Strick (1976) writes in his *Sight and Sound* review that *Face to Face* breaks with the 1960s films about "the artist's function in society". The new Bergman of the 1970s has turned away from social

---

* See Young 1971.
† In Swedish film critic Lasse Bergström's (1976) report from a preview screening of the film in New York, he summarises the talk about the tax evasion affair: "people comment on the [tax] authority's hunt for Bergman during the dark part of the year as if it was a parallel case to the Soviet Union versus Solzhenitsyn".

engagement to the psychological sphere of looking inwards: "The only art that concerns Bergman now, it seems, is that of survival, which means leaving society to its own unpleasant devices for a while and concentrating on oneself."

Generally, the press reviews and articles following the US cinema premiere on 5 April 1976 – including the ones that expressed reservations about the film itself – were in awe of Liv Ullmann's performance. In the *New Yorker*, Penelope Gilliatt described it as "an extraordinary physical depiction of a controlled and alert woman's fall into desuetude and neglect" (1976, p. 121). Vincent Canby called it "another tour-de-force for Miss Ullmann, who is nothing short of immense" (1976a).

Jay Cocks of *Time* avowed that "She has never been better", adding, "Hers is an intelligent, devastating performance." Roger Ebert of the *Chicago Sun-Times* considers Ullmann's performance "virtuoso". To him, she makes the film "a necessity for any serious filmgoer – we haven't seen such psychic depths on the screen since her debut in Bergman's *Persona* ten years ago – and yet the character she creates almost seems to exist apart from the universe he provides for her."

The film itself got a cooler reception, in contrast to the ovations for *Cries and Whispers* or *Scenes from a Marriage*. Gilliatt writes "magnificent", but nothing more. Canby calls it a "beautiful, agonizing film" and concludes his review with some ambiguous word of praise: "Mr. Bergman is more mysterious, more haunting, more contradictory than ever, though the style of his films has never been more precise, clear, level-headed."

Face to Face is, to Cocks, one of Bergman's minor films, one of his transitional works of the 1970s: "The new films lack the daunting, haunted intensity, the sheer stylistic brilliance of the earlier *Persona* (1966), *The Shame* (1968) and *The Passion of Anna* (1969)." Ebert notes that *Face to Face* is "a film that's not in itself among Bergman's greatest" since it at times becomes "embarrassingly literal".

The full spectrum of the mixed reception is summarised in a review essay by Charles Michener in *Film Comment*. He begins by making an auteurist case for the film: the austere style, the use of women protagonists and especially Liv Ullmann, the mask play, the camera's relation to the characters and Bergman's artistic presence: "the film's more compelling fascination lies in its implicit struggle between the camera and Ullmann, between Bergman and his mask". Ullmann's acting "must be one of the most valiant, generous performances ever recorded on film".

But something is bothering Michener: "Why then is the effect of *Face to Face* less like an adventure and more like a trip to the dentist?" He answers by pointing out the provincial character of Bergman's work and "a certain clumsiness at catching social nuance", perhaps most embarrassingly in "his characterization of a homosexual actor as a caricature of the peroxide-haired faggot". The dreams he thinks "are equally conscientious – and unpersuasive". Furthermore, he paraphrases a key line in *Face to Face* to characterise the finale as "a litany of psychiatric insights, of Bergman's words, *his* insights" (italics in original).

In Sweden, it was not only the tax evasion affair that blotted out the advance interest in the series. Only a week before the premiere of the TV series, Bergman announced his exile, effectively killing the media's interest in his upcoming production. The few interviews and articles printed in advance are mostly about Bergman's relation to women, on and off screen.

In an interview with Liv Ullmann, she talks about their unequal relationship under the telling headline "He Was Like a God to Me" (Garfinkel 1976). An article called "Bergman and All These Women" (Anon. 1976b) mixes quotes from Höök's biography with interviews featuring some of his leading women actors: Eva Dahlbeck, Inga Landgré, Maj-Britt Nilsson and Liv Ullmann. "Ingmar Bergman – A Career in Anxiety" (Melin 1976) sums up his life and work in one word and using selected quotes from Bergman and, again, from Höök's book.

The most ambitious journalistic works about the *Face to Face* TV premiere on 28 April were two interviews with Bergman made during the production. The first was Jörn Donner's filmed interview with Bergman in which the director talks about his life in the movies. It was broadcast in three half-hour parts on Swedish Television over the New Year's weekend of 1975–76. The second was Kajsa Harrysson's interview solely about *Face to Face*, published over two consecutive issues in the weekly *Röster i Radio TV* at the time of the premiere in late April.

In part one, Bergman again tries to generate interest by issuing a warning to oversensitive viewers. For everybody else he hopes that the series, like *Scenes from a Marriage*, will make people "sit down and talk with each other over a beer and a sandwich in the kitchen" (Harrysson 1976, p. 9). Part two is about the influence of primal therapy. Bergman claims that he wrote *Face to Face* before reading Janov's book, but as we have seen in his engagement planner this is not true, and it is revealing that he keeps talking about the series in relation to Janov's theories throughout the interview (ibid.).*

---

* In *The Magic Lantern* (1988, p. 231), however, he acknowledges that he was inspired to write the TV series after reading *The Primal Scream*.

After the premiere, the interest in the series rose significantly, although it came nowhere near the levels of *Scenes from a Marriage*. A text that set the tone for the reception was a pre-review titled "Her Performance Is Almost Beyond Belief" and printed in *Expressen* on 11 April. It was authored by the paper's leading film critic Lasse Bergström, one of Bergman's most reliable admirers.*

He wrote it after attending a preview screening of the film version at Paramount's office in the Gulf & Western building in New York. The text accounts for the successes of *Scenes from a Marriage* and *The Magic Flute* in the Big Apple, and how the tax affair is considered as an international scandal of great magnitude. It proceeds to praise the film as a confirmation of Ingmar Bergman as auteur and of Liv Ullmann as one of the internationally most important actors alive.

Bergman was at the height of his success in the 1970s, after gaining a wide popularity for his TV productions, and this paved the way for a generally favourable reception in extensive reviews. Thus, he was important with a capital I, and the reception responded accordingly. In *Aftonbladet*, for instance, *Face to Face* was announced as "The Most Upsetting Ever to Be Shown on Film…", and the article quotes selected US film critics to underscore that the headline was indeed no exaggeration (Rydén 1976).

The Swedish reviews largely followed the pattern of the US reception a few weeks earlier. There was unanimous praise for Liv Ullmann; see headlines such as "Liv Ullmann Emerges as a Miracle" (Schildt 1976). Most critics acknowledged that Bergman had made an important and emotionally powerful drama, perhaps the best he had ever made for TV (Janzon 1976a–d), although not as good as his greatest achievements in cinema (Hjertén 1976). And then there were a few voices of discontent, who talked about *Face to Face* as an artistic failure (Sten 1976) or at least a series of diminishing returns for every act in the drama (Donnér 1976a–d).

The audience's response, according to reports in the press, was mixed. A page in *Expressen* was divided in two: the upper half titled "Captivating", the lower half "Uninteresting" (Anon. 1976d). The supporters had praise for Liv Ullmann's acting abilities, for Bergman's realism in depicting the protagonist's psychological problems and for the series' willingness to raise the awareness for persons with psychiatric problems. The detractors saw the series as dull, too complicated or contrived and as a repeat take of Bergman's earlier productions (Anon. 1976c–g).

---

* *Images* (see Bergman 1995, pp. 440–441) was originally conceived as an interview project with Lasse Bergström as the interviewer and co-author of the book.

Face to Face did not become a cultural phenomenon like *Scenes from a Marriage*.* Some critics anticipated a big debate about mental problems and psychiatry. One headline stated, "The Bergman Series That Will Raise Hell" (Gustafson 1976), but it did not go beyond a few articles and a TV programme. In an interview, psychiatrist Dag Notini was supportive of Bergman's close-up of a mental breakdown (Eriksson 1976). He thought that the viewers' confrontation with anxiety could lead to something good since they would also witness the protagonist's recovery. Notably, he describes Jenny as a rather unconventional and gentle psychiatrist, and asserts that psychiatrists in general tend to be more guarded, more closed off.

His opposite was Madeleine Kats, who in a review in women's magazine *Femina* (Kats 1976a) and a polemical article in *Expressen* (Kats 1976b) attacked Bergman for having a sado-sexual interest in Jenny's breakdown but no interest in her recovery: "She has given him his orgasm and it brings him a moment of relief. Then he is not interested any more." She thought his portrait of psychiatry as a cynical con game was dangerous and warned people against believing in the powerful suggestions of the series.

If anything, its biggest impact was to raise the public attention to primal therapy. By 1976, Arthur Janov had become an international celebrity and the interest in his theories peaked at the time of *Face to Face*'s premiere. In Ana Maria Narti's review essay of *Face to Face* for *Chaplin*, Bergman becomes the prophet of Janov, even anticipating his ideas in the earlier films: "Many years before Janov's theory was known, Bergman made films that today easily can be regarded as moving images sprung from the American therapist's ideas" (1976, p. 94).

Jenny's nightmares about maltreating her patients and Tomas Jacobi's longing to be an authentic person with authentic feelings are mentioned as "Janov quotes". To Narti, this has implications beyond that of personal liberation. Ultimately, it is a question of changing "the way of life in the Western world – how to work, relax and communicate with each other" (1976, p. 95).

A fifty-minute special on *Face to Face* by TV programme *Kris* ("Crisis") followed on 24 May. Two formerly suicidal psychiatric patients confirm the accuracy of Bergman's staging, talking about the sense of detachment from the real world before the suicide attempt and their experiences of waking up afterwards in

---

* There are no audience statistics for the first transmission of the TV series, but the rerun attracted 14 per cent of the audience or about 700,000 viewers. Statistics from Audience & Programming Analysis, a department within Swedish Television in Stockholm, by email, 8 December 2016 from the head of the department, Thomas Lindhé.

intensive care. Over images of hospital equipment, the reporter-speaker claims that Swedish health care is good at "patching up the body, but we are not as skilful when it comes to the soul".

In agreement, the patients and reporter portray psychiatry as a dehumanised institution of medical treatment only; there is no conversational therapy. Two alternatives are discussed: psychiatrist and psychoanalyst Johan Cullberg's new method of complementing medicines with conversational therapy, and psychoanalyst Kjell Myrberg's treatment over several years. The last twenty minutes is an interview with Arthur Janov at the Grand Hotel in Stockholm. By intercutting with clips from *Face to Face*, Bergman artistry and Janov's theories seem to confirm one another.

The value of this product placement for primal therapy in *Face to Face* and *Kris* could not be overestimated, and that was duly noted by Svenska Primalföreningen. In their bimonthly newsletter *Primalbladet* (Anon. 1976h, pp. 6–7), they published a complete transcript of the Janov interview. *Face to Face* was regarded as an endorsement of primal therapy, and the organisation tried to arrange public screenings of the TV series two years after its original broadcast. By the time *Face to Face* was broadcast again on Swedish Television, in June and July 1979, the primal therapy vogue had all but faded away. The rerun went by without any attention in the media and to mediocre TV ratings.

A SUCCESS AND A FAILURE

Face to Face and Liv Ullmann received some prestigious awards and nominations in 1977. The film won in the Best Foreign Film category at the Golden Globes, the Los Angeles Film Critics Association Awards and the Brazilian SESC Film Festival, and it was nominated for an Academy Award. Liv Ullmann won in the Best Actress category at the New York Film Critics Circle Awards, Los Angeles Film Critics Association Awards and National Board of Review Awards. She was also nominated for a Golden Globe, a BAFTA and an Academy Award.

Still, for the last forty years *Face to Face* has probably been best remembered as the film Alvy Singer (Woody Allen) and Annie Hall (Diane Keaton) are late for in *Annie Hall* (1977), resulting in their decision to go and see another film. Not much of a reputation for a production generally praised at the time of its premiere. What happened? To answer this question, I think at least five concurrent factors that needs to be considered.

THE TAX EVASION AFFAIR AND EXILE

Although the affair could potentially have boosted the interest, it in effect drowned out the advance publicity for both the film and the TV premiere. *Face to Face* essentially became a sideshow to the spectacle, as noted above.

THE DOWNFALL OF PRIMAL THERAPY

Primal therapy fell out of fashion at the beginning of the 1980s. During the 1970s it had become the foremost of the many alternative psychotherapies, but that status became damaging when some of them were revealed to be close to religious cults or just simple scams. The most devastating scandal for Arthur Janov was about the Center for Feeling Therapy, an offshoot of primal therapy by therapists personally certified by Janov himself. When it collapsed in 1980, the centre's systematic abuse – both violent and sexual – was exposed and led to a major lawsuit.[*]

Moreover, Janov's scientific data was subjected to scrutiny and found wanting. Besides his outrageous claims that primal therapy could cure numerous diseases, have positive hormonal effects and even show results that would otherwise require plastic surgery or other medical treatment, many pointed to the absurdity in Janov's own assessment that nearly a hundred per cent of his patients were 'cured'. In 1983 Tomas Videgård's doctoral dissertation on primal therapy was published, and it showed that the outcome of primal therapy was only about half as good as Janov claimed it to be. Since then, several peer-reviewed articles have dismissed both Janov's theories and his practices, and primal therapy has faded into insignificance.[†]

The tarnished reputation of primal therapy undoubtedly affected *Face to Face*. Although Bergman did not make it as a propaganda piece for Janov's ideas, his public sympathies with the new-age cultural phenomenon nevertheless came to stain the work. Interestingly, Bergman never dissociated from Janov, but blamed the failure on the "enthusiastic but ill-digested fruit of my reading" (1988, p. 232).

BERGMAN'S DENOUNCEMENT

As mentioned in the introduction, Bergman himself has affected the assessment of his works, not least what came to be his canonical and apocryphal works respectively. *Face to Face* turned apocryphal in just a few years. Like *The Touch* and other 'failures', it is rarely mentioned in books, articles, reviews and interviews.

The wilful ignorance coincides with the elevation of Bergman from controversial theatre and film director in the 1960s to become a revered auteur in the 1970s and a cultural icon almost beyond criticism from the early 1980s onwards. Towards the end of his career, Bergman took control of his own reputation and was hardly ever challenged by critical questions in interviews. On the contrary, he was elevated to cinema royalty. Critics and academics alike have largely followed Bergman's opinions about his cinema oeuvre.

---

[*] For the history of the Center for Feeling Therapy, see Mithers (1994) and Ayella (1998).
[†] See Gardner 2001 and Williams and Edgar 2008 for a summary.

CHANGING AESTHETIC IDEALS

The mid-1970s marked the beginning of a new era: the rise of a new Hollywood increasingly committed to light entertainment – action, adventure, space opera, fantasy – in lavish blockbuster megapics. New European film directors like Jean-Jacques Beineix and Lars von Trier followed suit by breaking away from the austere art cinema style of Bergman and Antonioni, to tell rather traditional genre stories in an energetic and flamboyant style inspired by advertising photography, commercials and rock videos.

Following a string of commercial failures – *The Serpent's Egg* (1977), *Autumn Sonata* (*Höstsonaten*, 1978) and *From the Life of the Marionettes* (1980) – Bergman would return in 1982/83 with a lavish blockbuster of his own: *Fanny and Alexander*. This farewell to film was also a radical aesthetic departure, not only in its melodramatic family saga but also in its use of colour, moving camera, beautified images and just about everything he had dismissed from his audio-visual palette at the end of the 1960s.

It is a film that significantly takes place in a nineteenth-century bourgeois sanctuary. In the final scene, Alexander (Bertil Guve) listens to his grandmother reading Strindberg's *A Dream Play*, which forebodes the coming of twentieth-century modernism and its disrupting implications for this family. Bergman made his farewell with a prequel to his modernist films.

The main characters' family name is Ekdahl, an overt reference to the family living a lie in Ibsen's *The Wild Duck*. Like them, Bergman's film seemingly celebrates everything he has attacked during his career in film and theatre: the bourgeois family and its idealist values – the "small world", sentimentally praised by Gustav Adolf (Jarl Kulle) in a dinner speech. *Face to Face* belonged to another era, the one in which idealism was challenged.

THE WORK ITSELF

Face to Face is a problematic production. That is already apparent in Bergman's workbook for the screenplay. At the outset, he intended to follow his instincts and make a "yummy" film without beginning, middle or end. Inspired by Leonor Fini's painting and most likely by contemporary films like his friend Federico Fellini's *Satyricon* (1969), it would be a series of surreal and hallucinatory episodes, aiming to go beyond the already loose, dream-like structure of *Cries and Whispers* to ultimately dissolve storytelling as such. That would possibly be what he meant by "the film *as it ought to have been*".

Afraid that such a work might be too inaccessible and personal, Bergman starts working on a more coherent and realistic narrative leading up to the dreams, which become the arena in which the protagonist confronts the childhood roots to her real-life problems. The emotional experience of the confrontation triggers a primal scream, after which she becomes an authentic primal man. Thus, she is set free from the neurotic dreams and traumas that have haunted her.

Remember, Bergman saw the first, realistic part of the narrative as essentially solid when reflecting on the film in *Images*. But when looking at the finished TV series and film, the most damaging flaw of the narrative is in the first half: Jenny's lack of a background story.

Face to Face was planned as an emotionally charged tale of a psychologically troubled woman, who breaks down, tries to take her own life and finally relives her childhood traumas. Without any backstory to her emotionally stunted condition introduced in the first half, the implications of her behaviour are lost to us. Her reactions to Maria, the one-eyed phantom lady and Tomas' flirtations and the attempted rape bear no sign of a more serious mental condition, rooted in childhood traumas.

On the contrary, Jenny's childhood home at the grandparents' radiates warmth and emotional security. The few alarming signs are not supported by much. Maria's claim of Jenny being an emotional cripple is undermined in the filmed version by cutting out the few intelligent reflections she had in the screenplay. In the final TV and film versions, the psychotic Maria is hardly credible as a person of emotional insight.

When Jenny moves back to her childhood room in her grandparents' apartment, there is first a cut to Grandfather looking worried then to a close-up of Jenny with a similar expression. It could be a remnant of Bergman's early sketches for an incestuous backstory between the two as the hidden secret of the 'doll's house'. That would also explain the dialogue about Jenny being "Daddy's little girl" and why she has chosen a husband just as infantile, weak, emotionally stunted and at a loss for words as both her father and Grandfather.

But there are no echoes of anything incestuous in the dreams, nor in the final breakdown and primal scream. Instead, Grandmother suddenly appears out of nowhere as the monster of repression, something we would never have guessed from our impression of her in the realistic half. To really hammer home the suggestion that Jenny suffered a bad childhood, Bergman has Grandmother tell a "Cinderella"-like fairy tale of a girl being robbed of everything by her evil guardians. But, again, there is little to support it, which undermines the traumatic scenario leading up to the primal scream.

When Jenny has her final breakdown, wrestling demons and speaking in other people's voices like a sanitised version of Regan in *The Exorcist* (1973), her emotional state seems overwrought. Is Jenny perhaps delusional, even psychotic? Is she putting on a show? Though it is no fault of Liv Ullmann, the scene that should reveal the true, authentic Jenny, breaking out of her theatrical shell, becomes yet another theatrical moment in the film. This in a project that was intended to critique theatricality, dissolve storytelling and even mark the end of art.

CODA: THE END OF ART?

In his letter to Liv Ullmann before shooting *Face to Face*, Bergman wrote about the transformation of Jenny's exterior to reflect her inner revolution after the primal scream. She was to be "only dressed in a sweater and a pair of old jeans" and "unaware of her looks" for the first time in her life. Here, Bergman connects with Ibsen's ending of *A Doll's House*, in which Nora signals her new-found freedom by ridding herself of the 'doll outfit' to dress in her everyday clothes before taking her leave of the bourgeois golden cage.

Jenny not only is about to break away from her home and marriage, but is possibly leaving psychiatry – at least the institutionalised variety she currently works within. At the end of *Face to Face*, we find her at the same point in life as Elisabet was at the beginning of *Persona*: realising the theatricality of both private life and work. They both confront the "tangle of lies" that has kept them imprisoned in a sanctuary associated with 'the good things in life' and closed off from authentic life in the real world.

In both cases, the outcome is uncertain as the final scene does not present any resolution to the conflict. Does Elisabet go back to the theatre and her marriage? We will never know. Does Jenny go back to psychiatry and to her family? Yes, but perhaps only temporarily.

In the TV version of *Face to Face*, we are informed by a text that she quits her job, divorces her husband and starts over by doing research in the US – at the Primal Institute, maybe? In the film version, she just leaves her childhood home, destination unknown. In neither version has she rid herself of her old 'doll's clothes'; she still wears the very same garments she wore in the opening scene. The only difference is that she has let her hair hang down.

Moreover, the two films can be regarded as metaphors for Bergman's reflections on his own life and art. In *Persona*, Bergman (as Elisabet) and his art stirs repressed thoughts, feelings and impulses in the collective unconscious of his audience (as Alma). In *Face to Face*, Bergman (as Jenny) himself comes face to face with repressed fears and doubts about himself and his art, using psychiatry as a metaphor.

What attracted him and many others in the mid-1970s to primal therapy was the promise of a cure for neurosis and, by implication, the end of psychiatry. Arthur Janov describes in *The Primal Scream* how his patients' dreams became less symbolic and more real as his therapy progressed: "Mother was mother, children were children, and New York was New York". To him, "this is logical since symbols arise to mask *old* feelings from childhood" (Janov 1970, p. 281; italics in original).*

For primal man, the real world is real, both in life and in imagination. *Face to Face* ends with Jenny realising that Grandmother is not a demon. She is a real person:

> Jenny stops herself and looks at Grandmother. It is as if she saw her for the first time. The old woman has seated herself on a chair by the wall and the sun is shining on her face. She now discovers that her grandmother is very old, that the clear blue-grey eyes are sad, that the determined mouth is no longer as determined, that the straight posture is not so straight, that Grandmother in some way has become smaller, not very much, but discernible. And when she turns her face towards Jenny with an inquisitive smile, her head shakes almost imperceptibly, but it shakes just the same and the strong broad hands, the capable, active hands, lie tired and numb in her lap. (Bergman 1976a, p. 103)

The project of leaving art to step into the real authentic life is also suggested in Toril Moi's book on Ibsen. The last chapter discusses the author's last play *When We Dead Awaken* (*Når vi døde vågner*, 1899). In the final scene, the female protagonist "makes her way down from the cold heights of idealist ecstasy to the valleys and plains of ordinary life" while singing a simple song of freedom. Toril Moi takes it as a farewell also "to idealism and its ecstatic celebration of art and artists" and she

---

* A few pages on, he suggests that his patients stopped dreaming altogether and even lost their unconscious, since for the post-primal man "nothing is unconscious anymore" (1970, p. 290).

concludes, "Ibsen saw that without idealism, it is hard to feel *that* sanguine about a life spent in the service of art" (2008, p. 324; italics in original).

When Bergman set out to write a film that promised to ultimately dissolve storytelling as such, was he perhaps also contemplating making it his final work? Was he planning to leave his life in the arts, his own sanctuary? After all, he had already referred to art as a hollow but still twitching snakeskin – an imitation of life (Bergman 1966, pp. 7–13). In *Persona*, the film that more than any other of his works challenged conventional storytelling, he breaks the film strip, shows the apparatus and disrupts the illusory effect of film in other ways.

In my proposed Djursholm trilogy, Bergman starts an Ibsenian project by portraying the interiors of three modern doll's houses. In the last part, *Face to Face*, he even suggests a life after the fall of bourgeois idealism: a free woman of the modern world. But he still cannot or will not envision it. The reason might be that he considered it to be outside his artistic realm – that is, where art ends and life begins.

Instead, he leaves Jenny and himself with three possible alternatives at the curtain-fall: 1. Stay the same. 2. Become primal man. 3. Put out the light. From what we can tell by her appearance and by her promise to go back to work, Jenny largely stays the same. If for no other reason, then out of a sense of duty.

Her choice is not unprecedented in Bergman's oeuvre. When faced with doubts about his religious conviction, the priest Thomas in *Winter Light* still decides to continue his work as a priest. In *Persona*, Alma's life in lies is challenged to the point where her language and identity break down. Even so, she goes back to her old life and work. Anna in *The Lie* hesitates with a "No", and Marianne in *Scenes from a Marriage* is haunted by demons.

Have any of them changed? If so, apparently not enough to become authentic people in Bergman's mind. And what about Bergman himself? He obviously did not step out of his sanctuary in the arts. Like Thomas, Alma and Jenny, he continued to dwell on his autobiographical themes and motifs, although the subsequent representations of his parents took the form of more complicated and hence more real people in *The Best Intentions*, *Sunday's Children* and *Private Confessions*. Still, he kept holding on to his *traums* and traumas, the dwelling of the demons that he needed in the harnesses of his artistic chariot.

REFERENCES

Note: where entries list more than one edition or printing for a publication, the most recent edition or printing was the one consulted for the purposes of providing citation page numbers.

PRINTED MATERIAL

Aare, Leif. 1975. "Mozart förlöste Bergman, men allting har sitt pris." *Dagens Nyheter*, 2 January.

Aghed, Jan. 1969. "Samtal med Bergman: 'Men vad fan gör det?'" *Sydsvenska Dagbladet*, 9 February.

———. 2002. "Encounter with Ingmar Bergman." Reprinted in Raphael Shargel (ed.). 2007. Ingmar Bergman: Interviews. Jackson, MS: University Press of Mississippi, pp. 190–200.

Alvarez, A. 1975. "A Visit with Ingmar Bergman." *New York Times Magazine*, no. 36, 7 December, pp. 37, 90–106. Reprinted in Raphael Shargel (ed.). 2007. *Ingmar Bergman: Interviews*. Jackson, MS: University Press of Mississippi, pp. 113–125.

Andersson, Bibi. 1971. "Det banala ej ointressant." *Dagens Nyheter*, 4 July.

Andersson, Carl V. 2007. "Bergman sörjde drömprojektet som sprack." *Expressen*, 31 July.

Andersson, Elisabet. 2014. "Roy Andersson öser galla över Bergman." *Svenska Dagbladet*, 10 October.

Andersson, Jan. 1971. "Socialisera hela filmindustrin!" *Aftonbladet*, 3 December.

———. 1975. "Det var nästan så att man blev operafrälst!" *Aftonbladet*, 2 January.

Anon. 1796. *Das ältste Systemprogramm des deutschen Idealismus.* http://www.hs-augsburg.de/~harsch/germanica/Chronologie/18Jh/Idealismus/ide_fra0.html (accessed 2016-06-10)

———. 1878. Samhällslärans grunddrag eller fysisk, sexuel och naturlig religion. Stockholm: Associationsboktr.

———. 1969a. "Bergman varnar för TV-pjäsen ikväll: 'Ni hinner gå på bio!'" *Expressen*, 25 March.

———. 1969b. "Ingen begrep Ingmar Bergman." *Expressen*, 26 March.

———. 1969c. "*Riten* fick lysande recensioner i hela Skandinavien." *Kvällsposten*, 27 March.

———. 1969d. "Undran och beundran efter *Riten* i TV." *Svenska Dagbladet*, 27 March.

———. 1970a. "Bergman lägger ner Amerikaprojektet." *Dagens Nyheter*, 2 January.

———. 1970b. "*Skammen* topprankad i Amerika." *Dagens Nyheter*, 2 January.

———. 1970c. "En 'lätt' Ingmar Bergman!" *Kvällsposten*, 28 October.

———. 1970d. "*Reservatet* är en ovanlig Ingmar Bergman-pjäs." *Dagens Nyheter*, 28 October.

———. 1971a. "Disappointing Bergman." *Time*, vol. 98, no. 4, 26 July.

———. 1971b. "Ingmar Bergman och alla hans kvinnor." *Aftonbladet*, 19 September.

———. 1973a. "12 av 16 familjer såg Bergmans pjäs." *Expressen*, 3 May.

———. 1973b. "Johan och Marianne kan inte leva utan varandra!" *Aftonbladet*, 16 May.

———. 1973c. "Oss fotografer emellan." *Chaplin*, no. 5, pp. 183–191.

———. 1974. "Det blev mindre skamligt att ha det svårt med varann." *Svenska Dagbladet*, 29 August.

———. 1975. "*Trollflöjten* igen! Den blev en världssuccé." *Röster i Radio TV*, no. 17, 16–22 April.

———. 1976a. "American Film Institute Dialogue on Film: Ingmar Bergman." *American Film*, no. 1, January–February, pp. 33–48. Reprinted in Raphael Shargel (ed.). 2007. *Ingmar Bergman: Interviews*. Jackson, MS: University Press of Mississippi, pp. 126–139.

———. 1976b. "Bergman och alla dessa kvinnor." *Aftonbladet*, 26 April.

———. 1976c. "Fantastisk Liv Ullmann skakade om TV-tittarna!" *Kvälls-Posten*, 29 April.

———. 1976d. "Första avsnittet av *Ansikte mot ansikte*: Fängslande/Ointressant." *Expressen*, 29 April.

———. 1976e. "Jodå, du är uppskattad, Bergman." *Göteborgs-Tidningen*, 29 April.

———. 1976f. "Ris och ros för Liv och Ingmar." *Expressen*, 13 May.

———. 1976g. "Ansiktet som skakade oss." *Kvälls-Posten*, 20 May.

———. 1976h. "TV-intervjun med Arthur Janov." *Primalbladet* (newsletter for Svenska Primalföreningen), no. 4, July, pp. 6–7.

———. 1976i. "'Nu börjar jag om': Bergman till USA, nytt skatteutspel." *Dagens Nyheter* 23 April.

———. 1980. *Prostitutionen i Sverige, del II*. DS S 1980:09. Stockholm: Socialdepartementet.

———. 1999. "Bergman Admits Nazi Past." BBC News, 7 September. See http://news.bbc.co.uk/2/hi/entertainment/441057.stm (accessed 29 January 2016).

Archer, Eugene. 1967. "Bergman: 'I Try to Write Subconsciously, to Let My Dreams Flow'." *New York Times*, 2 April.

Asplund, Uno (pen name: Big Ben). 1973. "Äktenskap och relationer i Bergmans nya TV-serie." *Göteborgs-Posten*, 11 April.

Åstrand, Hans. 1975. "Förtrollad TV-flöjt – en bild av skönhet och behag." *Kvällsposten*, 2 January.

Ayella, Marybeth F. 1998. *Insane Therapy: Portrait of a Psychotherapy Cult*. Philadelphia, PA: Temple University Press.

Baehrendtz, Maj-Britt. 1973. "Johan är ingen knöl." *Expressen*, 11 May.

Baldwin, James. 1960. "The Northern Protestant." Reprinted in Raphael Shargel (ed.). 2007. *Ingmar Bergman: Interviews*. Jackson, MS: University Press of Mississippi, pp. 10–20.

Balio, Tino. 2010. *The Foreign Film Renaissance on American Screens 1946–1973*. Madison, WI: University of Wisconsin Press.

Barrow, John. 1973. "How Do You Photograph a Cry or a Whisper?" *New York Times*, 14 January.

Behring, Bertil. 1970a. "Ingmar Bergman – mästerreporter: I härnad för sitt Fårö." *Kvällsposten*, 2 January.

———. 1970b. "En äktenskaplig deckarserie." *Kvällsposten*, 12 April.

———. 1973. "En slags äktenskaplig deckarserie." *Kvällsposten*, 12 April.

Bergman, Ingmar. 1966. *Persona*. Stockholm: P. A. Norstedts.

———. 1973a. *Filmberättelser 3: Riten, Reservatet, Beröringen, Viskningar och rop*. Stockholm: Norstedts.

———. 1973b. *Scener ur ett äktenskap*. Stockholm: Norstedts.

———. 1975. "A Briefing for a Film, By Ingmar Bergman." *New York Times*, 24 September.

———. 1976a. *Ansikte mot ansikte*. Stockholm: Norstedts.

———. 1976b. "Ingmar Bergman: 'Nu lämnar jag Sverige'." *Expressen*, 22 April.

———. 1988. *The Magic Lantern: An Autobiography*. Translated by Joan Tate. Chicago, IL: University Press of Chicago.

———. 1995. *Images: My Life in Film*. Translated by Marianne Ruuth. London and Boston, MA: Faber and Faber.

———. 2000. *Föreställningar*. Stockholm: Norstedts.

Bergom-Larsson, Maria. 1977. *Ingmar Bergman och den borgerliga ideologin*. Stockholm: Norstedts.

———. 1978. *Ingmar Bergman and Society*. Translated by Barrie Selman. New York, NY: A. S. Barnes.

Bergström, Lasse. 1971. "Bergman's *Love Story*." *Expressen*, 27 June.

———. 1973. "En av hans rikaste filmer." *Expressen*, 6 March.

———. 1976. "Hennes insats är närmast ofattbar." *Expressen*, 11 April.

Berlioz, Jacques. 2007. "Il faut sauver 'Le petit chaperon rouge'." Les Collections de L'Histoires, no. 6, September, p. 63. See http://www.lhistoire.fr/il-faut-sauver-le-petit-chaperon-rouge (accessed 11 October 2016).

Beyer, Nils. 1970. "Stor kväll för TV-teatern." *Arbetet*, 29 October.

———. 1976. "Ansikte mot ansikte med Ingmar Bergman." *Arbetet*, 29 April.

Björkman, K. G. 1970. "Ingmar Bergman ville ha Dustin Hoffman som stjärna i sin nya film." *Aftonbladet*, 23 August.

———. 1973. "Såg ni Liv i TV igår?". *Aftonbladet*, 12 April.

Björkman, Stig. 1969. "*En passion*." *Chaplin*, vol. 11, no. 9, pp. 321–322.

Björkman, Stig, Torsten Manns and Jonas Sima. 1973. *Bergman on Bergman: Interviews with Ingmar Bergman*. Translated by Britten Austin. New York, NY: Simon and Schuster.

Björkstén, Ingmar. 1970. "Skrapa på samhället och förnedringsritualen skiner igenom." *Vecko-Journalen*, no. 19, pp. 24–27.

Blackwell, Marilyn Johns. 1997. *Gender and Representation in the Films of*

Ingmar Bergman. Columbia, SC: Camden House.

Bloom, John. 2012. "J.R. Takes Another Shot." *D Magazine*, June. See http://www.dmagazine.com/publications/d-magazine/2012/june/as-dallas-returns-to-tv-jr-ewing-takes-another-shot?single=1 (accessed 30 January 2016).

Boëthius, Maria-Pia. 1991. *Heder och samvete: Sverige och andra världskriget*. Stockholm: Norstedts.

———. 1999. *Heder och samvete: Sverige och andra världskriget*. Stockholm: Ordfront.

———. 2007. "Ingmar Bergman beundrade Hitler." *Svenska Dagbladet*, 12 August.

Bordwell, David. 2008. *Poetics of Cinema*. New York, NY: Routledge.

Borger-Bendergard, Lisbeth. 1971. "Ingmar Bergman – Hur kan du förföra så?" *Femina*, no. 45, 7 November.

Bransmo, Gunnel. 1969. "TV-chock ikväll!" *Kvällsposten*, 25 March.

Branting, Jacob. 1970. "Genialisk tolkning av Gunnel Lindblom." *Aftonbladet*, 29 October.

Byron, Stuart. 1975. "Don Rugoff: Ballyhoo with a Harvard Education." *Film Comment*, vol. 11, no. 3, May–June, pp. 20–27.

Canby, Vincent. 1971a. "*The Touch*." *New York Times*, 15 July.

———. 1971b. "Getting Hustled by the Big Bustle." *New York Times*, 25 July.

———. 1972. "*Cries and Whispers*." *New York Times*, 22 December.

———. 1974. "Scenes from a Marriage." *New York Times*, 16 September.

———. 1976a. "In Bergman Film, Beauty and Agony." *New York Times*, 6 April.

———. 1976b. "Bergman Explores the Terror of Blandness." *New York Times*, 18 April.

Childs, Peter. 2008. *Modernism*. New York, NY: Routledge.

Chabrol, Claude. 1954. "Story of an Interview." Sidney Gottlieb (ed.). 2003. *Alfred Hitchcock: Interviews*. Jackson, MS: University Press of Mississippi, pp. 39–43.

Cocks, Jay. 1973. "Four Women." *Time*, vol. 101, no. 2.

———. 1976. "Over the Edge." *Time*, vol. 107, no. 15.

Corman, Roger, with Jim Jerome. 1990. *How I Made a Hundred Movies in Hollywood and Never Lost a Dime*. New York, NY: Delta.

Corsini, Raymond J. 1981. *Handbook of Innovative Psychotherapies*. New York, NY: John Wiley & Sons.

Cowie, Peter. 1992. *Ingmar Bergman: A Critical Biography*. New York, NY: Limelight Editions.

———. 1988. "Ingmar Bergman: A Chronology." Ingmar Bergman. *The Magic Lantern*. Translated by Joan Tate. Chicago, IL: University Press of Chicago, pp. 291–303.

Cushman, Philip. 1995. *Constructing the Self, Constructing America: A Cultural History of Psychotherapy*. Boston, MA: Da Capo Press.

Davies, Hunter (ed.). 2012. *The John Lennon Letters*. London: Weidenfeld & Nicholson.

Dawson, Jan. 1970. "*A Passion*." *Monthly Film Bulletin*, vol. 37, no. 440, p. 181.

Domarchi, Jean. 1960. "*La Source*: Décline de Bergman." *Arts*, 14–20 December, p. 7.

Donnér, Jarl W. 1970. "Miljöskyddade enslingar." *Sydsvenska Dagbladet*, 29 October.

———. 1973a. "Kontrastrikt." *Sydsvenska Dagbladet*, 12 April.

———. 1973b. "Begynnande sprickor." *Sydsvenska Dagbladet*, 19 April.

———. 1973c. "Spänningsrikt." *Sydsvenska Dagbladet*, 3 May.

———. 1973d. "Snopet och resignerat." *Sydsvenska Dagbladet*, 17 May.

———. 1976a. "Bergmans spelöppning." *Sydsvenska Dagbladet*, 29 April.

———. 1976b. "Mot en gräns." *Sydsvenska Dagbladet*, 6 May.

———. 1976c. "Sviktande drömspel." *Sydsvenska Dagbladet*, 13 May.

———. 1976d. "En sjunkande kurva." *Sydsvenska Dagbladet*, 20 May.

Donner, Jörn. 1964. *The Personal Vision of Ingmar Bergman*. Bloomington, IN: University of Indiana Press.

———. 1973. "Det måste finnas en förtröstan." *Femina*, no. 38, 23 September, pp. 22–25.

Donner, Jörn, and Berit Nordin. 1977a. "Nattvardsgästerna." Jörn Donner (ed.). *Svensk Filmografi, 1960–1969*. Stockholm: Svenska Filminstitutet, pp. 135–137.

———. 1977b. "Tystnaden." Jörn Donner (ed.). *Svensk Filmografi, 1960–1969*. Stockholm: Svenska Filminstitutet, pp. 152–154.

———. 1977c. "491." Jörn Donner (ed.). *Svensk Filmografi, 1960–1969*. Stockholm: Svenska Filminstitutet, pp. 171–174.

Dundes, Alan. 1991. "Bruno Bettelheim's *Uses of Enchantment* and Abuses of Scholarship." *Journal of American Folklore*, vol. 104, no. 411, pp. 74–83.

Ebert, Roger. 1973. "*Cries and Whispers.*" *Chicago Sun-Times*, 12 February.

———. 1974. "*Scenes from a Marriage.*" *Chicago Sun-Times*, 15 September.

———. 1976. "*Face to Face.*" *Chicago Sun-Times*, 6 August.

Edlund, Birgitta. 1971. "Många filmare starkt kritiska: 'Satsa på de icke etablerade!'" *Dagens Nyheter*, 15 October.

Edström, Mauritz. 1970. "Bergmans film om Fårö." *Dagens Nyheter*, 2 January.

———. 1971. "Skicklig och lätt kärlekshistoria om saknaden efter." *Dagens Nyheter*, 31 August.

———. 1973a. "Bergmans TV-serie: Rasande diskussioner i raka, enkla bilder." *Dagens Nyheter*, 12 April.

———. 1973b. "En av Bergmans finaste människoskildringar." *Dagens Nyheter*, 17 April.

Edvardson, Cordelia. 1973. "Jag tror på det heliga i människan." *Vecko-Journalen*, no. 15, 11 April.

Ennis, Bruce J. 1972. *Prisoners of Psychiatry: Mental Patients, Psychiatrists and the Law*. 1974 Discus edition. New York, NY: Avon and Discus Books.

Eriksson, Ingalill. 1976. "Är det farligt att se *Ansikte mot ansikte?*" *Expressen*, 9 May.

Eriksson, Ingmari, and Sölve Skagen. 1973a. "Bergman och vampyrerna." *Dagens Nyheter*, 6 April.

———. 1973b. "Film som finkultur." *Dagens Nyheter*, 12 May.

Evander, Per Gunnar. 1969. *Uppkomlingarna: En personundersökning*. Stockholm: Albert Bonniers.

Fahlgren, Margareta. 2009. "Strindberg and the Woman Question." Michael Robinson (ed.). *The Cambridge Companion to August Strindberg.* Cambridge: Cambridge University Press, pp. 20–33.

Falk, Bertil. 1969. "'Stoppa Ingmar Bergman': Våldsam Svensk reaktion efter TV-pjäsen." *Kvällsposten,* 26 March.

Feltham, Colin (ed.). 1999. *Controversies in Psychotherapy and Counselling.* London: Sage.

Ferguson, Robert. 1996. *Henrik Ibsen: A New Biography.* London: Richard Cohen Books.

Fornäs, Johan. 1977. "Det inre förtrycket." *Tekla,* no. 1, March. Digitally reprinted at Marxists Internet Archive: https://www.marxists.org/svenska/tidskrifter/tekla/77-1/c.htm#h7 (accessed 31 July 2016).

Forslund, Bengt (ed.). 1960. "Bergmans ansikte". *Chaplin,* vol. 2, no. 2, pp. 189–195.

———. 2003. *Molander, Molander, Molander.* Stockholm: Carlssons.

———. 2006. *Dramatik i TV-soffan: Från "Hamlet" till "Svensson Svensson".* Stockholm: Bokförlaget Arena.

Forssell, Lars. 1968. "*Skammen.*" *BLM,* no. 8, pp. 605–607.

Friedland, Ronald. 1973. "If We Understood Bergman, We'd Stone Him." *New York Times,* 27 May.

Furhammar, Leif. 2003. *Filmen i Sverige.* Stockholm: Dialogos.

Gado, Frank. 1996. *The Passion of Ingmar Bergman.* Durham, NC: Duke University Press.

Gårdlund, Torsten. 1956. *Knut Wicksell: Rebell i det nya riket.* Stockholm: Bonniers.

Gardner, Martin. 2001. "Primal Scream: A Persistent New Age Therapy." *Skeptical Inquirer,* no. 25, pp. 17–19.

Garfinkel, Bernie. 1976. "Han var som en gud för mig." *Aftonbladet,* 19 April.

Geber, Nils-Hugo. 1977a. "*Vargtimmen.*" Jörn Donner (ed.). *Svensk Filmografi, 1960–1969.* Stockholm: Svenska Filminstitutet, pp. 366–368.

———. 1977b. "*Skammen.*" Jörn Donner (ed.). *Svensk Filmografi, 1960–1969.* Stockholm: Svenska Filminstitutet, pp. 399–401.

———. 1977c. "*En passion.*" Jörn Donner (ed.). *Svensk Filmografi, 1960–1969.* Stockholm: Svenska Filminstitutet, pp. 492–494.

———. 1983. "*Gycklarnas afton.*" Lars Åhlander (ed.). *Svensk Filmografi, 1950–1959.* Stockholm: Svenska Filminstitutet, pp. 302–305.

Georgsson, Lars-Olof. 1970. "Bergman-pjäs på världens största teater: Ses av 50 miljoner." *Arbetet,* 28 October.

Gilliatt, Penelope. 1971. "Bergman About Love." *New Yorker,* 24 July.

———. 1974. "Of Dreaming and Mayhem." *New Yorker,* 23 September, pp. 95–98.

———. 1976. "Trapdoor." *New Yorker,* 5 April, pp. 121–123.

Godard, Jean-Luc. 1958. "Bergman-orama." *Cahiers du cinéma,* no. 85, pp. 1–5.

Goodman, Jane E. 2005. *Berber Culture on the World Stage: From Village to Video.* Bloomington, IL: Indiana University Press.

Granath, Gunilla, Annika Persson and Ebba Witt-Brattström. 1973. "Manligt kvinnoideal i svensk film: Gengångare från den viktorianska epoken." *Film & TV*, nos. 5–6, pp. 11–19.

Gräslund, Tau. 1973. "Så här tyckte tre vanliga par om Bergmans äktenskapspjäs." *Expressen*, 12 April.

Greer, Germaine. 1970. *The Female Eunuch*. London: Harper Perennial.

Grenier, Cynthia. 1964. "Ingmar Bergman." *Playboy*, vol. 11, no. 6, pp. 61–68.

Grönberg, Staffan. 1980. "*Kris.*" Lars Åhlander (ed.). *Svensk Filmografi, 1940–1949*. Stockholm: Svenska Filminstitutet, pp. 512–514.

Gustafson, Stig Göran. 1976. "Bergmanserien som det kommer att bli ett helsickes liv om." *Kvälls-Posten*, 28 April.

Gutman, Robert W. 2001. *Mozart: A Cultural Biography*. London: Pimlico.

Hagen, Cecilia. 2004. "Hon är Ingmar Bergmans hemliga dotter." *Expressen*, 15 October.

Hallam, Lindsay Anne. 2012. *Screening the Marquis de Sade: Pleasure, Pain and the Transgressive Body in Film*. Jefferson, NC: McFarland.

Harrysson, Kajsa. 1974. "Trollflöjten, en makalös operakväll." *Röster i Radio TV*, nos. 1–2, 30 December 1974 – 9 January 1975, pp. 4–5, 31, 67.

———. 1976. "Ansikte mot ansikte: ett samtal med Ingmar Bergman." *Röster i Radio TV*, no. 18, 23–29 April, pp. 8–9. Continued under the same heading in *Röster i Radio TV*, no. 19, 30 April – 6 May, pp. 10–11, 61.

Hedberg, Birgit. 1975. "Decenniets stora framgång för TV." *Göteborgs-Posten*, 2 January.

Hellbom, Thorleif. 1972. "Bergman i sin nya filmstad." *Dagens Nyheter*, 30 August.

Henttonen, Anita. 1969. "Är du ett geni, Ingmar Bergman?" *Aftonbladet*, 26 April.

Heurling, Bo. 1983a. "*En lektion i kärlek.*" Lars Åhlander (ed.). *Svensk Filmografi, 1950–1959*. Stockholm: Svenska Filminstitutet, pp. 384–387.

———. 1983b. "*Ansiktet.*" Lars Åhlander (ed.). *Svensk Filmografi, 1950–1959*. Stockholm: Svenska Filminstitutet, pp. 727–730.

———. 1988. "*Trollflöjten.*" Lars Åhlander (ed.). *Svensk Filmografi, 1970–1979*. Stockholm: Svenska Filminstitutet, pp. 290–291.

Hitchcock, Alfred. 1937. "Direction." Reprinted in Sidney Gottlieb (ed.). 1995. *Hitchcock on Hitchcock*. London: Faber and Faber, pp. 253–261.

Hjertén, Hanserik. 1973. "Ingmar Bergmans märkligaste film." *Dagens Nyheter*, 6 March.

———. 1976. "Naket och instängt." *Dagens Nyheter*, 28 April.

Holm, Hans Axel. 1971. "Stark Forssell på Dramaten: Edwall fascinerar från första scen." *Dagens Nyheter*, 21 March.

Holmqvist, Mikael. 2015. *Djursholm: Sveriges ledarsamhälle*. Stockholm: Norstedts.

Höök, Marianne. 1962. *Ingmar Bergman*. Stockholm: Wahlström & Widstrand.

———. 1969. "Publiken ska känna det som om den fått en elektrisk stöt." *Vi*, no. 12, 22 March.

———. 2008. *Får man vara lite tilltalande i det här samhället?* Edited by Anette Kullenberg. Stockholm: Atlas.

Humble, Kristina, and Gitte Settergren-Carlsson. 1974. "Unga lagöverträdare: Personlighet och relationer i belysning av projektiva metoder." SOU, no. 31.

Ibsen, Henrik (ed.). 1971. *Ibsens dramatik*. Edited by Egil Törnqvist. Stockholm: Wahlström & Widstrand.

Isaksson, Ulla. 1973. *Paradistorg*. Stockholm: Albert Bonniers.

Jahnsson, Bengt. 1970. "Bergmans 'Reservatet': Tveksam regi tog bort den satiriska skärpan." *Dagens Nyheter*, 29 October.

Janov, Arthur. 1970. *The Primal Scream*. London: Sphere Books.

———. 1974. *Primalskriket*. Stockholm: Wahlström & Widstrand.

Janzon, Åke. 1970. "Vårt komfortabla reservat." *Svenska Dagbladet*, 29 October.

———. 1971. "Ett drömspel på drift." *Svenska Dagbladet*, 21 March,

———. 1973a. "Äktenskapets lektion nr 1." *Svenska Dagbladet*, 12 April. Janzon, Åke. 1973b. "Scener ur ett äktenskap II: Relationer och psykologi." *Svenska Dagbladet*, 19 April.

———. 1973c. "Den stora vreden." *Svenska Dagbladet*, 26 April.

———. 1973d. "Subtilt möte." *Svenska Dagbladet*, 3 May.

———. 1973e. "Driva ut onda andar." *Svenska Dagbladet*, 10 May.

———. 1973f. "Frågandet fullbordat." *Svenska Dagbladet*, 17 May.

———. 1976a. "Suggestionsteknikens triumf." *Svenska Dagbladet*, 29 April.

———. 1976b. "Känsloladdade scener, psykologiska luckor." *Svenska Dagbladet*, 6 May.

———. 1976c. "Vägen till skärselden." *Svenska Dagbladet*, 13 May.

———. 1976d. "Vackra och begåvade skådespelare." *Svenska Dagbladet*, 20 May.

Jebb, Julian. 1975. "*Scenes from a Marriage*." *Sight and Sound*, vol. 44, no. 1, winter 1974–75, pp. 57–58.

Jones, Evelyn. 2016. "Kvinnor mer kulturellt aktiva än män." *Dagens Nyheter*, 19 January.

Josefsson, Jan, and Mats Zetterberg. 1976. *Behöver vänstern gå i terapi?* Lund: Forum.

Judt, Tony. 2005. *Postwar: A History of Europe Since 1945*. London: Vintage.

Jung, Carl. 1916. "The Relations Between the Ego and the Unconscious." Joseph Campbell (ed.). 1976. *The Portable Jung*. New York: Viking Press, p. 70–138.

———. 1934–54. *The Archetypes and the Collective Unconscious. The Collected Works of C.G. Jung, Vol. 9, Part 1*. Translated by R.F.C. Hull. Princeton, NJ: Princeton University Press.

Kant, Immanuel. 1922. *Critique of Pure Reason*. Translated by F. Max Müller. London: MacMillan.

———. 2002. *Groundworks for the Metaphysics of Morals*. Edited and translated by Allen W. Wood. New Haven, CT: Yale University Press.

Kael, Pauline. 1968. "A Sign of Life." *New Yorker*, 28 December. Reprinted in Pauline Kael. 1970. *Going Steady: Film Writings 1968–1969*. New York, NY: Marion Boyars, pp. 214–221.

———. 1971a. "Raising *Kane.*" *New Yorker*, 20 February. Reprinted in Pauline Kael. 2002. *Pauline Kael on the Best Film Ever Made* (booklet). London: Sight and Sound.

———. 1971b. "A Note on New Actors, New Movies." *New Yorker*, 4 December. Reprinted in Pauline Kael. 1975. *Deeper into Movies.* New York, NY: Marion Boyars, pp. 348–349.

———. 1973. "Flesh" . *New Yorker*, 6 January. Reprinted in Pauline Kael. 1977. *Reeling.* New York, NY: Marion Boyars, pp. 89–94.

Kant, Immanuel. 2002. *Groundwork for the Metaphysics of Morals*. Edited and translated by Allen W. Wood. New Haven, CT: Yale University Press.

Kats, Madeleine. 1976a. "Vi kommer varje gång han ropar." *Femina*, no. 19, 9 May.

———. 1976b. "Bergman – rädd, rädd, rädd." *Expressen*, 20 May.

Kinder, Marsha. 1974. "*Scenes from a Marriage.*" *Film Quarterly*, vol. 28, no. 2, winter 1974–75, pp. 48–53.

Klynne, Keity. 1972. "Ingmar Bergmans kvinnosyn." *Chaplin*, no. 1, pp. 28–29.

Koskinen, Maaret. 1993. *Spel och speglingar: En studie i Ingmar Bergmans filmiska estetik.* Stockholm: Department of Theatre and Cinema Arts.

———. 2001. *"Allting föreställer, ingenting är": Filmen och teatern – en tvärestetisk studie.* Nora: Nya Doxa.

———. 2002. *I begynnelsen var ordet: Ingmar Bergman och hans tidiga författarskap.* Stockholm: Wahlström & Widstrand.

Kullenberg, Annette. 2009. *Jag var självlockig, moderlös, gripande och ett monster av förljugenhet: En biografi om Marianne Höök.* Stockholm: Atlas.

Lader, Robert S. 1973. "What Is Ingmar Bergman's Answer to Death?" *New York Times*, 11 February.

Laing, Adrian. 1994. *R. D. Laing: A Biography.* New York: Thunder's Mouth Press.

Larsson, Ann-Hjördis. 1973. "Johan och Marianne räddar hundratals äktenskap!" *Expressen*, 27 May.

Larsson, Janerik. 1976. "Bergman och byråkraterna." *Sydsvenska Dagbladet* 29 April.

Leahey, Thomas Hardy. 2013. *A History of Psychology: From Antiquity to Modernity.* Boston, MA: Pearson.

Lennerhed, Lena. 1994. *Frihet att njuta: Sexualdebatten i Sverige på 1960-talet.* Stockholm: Norstedts.

Lessing, Doris. 1969. *The Four-Gated City.* New York, NY: Knopf.

———. 1971. *Briefing for a Descent Into Hell.* London: Cape.

Lewis, Jon. 2000. *Hollywood v. Hardcore: How the Struggle over Censorship Saved the Modern Film Industry.* New York, NY: New York University Press.

Lidman, Sara. 1968. "Sara Lidman angriper Bergman – *Skammen.*" *Aftonbladet*, 6 October.

Linton-Malmfors, Birgit. 1992. *Den dubbla verkligheten: Karin och Erik Bergman i dagböcker och brev 1907– 1936.* Stockholm: Carlssons.

LoBrutto, Vincent. 1997. *Stanley Kubrick: A Biography.* New York, NY: Donald I. Fine Books.

Löfgren, Lars. 1972. "Förord." Stefan Valmin. *TV-teater.* Stockholm: Sveriges Radio, pp. 3–4.

Löthwall, Lars-Olof. 1972. "Väsentligt och oväsentligt." *Chaplin*, vol. 13, no. 3, pp. 88–99.

———. 1976. "Introduktion." *Chaplin*, vol. 18, no. 3, p. 3.

Marowitz, Charles. 1973. "The Man of *Cries and Whispers*: As Normal as Smorgasbord." *New York Times*, 1 July.

Matteson, Leif. 1971. "Kvinnorna kring Bergman satsar pengar och sig själva för att hjälpa honom med en ny film." *Kvällsposten*, 7 September.

Mehr, Stefan. 1971. "Hur känns det idag då, Ingmar Bergman?" *Aftonbladet*, 28 June.

Melin, Bengt. 1976. "Ingmar Bergman – en karriär i ångest." *Aftonbladet*, 25 April.

Mellen, Joan. 1973. "Bergman and Women: *Cries and Whispers*." *Film Quarterly*, vol. 27, no. 1, pp. 2–11.

Mellen, Joan. 1974. *Women and Their Sexuality in the New Film*. New York, NY: Horizon Press.

Michener, Charles. 1976. "Two Faces of Bergman: The Man in the Ironic Mask." *Film Comment*, vol. 12, no. 3, pp. 44–45.

Milne, Tom. 1973. "*Viskningar och rop* (*Cries and Whispers*)." *Monthly Film Bulletin*, vol. 40, no. 470, pp. 61–62.

———. 1976. "*Ansikte mot ansikte* (*Face to Face*)." *Monthly Film Bulletin*, vol. 43, no. 515, p. 247.

Mithers, Carol Lynn. 1994. *Therapy Gone Mad: The True Story of Hundreds of Patients and a Generation Betrayed*. Reading, MA: Addison-Wesley.

Moi, Toril. 2008. *Henrik Ibsen and the Brith of Modernism: At, Theater, Philosophy*. Oxford: Oxford University Press.

Monaco, James. 1980. "Kenneth Loach." Richard Roud (ed.). *Cinema: A Critical Dictionary. The Major Filmmakers*. New York, NY: The Viking Press, pp. 630–631.

Narti, Ana Maria. 1973. "Den politiska dödsångesten." *Dagens Nyheter*, 21 April.

———. 1976. "*Ansikte mot ansikte*." *Chaplin*, vol. 18, no. 3, pp. 94–95.

Nilsson, Björn. 1971. "En mycket stor smärta." *Expressen, 21 March*.

Norcross, John C., Gary R. Vandenbos and Donald K. Freedheim (eds). 2011. *History of Psychotherapy: Continuity and Change*. Washington, DC: American Psychological Association.

Nordberg, Carl-Eric. 1971. "*Beröringen*." *Vi*, no. 31, 11 September.

Nordmark, Carlösten. 1974. "Bergman och Streisand överens: Vi *ska* göra film ihop." *Aftonbladet*, 23 March.

Norström, Björn. 1970. "*En passion*." *Filmrutan*, no. 1, pp. 36–37.

Nykvist, Sven. 1997. *Vördnad för ljuset: Om film och människor*. Stockholm: Albert Bonniers Förlag.

Ollén, Gunnar. 1984. "Tillkomst och mottagande: *Fröken Julie*." August Strindberg. *Fadren/Fröken Julie/Fordringsägare*. Nationalupplagan. Stockholm: Almqvist & Wiksell, pp. 292–321.

Olsson, Sven E. 1971. "Apropå Bergmans film och kritikernas katekes." *Arbetet*, 15 July.

———. 1973. "*Viskningar och rop*: Ett svårt mästerverk." *Arbetet*, 6 March.

Örnberg, Sune. 1970. "Bergman med en utsökt enkelhet i berättandet." *Göteborgs-Tidningen*, 29 October.

Orr, Christopher. 2000. "Scenes from the Class Struggle in Sweden." Lloyd Michaels (ed.) *Ingmar Bergman's "Persona"*. Cambridge: Cambridge University Press, pp. 86–109.

Pavey, Don. 2009. *Colour Symbolism: From Prehistory to Modern Aesthetics, Psychology & IT*. Edited by John Osborne. London: Amazon.

Penley, Constance. 1976. "*Cries and Whispers.*" Bill Nichols (ed.). *Movies and Methods*. Berkeley, CA: University of California Press, pp. 204–208.

Perlström, Åke. 1970. "Bergman och välfärden." *Göteborgs-Posten*, 29 October.

Plath, Sylvia. 1963. *The Bell Jar*. London: Faber.

Pryser, Tore, and Anders Thunberg. 2007. "En sfinx, en gåta." *Dagens Nyheter*, 15 November.

Raphael, Frederic. 1999. "Introduction." Arthur Schnitzler. 1926. *Dream Story*. Translated by J. M. Q. Davis. London: Penguin.

Raphaelson, Samson. 1976. "Two Faces of Bergman: II That Lady in Bergman." *Film Comment*, vol. 12, no. 3, pp. 46–49.

Richman, Larry. 1973. "What Was Bergman Really Crying and Whispering About?" *New York Times*, 8 July.

Riffe, Ernest (pseudonym for Ingmar Bergman), Viveka Heyman Hanserik Hjertén and Erland Törngren. 1960. "Bergmans ansikte. *Chaplin*, no. 8, pp. 188–195.

Roth-Lindberg, Örjan. 1977. "*Skammen* 1968." Jörn Donner (ed.). *Svensk Filmografi, 1960–1969*. Stockholm: Svenska Filminstitutet, pp. 401–406.

Russo, Vito. 1981. *The Celluloid Closet*. New York, NY: Quality Paperback Book Club.

Rydén, Carl-Olof. 1976. "Det mest skakande som visats på film…" *Aftonbladet*, 28 April.

Rying, Matts. 1969. "Ingmar Bergmans första TV-film." *Röster i Radio TV*, no. 13, 22–28 March, pp. 12–15.

Sarris, Andrew. 1971. "Focus on Film". *The Village Voice*, April 15.

———. 1976. "Nothing Is Certain with Bergman Except Death and Taxes." *Village Voice*, 5 April, p. 134.

Schein, Harry. 1971. "Bergmans pengar." *Expressen*, 20 October.

———. 1980. *Schein*. Stockholm: Bonniers.

Schildt, Jurgen. 1971. "Triangelspel i Tomtebos ruiner." *Aftonbladet, 31 August*.

———. 1973a. "En mycket stor Bergmanfilm." *Aftonbladet*, 6 March.

———. 1973b. "Ikväll börjar Ingmar Bergmans TV-serie." *Aftonbladet*, 11 April.

———. 1976. "Liv Ullmann tonar fram som ett mirakel." *Aftonbladet*, 29 April.

Schnitzler, Arthur. 1926. *Dream Story*. Translated by J. M. Q. Davis. London: Penguin.

Sellermark, Aino, and Arne Sellermark. 1974. "Det började på min soffa." *Allers*, no. 39, 29 September.

Sellermark, Arne. 1974. "Kvinnor behagar med att hålla käften." *Femina*, no. 39, 29 September.

Shargel, Raphael (ed.). 2007. *Ingmar Bergman: Interviews*. Jackson, MS: University Press of Mississippi.

Shaw, Bernard. 1891. "The Quintessence of Ibsenism." Bernard Shaw. *Major Critical Essays*. London: Penguin,

pp. 23–176.
Sima, Jonas. 1971a. "Ny godbit för Bergman-ätarna?" *Expressen*, 6 July.
____. 1971b. "Beröringen, en av mina intressantaste filmer." *Expressen*, 29 September.
____. 1971c. "Ingmar Bergman om censuren: Befängt att sätta in en gammal stöt som censurchef." *Expressen*, 29 September.
Simon, John. 1972. *Ingmar Bergman Directs*. New York, NY: Harcourt Brace Jovanovich.
Sjöman, Vilgot. 1963. *L136: Dagbok med Ingmar Bergman*. Stockholm: Norstedts.
____. 1998. *Mitt personregister: Urval 98*. Stockholm: Natur och Kultur.
Skoglund, Crister. 1991. *Vita mössor under röda fanor: vänsterstudenter, kulturradikalism och bildningsideal i Sverige 1880–1940*. Stockholm: Almqvist & Wiksell International.
____. 1993. "Kulturradikalismen – arvet och förnyelsen." Bertil Nolin (ed.). *Kulturradikalismen: Det moderna genombrottets andra fas*. Stockholm and Stehag: Brutus Östlings Bokförlag Symposion, pp. 103–131.
Skoglund, Erik. 1971. *Filmcensuren*, Stockholm: Svenska Filminstitutet/ Norstedts.
Smith, Roger. 2013. *Between Mind and Nature: A History of Psychology*. London: Reaktion Books.
Sörenson, Elisabeth. 1970a. "Ingmar Bergmans *Reservatet* tar form." *Svenska Dagbladet*, 18 February.
____. 1970b. "Universum kan få se Bergmans kärleksfilm." *Svenska Dagbladet*, 6 September.

____. 1972. "Bergman gör *Spöksonat* no. 3." *Svenska Dagbladet*, 12 December.
Steene, Birgitta. 1996. *Måndagar med Bergman: En svensk publik möter Ingmar Bergmans filmer*. Stockholm: Stehag.
____. 2000. "Bergman's *Persona* Through a Native Mindscape." Lloyd Michaels (ed.). *Ingmar Bergman's 'Persona'*. Cambridge: Cambridge University Press, pp. 24–43.
____. 2005. *Ingmar Bergman: A Reference Guide*. Amsterdam: Amsterdam University Press.
____. 2008. "Un-Swedish." Paul Duncan and Bengt Wanselius (eds). *The Ingmar Bergman Archives*. Hong Kong/Cologne/London/Los Angeles/Madrid/Paris/Tokyo: Taschen, pp. 324–325.
Sten, Hemming. 1970. "Gripande, djupt engagerande." *Expressen*, 29 October.
____. 1973. "Ingmar Bergman: Mitt livs roligaste jobb." *Expressen*, 17 May.
____. 1976. "Ett sus av besvikelse." *Expressen* 29 April.
Stenström, Urban. 1970. "Politisk Bergman." *Svenska Dagbladet*, 2 January.
Strick, Philip. 1970. "*A Passion.*" *Sight and Sound*, vol. 39, no. 4, pp. 216–217.
____. 1976. "*Face to Face.*" *Sight and Sound*, vol. 46, no. 1, p. 55.
Strindberg, August. 1879. *Röda rummet*. 1981 reprinted text annotated and commented by Carl Reinhold Smedmark. Stockholm: Norstedts.
____. 1907. *Ett drömspel*. 1988 reprint, text annotated by Gunnar Ollén. Stockholm: Norstedts.
Strömstedt, Bo. 1973. "Ingmar Bergman petar på dig." *Expressen*, 19 April.

———. 1974. "Ingmar Bergman: Ge kvinnorna en chans!" *Expressen*, 18 February.
Struck, Rune. 1970. "Bergmans Fårö." *Aftonbladet*, 2 January.
Sullivan, Harry Stack. 1970. *The Psychiatric Interview*. New York, NMY: W. W. Norton.
———. 1996. *Interpersonal Theory and Psychotherapy*. London: Routledge.
Swedberg, Ulla. 1973a. "Han låter upptäcka sanningen om oss!" *Göteborgs-Tidningen*, 11 April.
———. 1973b. "Trodde ni Bergman om detta?" *Göteborgs-Tidningen*, 12 April.
———. 1973c. "Bergmans gränslösa kvinnokraft." *Göteborgs-Tidningen*, 17 May.
Szasz, Thomas S. 1961. *The Myth of Mental Illness: Foundations of a Theory of Personal Conduct*. New York, NY: Harper Perennial.
Tapper, Michael. 2014. *Swedish Cops from Sjöwall & Wahlöö to Stieg Larsson*. Bristol: Intellect.
Thoor, Alf. 1975. "Här flyger världens bästa musical!" *Expressen*, 2 January.
Thunberg, Anders. 2008. *Karin Lannby: Ingmar Bergmans Mata Hari*. Stockholm: Natur och Kultur.
Timm, Mikael. 2008. *Lusten och dämonerna: Boken om Bergman*. Stockholm: Norstedts.
Tirén, Sverker. 1976. "'Jag visste mer om LM än om mig själv'." *Femina*, no. 2, 11 January. Reprinted in *Primalbladet* (newsletter for Svenska Primalföreningen), no. 3, March 1976, p. 9.
Tockenström, Göran. 2009. "Crisis and Change: Strindberg the Unconscious Modernist." Michael Robinson (ed.). *The Cambridge Companion to August Strindberg*. Cambridge: Cambridge University Press, pp. 79–92.
Tolstoy, Leo. 1897. *What Is Art?* 1995 paperback edition. Translated by Richard Pevear and Larissa Volokhonsky. London: Penguin.
Törnqvist, Egil. 1995. *Between Stage and Screen: Ingmar Bergman Directs*. Amsterdam: Amsterdam University Press.
———. 2000. *Strindberg's 'The Ghost Sonata'*. Amsterdam: Amsterdam University Press.
———. 2003. *Bergman's Muses*. Jefferson, NC: McFarland.
———. 2009. "Bergman's Strindberg." Michael Robinson (ed.). *The Cambridge Companion to August Strindberg*. Cambridge: Cambridge University Press, pp. 149–163.
Torrey, E. Fuller. 1976. "The Primal Therapy Trip: Medicine or Religion?" *Psychology Today*, vol. 10, no. 7, pp. 62–68.
Ullmann, Linn. 2016. *De oroliga*. Translated by Urban Andersson. Stockholm: Albert Bonniers Förlag.
Ullmann, Liv. 1976. *Changing*. London: Star.
Usai, Paolo Cherchi. 2000. *Silent Cinema: An Introduction*. London: British Film Institute.
Valmin, Stefan. 1972. *TV-teater*. Stockholm: Sveriges Radio.
Videgård, Tomas. 1973. "Primal Therapy – revolution inom psykoterapin?" *Psykolog-Nytt*, no. 7, pp. 13–14.
———. 1983. *The Success and Failure of Primal Therapy*. Stockholm: Almqvist & Wiksell International.

Vinberg, Björn. 1968. "Startar eget bolag – och gör TV film." *Expressen*, 3 February.

———. 1974. "Hela världen får se halva 'Äktenskapet'." *Expressen*, 27 August.

von Essen, Ebba. 1972. "Ingmar Bergman berättar om sitt ensamma liv på Fårö." *Aftonbladet*, 6 January.

———. 1973. "Jag har struntat i mina barn." *Aftonbladet*, 23 April.

Wells, Jerry. 1969. "I. Bergman åtalad. 'Ofredade Jahnsson.'" *Kvällsposten*, 25 March.

Werner, Gösta. 1973. "Traditionen i svenskt filmfoto." *Chaplin*, no. 5, pp. 176–182.

West, Britt. 1973. "Hitta på nåt nytt, Bergman!" *Aftonbladet*, 2 May.

Wester, Maud. 1970. "Bergman om Bergman: 'Jag har ett oerhört kontaktbehov'." *Veckojournalen*, no. 18, 29 April, pp. 22–25.

White, Rob. 2008. *Freud's Memory: Psychoanalysis, Mourning and the Foreign Body*. London: Palgrave Macmillan.

Widegren, Björn. 1972. "Är Bergman slut som konstnär?" *Chaplin*, vol. 14, no. 2, p. 66.

Widerberg, Bo. 1962. *Visionen i svensk film*. Stockholm: Bonniers.

Williams, Linda. 1999. *Hard Core: Power, Pleasure and the "Frenzy of the Visible"*. Berkeley, CA: University of California Press.

Williams, Paul, and Brian Edgar. 2008. "Up Against the Wall: Primal Therapy and 'the Sixties'." *European Journal of American Studies*, vol. 3, no. 2. See http://ejas.revues.org/3022 (accessed 4 December 2016).

Wood, Robin. 2000a. "'I Just Went Gay All of a Sudden': Bögar i 1990-talets amerikanska komedier." *Filmhäftet*, vol. 28, no. 109, pp. 36–45.

———. 2000b. "*From the Life of the Marionettes*: Bergman, Sweden and Me." *Filmhäftet*, vol. 28, no. 3, pp. 12–20. Reprinted in Robin Wood. 2013. *Ingmar Bergman*. Edited by Barry Keith Grant. Detroit, MI: Wayne State University Press, pp. 275–306.

Wrangsjö, Björn. 1974. "Arthur Janov: *Primalskriket*" (review). *Psykolog-Nytt*, no. 15, pp. 24–25.

Wright, Rochelle. 1998. *The Visible Wall: Jews and Other Ethnic Outsiders in Swedish Film*. Uppsala: Acta Universitatis Upsaliensis.

Young, Vernon. 1971. *Cinema Borealis: Ingmar Bergman and the Swedish Ethos*. New York, NY: Avon Books.

Yumibe, Joshua. 2015. "Techniques of the Fantastic." Tom Gunning, Joshua Yumibe, Giovanna Fossati and Jonathon Rosen. *Fantasia of Color in Early Cinema*. Amsterdam: Eye Filmmuseum and Amsterdam University Press.

FROM THE INGMAR BERGMAN ARCHIVE

Engagement planners, 1971–76.

Handbook of Production Information: *Face to Face*. Paramount Pictures.

Letter dated 18 April 1975 from Ingmar Bergman to Liv Ullmann regarding her part in *Face to Face*.

Schedules for press and industry screenings of *Scenes from a Marriage* and *Face to Face*.

Texts for voice-over narration to both the Swedish TV trailer and the American cinema trailer.

Workbook no. 24, 1967–68 (last days of 1967 – 30 September 1968): *A Passion. The Plan. The Border.* Conversations. Notes. *Maria. The Collage. The Hands Amen Amen. Annandreas.*

Workbook no. 26, 1970–71 (16 April 1970 – 10 May 1971): *Cries and Whispers, I. Karin, The Touch.*

Workbook no. 27, 1971–72 (Tuesday, 11 May 1971 – Thursday, 20 April 1972): *Cries and Whispers, II. Scenes from a Marriage, II. Marital Games.*

Workbook no. 29, 1974–75 (13 April 1974 Easter Eve – Tuesday, 1 July 1975): *The Psychiatrist. Face to Face. The Living Room. The Clouds. The Beach. Grandfather's House. The Understanding.*

Workbook no. 30, 1975 (Wednesday, 2 July 1975 – Thursday, 13 November 1975): *The Defeat. The Experiment. The Laboratory. The Prince. The Serpent's Egg. Seven Six. Porno Film. The Paralyzed Sovereign. 48 Hours in the Life of Jesus.*

Workbook no. 33, 1975–76 (Saturday, 8 November 1975 – 30 March 1976): *Love without Lovers. The Experiment. The Serpent's Egg. Autumn Sonata.*

TV SHOWS, RADIO, FILMS, PROGRAMMES

1971. *Presskonferens*, Swedish Radio, broadcast on TV1, 26 February.

1971. *Kvällsöppet*, Swedish Radio, broadcast on TV2, 9 April.

1971. *På parkett*, Swedish Radio, broadcast on TV2, 12 June.

1971. *På parkett extra*, Swedish Radio, broadcast on TV2, 14 August.

1972. *The Dick Cavett Show*, broadcast on ABC, 19 January.

1973. *Filmkrönika*, broadcast on Swedish radio, TV1, 4 March.

Donner, Jörn. 1975–1976. *Tre scener med Ingmar Bergman*. Swedish Radio, broadcast on TV1, 28 and 30 December 1975, 1 January 1976.

1976. *Kris*, Swedish Radio, broadcast on TV2, 24 May.

Bergman, Ingmar. 2004. *Sommar*. Swedish Radio, broadcast on, P1, 18 July. See http://sverigesradio.se/sida/avsnitt/373942?programid=2071 (accessed 31 July 2016).

AUTHOR'S INTERVIEWS

Interview with Rolf Holmqvist, 14 June 2015.

Interview with Tomas Videgård, 29 June 2015.

INDEX

ABC Pictures Corporation 17, 18
abortion 47, 56, 108–9
Aftonbladet 8, 13, 25, 30, 32, 34, 36, 206
All These Women (aka *Now About These Women*) 16, 91
Alma *see Persona*
Älskarinnan see Mistress, The
Aminoff, Marianne 192
Andalusian Dog, The 118
Andersson, Bibi 16–18, 54, 55, 60, 85, 92; *see also Persona*
Andersson, Harriet 17, 30, 63, 97, 100, 102
Andersson, Roy 11, 15
Aniara children/generation 153, 154, 158, 159, 166, 168, 193
Annandreas: Scenes from a Marriage (screenplay) 77
Annie Hall 209
Ansikte mot ansikte see Face to Face
Ansiktet see Magician, The
Arbetaren 9
Assault, The 15
Återkomsten *see Return, The*
Att älska see To Love
audience: adult audience 108; angry audience 25; bourgeois critics/ audience 63; contemporary audience 167, 183; failure to connect with the audience 10; international audience 92; mainstream audience 26, 76; male audience 38; mass audience 26, 35, 37–9, 45; new audience 22, 201; TV audience 24, 29, 181; working-class audience 38
Aus dem Leben der Marionetten see From the Life of the Marionettes
auteur 9, 14, 31–2, 110, 151, 204, 206, 210
Autumn Sonata 211
awards: Academy Award 7, 69, 209; BAFTA 209; Brazilian SESC Film Festival 209; Erasmus Prize 54, 149; Golden Globes 209; Guldbaggegalan Awards 14; Irving Thalberg Memorial Award 28; Los Angeles Film Critics Association Awards 209; National Board of Review Awards 209; New York Film Critics Circle Awards 209

Background Notes 201
Barnvagnen see Pram, The
Baumgarten, Alexander Gottlieb 51
Beineix, Jean-Jacques 211
Bell Jar, The, 71, 112

Bergman, Ellen 89–90
Bergman, Erik 65–6, 103, 120, 143
Bergman, Hjalmar 22, 61
Bergman, Karin 65, 66–7, 70, 89, 95, 102, 137
Berlin festival 18
Beröringen see Touch, The
Best Intentions, The 65, 147, 216
Best Intentions, Sunday's Children, The 147, 2216
Bettelheim, Bruno 189
bisexuality 159, 201
Björnstrand, Gunnar 39, 61, 63, 66, 138, 181
black-and-white film 41, 91
Blessed Ones, The 69, 137, 153
BLM 9, 13
Border, The 151, 156–61, 184
bourgeoisie: bourgeois cinema 45; bourgeois critics/audience 63; bourgeois doll's house 102, 198; bourgeois family 60, 62, 66, 76, 78, 80, 84, 86, 87, 95, 211; bourgeois idealism 88, 216; bourgeois life style 130; bourgeois sanctuaries 120, 133, 154, 159, 194, 211; bourgeois society 47; bourgeois wife 90; Swedish bourgeoisie 65, 85; Western bourgeois culture 47
Bout du monde, Le see End of the World, The
Breakup, The 151–56, 177
Bresson, Robert 60
Briefing for a Descent into Hell 112, 150
Brink of Life 68

Cabinet des Dr. Caligari, Das see Cabinet of Dr. Caligari, The
Cabinet of Dr. Caligari, The 118
censorship 8, 10, 24, 25, 37, 86, 108
Changing 174
Chaplin 9, 18, 40, 110, 207
Chicago Sun-Times 35, 204

chien andalou, Un see Andalusian Dog, The
childhood 61, 66, 89, 99, 100, 116, 128, 129, 130, 156, 160, 166, 167, 169, 212, 215; childhood memories 71, 99, 129; childhood rooms 103, 126, 130, 131, 155, 182, 212; *see also* trauma
Christianity 62, 78, 177; Christian fundamentalists 145; Christian symbolism 101; patriarchal Christianity 56
Cinematograph 2, 4, 12, 15, 22, 23, 26, 30, 33, 87, 127, 148, 171, 174, 178, 197, 199
claustrophobia 61
Clockwork Orange, A 153
close-ups: extreme close-ups 193, 196; grey and grainy close-ups 42; in and out of close-ups 193; medium close-ups 185, 196; signature close-ups 185
colour: 16, 42, 68 , 91–3, 100, 211; beige 92, 96; bland colour 90; cold colours 96; colour TV 39; colour film 41, 90, 91; green 95; primary colours 91; saturated colours 41; yellow 96, 97; *see also* symbolism
Comedy About Jenny, The (screenplay) 133
Corman, Roger 31, 35
Cries and Whispers 2, 4, 30–4, 36, 40, 45–50, 57, 66–8, 75, 77, 88, 92, 98, 99–100, 104, 107, 117, 118, 120, 122, 127, 131, 134, 136, 143, 149, 150, 159, 162, 182, 194, 202, 204, 211; Pietà scene 101, 136, 162, 191; static camera 40; *see also* dreams and feminism/women
Crisis 8, 68, 133, 184, 207
cultural radicalism 59, 60, 107, 108–9; *see also* politics and sexuality

Dagens Nyheter 8, 24, 47

dåres försvarstal, En see Defence of a Fool, The
Day Ends Early, The 133
Deadly Affair, The 17
Deep Throat 2, 110
Defence of a Fool, The 127, 148
De Laurentiis, Dino 4, 110, 171, 175, 201
depression 70, 113, 160, 174; *see also,* Marianne Höök and mental health/illness
Det regnar på vår kärlek see It Rains on Our Love
Devil in Miss Jones, The 110
Dick Cavett Show, The 29
Djursholm trilogy 3, 65, 70, 73–103, 120, 159, 163, 216
Dödsknullet i Eldoradodalen see Fuck of Death in Eldorado Valley, The
doll's house 96, 97, 103, 104, 120, 131, 161, 182, 198, 212; bourgeois doll's house 102; modern doll's houses 216; *see also* sanctuary
Doll's House, A 50–3, 55, 84, 85, 86, 93, 95, 98, 101, 189, 214
Dom kallar oss mods see They Call Us Misfits
Donner, Jörn 10–11, 61, 65, 109, 126, 205
Dramaten 14, 22, 38, 58, 82, 148, 176
Dream Play, A 49, 99, 100, 118, 211
dream: dream masquerade 121, 122, 142; dream narrative 32, 121–2, 126, 149; dream within a dream 100; post-suicide-attempt dream 198; reality/dream narrative 122; utopian dreams 67; *see also Cries and Whispers, Face to Face, Persona* and symbolism
Dreams 1
Dream Story (aka *Rhapsody: A Dream Novel*) 121, 127
Dr Wankel/Helmuth Wankel *see Face to Face*

Drysdale, George 101, 107

Eklund, Bengt 184
Ekman, Gösta 184
Ekman, Hasse 97, 119, 139
Elisabet *see Persona*
Elvira Madigan 18
Emmanuelle 2, 110, 171
End of the World, The 123
Enlightenment 60, 150
Ennis, Bruce J. 113, 146, 182
Enskilda samtal see Private Confessions
Et dukkehjem see Doll's House, A
Ett drömspel see Dream Play, A
European Broadcasting Union (EBU) *see* Eurovision
Eurovision 26, 27
exile 205, 209
Exorcist, The 213
Experiment, The (screenplay) 175, 176
Exponerad see Exposed
Exposed 110, 172
Expressen 34, 176, 206, 207

Face to Face (film) 1–4, 24, 36, 58–61, 68, 69, 71, 104, 107–216; Dr Wankel/Helmuth Wankel 133, 139, 142, 143, 145, 150–1, 155, 162, 164, 166, 172, 183, 190, 197; *Face to Face* (TV version) 1–4, 75, 85 199, 92, 93, 96, 151, 175, 188, 199; Grandfather 118, 119, 124, 128, 130, 134, 135, 139, 140, 142, 148, 158–64, 166, 172, 173, 181, 182, 189, 198, 212; Grandmother 118, 119, 124, 129, 130, 133–6, 139, 140, 142, 147, 154, 155, 158–64, 167, 169, 173, 181, 182, 189–91, 195, 197, 212, 215; Jenny/Jenny Isaksson 59, 68–9, 96, 104, 117, 130–98, 201, 203, 207, 212–16; *see also* depression, dreams, primal scream, rape and The Psychiatrist

Fadren see Father, The
Fall of the House of Usher, The 161
Family Life 115
Fängelse see Prison
Fanny and Alexander 1, 11, 53, 66, 69, 70, 122, 129, 131, 139, 147, 192, 211
Fanny och Alexander see Fanny and Alexander
Fantasia in C minor, K. 475   141, 159, 186, 195, 199
Far Away and Close 126
Farmor och vår herre see Thy Rod and Thy Staff
Fårö   12, 16, 22, 25, 33, 92, 172, 174
Fårö Document   25, 26, 29, 40, 42
Fårödokument see Fårö Document
Fårö trilogy   75
Fassbinder, R.W.   165
Father, The   82, 83
Faustrecht der Freiheit see Fox and His Friends
Feeling Child, The   175
Femina   115, 207
feminism/women: American radical feminists   109; anti-feminist mark 47; champion of feminism   202; de-idealisation of women   51; female body   48; female sacrifice   57; female subjectivity   48; feminist propaganda 98; femme fatale stereotype   68; self-sacrificing woman   55; sexual revolution for women   109; upper-class women   181, 192; view on women   46, 50; *see also* Other, pornography, sexuality and womb
FilmCentrum   15
Film Comment   204
Film Quarterly   35, 46
Filmson   8, 9
Fini, Leonor   122, 123, 162, 211
Fischer, Gunnar   42
Fisher, Else   68

Flossie   110, 172
Forandringen see Changing
För att inte tala om alla dessa kvinnor see All These Women (aka *Now About These Women*)
Forman, Milos   114
Forssell, Lars   13, 14, 29
Foucault, Michel   113, 114
Four-Gated City, The   112
491   108
Fox and His Friends   165
French New Wave   10
Frenzy   10, 83
Freud, Sigmund   3, 108, 115, 127, 147, 180
Friberg, Helene   192, 194, 201
From the Life of the Marionettes   58, 67, 71, 75, 110, 128, 138, 145, 160, 165, 211; *see also* homosexuality
Fuck of Death in Eldorado Valley, The   124

Godard, Jean-Luc   9
goda viljan, Den see Best Intentions, The
Grandfather *see Face to Face*
Grandmother *see Face to Face*
Gränsen see Border, The
Greer, Germaine   60, 99, 100
Grevenius, Herbert   68
Gycklarnas afton see Sawdust and Tinsel

Hagrann, Kenneth   171
Halldoff, Jan   186
hallucinations   141, 201
Hedda Gabler   52-3, 54-5, 85, 101
Hemsöborna see People of Hemsö, The
Herr Sleeman kommer see Mr Sleeman Cometh
Hets see Frenzy
Histoire de la folie à l'âge see Madness and Civilisation
Hitchcock, Alfred   41, 60, 91, 95
Hjortzberg, Lenn   165

homosexuality   108, 116, 144, 145,
    165, 168, 201, 205; decriminalisation
    of homosexuality   145; repressed
    homosexuality   158; *see also* sexuality
Horney, Karen   115
Höök, Marianne   24, 25, 45–7, 65, 68,
    69–71, 80, 89–90, 94, 113, 131, 134,
    138, 150, 161, 167, 190, 205
Höstsonaten see Autumn Sonata
Hour of the Wolf, The   13, 14, 16, 63, 68 ,
    75, 121, 134, 147, 158, 166, 183
How to Save Your Own Life   176
Huis clos see No Exit (aka *Behind Closed Doors*)
humiliation   62, 63, 65, 82, 83, 90,
    113, 121, 127, 146, 164; humiliating
    exploitation   63; humiliation dream
    121; sexual humiliation   88, 121, 143
hysteria   68, 160, 187; womb of hysteria
    100

Ibsen, Henrik   3, 29, 50–5, 57–9, 69,
    76, 77, 84, 85–6, 88, 95, 96, 98,
    101, 104, 131, 163, 167, 181, 211,
    214–16; attack on idealism   53, 80;
    Ibsenian doll's house   161; Ibsenian
    feminist deconstruction   99; Ibsenian
    landscape   54; *see also* modernism
idealism: absurdity of idealism   67;
    bourgeois idealism   88, 216; defeat
    of idealism   57; disease of idealism
    104; dismiss idealism   51; hypocrisy
    of idealism   56; radical idealism   85;
    representation of idealism   181;
    repressive idealism   42; self-deceiving
    idealism   80
Illicit Interlude see Summer Interlude
Images   1, 9, 17, 61, 75, 117, 194, 210, 212
Images: My Life in Film   75
incest   69, 161, 162, 164, 201, 212
Ingmar Bergman Archive   174, 199

Ingmar Bergman gör en film see Ingmar Bergman Makes a Movie
Ingmar Bergman Makes a Movie   11
In the Presence of a Clown   162
Isaksson, Ulla   65, 68– 9, 131, 137, 152,
    153
It Rains on Our Love   1, 65

Jack   186
Jag är nyfiken – gul see I Am Curious – Yellow
Jahnsson, Bengt   24–5, 27
Janov, Arthur   3, 111, 112–16, 131,
    144–6, 169, 175, 205, 207–8, 210, 215
Janus Films   7, 8, 17
Jenny/Jenny Isaksson *see Face to Face*
Johanson, Ulf   183
Jong, Erica   2, 176
Josephson, Erland   2, 34–5, 42, 61, 63,
    68, 80, 85, 87, 90, 103, 138, 148, 157,
    175, 184–5, 193, 200
Jung, Carl   55, 178, 180
Jungfrukällan see Virgin Spring, The

Kael, Pauline   18, 31, 32
Kant, Immanuel   129, 178
kärlekshistoria, En see Love Story, A
Katz, Madeleine   207
Kjellgren, Lars-Eric   10
Kohner, Paul   31, 171
Körkarlen see Phantom Carriage, The
Kremlin Letter, The   17
Kris see Crisis
Kristen Demokratisk Samling (KDS)
    108
Kubrick, Stanley   110, 153
Kvarteret Korpen see Raven's End
Kvinna utan ansikte see Woman Without a Face
Kvinnodröm see Dreams

Lacan, Jacques   113

Laing, R.D. 113, 115, 152
Långt borta och nära see Far Away and Close
Lannby, Karin 65, 67–8, 127
L'Année dernière à Marienbad see Last Year at Marienbad
Laretei, Käbi 66, 70, 76, 159
Larmar och gör sig till see In the Presence of a Clown
Last Adventure, The 186
Last Tango in Paris 110, 128
Last Year at Marienbad 118
lektion i kärlek, En see Lesson in Love, A
Lennon, John 116
Lessing, Doris 112, 150
Lesson in Love, A 61, 66, 89
Lie, The 4, 26, 27, 29, 67, 70, 71, 75–9, 81, 83, 85, 88–9, 98–99, 104, 120, 128, 149, 157, 161, 166, 184, 216
Life 41
Light of the Night 10
Lindberg, Sven 191
Lindblom, Gunnel 27, 69, 81, 83, 88
Lindqvist, Jan-Erik 192, 201
Lindström, Jörgen 54
Little Red Riding Hood 161, 189, 191
Löfgren, Lars 22, 37, 175
L136 39
Look 41
Love Story, A 15
Love Without Lovers (screenplay) 165

madness 69, 95, 129, 137, 140
Madness and Civilisation 114
Magic Flute, The (opera) 35, 60
Magic Flute, The (TV production) 2, 36, 41, 60, 112, 119–20, 141–3, 148, 189, 192, 194, 201, 206
Magician, The 25, 62, 63, 152
Magic Lantern, The 1, 11, 17, 18, 23, 28, 61, 65, 68, 75, 102, 117, 126, 165, 205, 210

Magnum Photos 41
Malmsten, Birger 185, 186
Marianne *see Scenes from a Marriage*
Marxism 47, 51
Marx, Karl 3, 108
masculine ideology 48
masquerade: erotic masquerade 121, 127, 128; masquerade dream 121, 122, 142; masquerade sex orgy 162; masquerade and suicide 143; *see also Face to Face*
Medan staden sover see While the City Sleeps
melodrama 55, 57, 75, 76; idealist melodrama 110; soap-opera-like melodramas 75, 76; women in melodramas 80; *see also Persona*
mental health/illness 108, 112, 113, 116, 134, 138, 145, 150, 152, 194, 202, 207, 212; mental breakdown 82, 168, 186, 207; *see also Face to Face*
mental institutions 113, 114
Merry Widow, The 30, 114, 118
metaphor 63, 104, 144, 166, 177, 178; Freudian metaphor 180; intentional metaphor for Sweden 203; metaphor for modern society 114; psychiatry as a metaphor 215
Mig till skräck see Unto My Fear
Mill, John Stuart 108
mirror images 180, 186
misogyny 45, 49–50, 96, 103, 109; *see also* feminism/women
Misshandlingen see Assault, The
Miss Julie 50, 71, 82
Mistress, The 11, 60
modernism: Ibsen's modernism 51–2; modernism as opposed to idealism 51, 56, 57; modernism in theatre 48; modernism in Swedish cultural debate 60; modernist aesthetics 3, 51;

modernist artist 48; modernist films 211; modernist strategies 57
Molander, Jan 26–7, 68, 76, 83
Monika: The Story of a Bad Girl see Summer with Monika
Monthly Film Bulletin 110, 203
Moral Re-Armament (MRA) 108
Morgon-Tidningen 9
Mr Sleeman Cometh 22
Music in Darkness 10
Musik i mörker see Music in Darkness

Naked, Joakim 134
Nära livet see Brink of Life
När vi döde vågner see When We Dead Awaken
Nattens ljus see Light of the Night
Nattlek see Night Games
Nattvardsgästerna see Winter Light
Nazism 23, 60, 65, 153
Nedstigandet *see* Descent, The
New Left 10–14, 31, 86, 115
New World Pictures 31
New Yorker, The 18, 32, 35, 204
New York Times, The 18, 32, 35, 59, 109, 202, 203, 204
New York Times Magazine, The 202
nihilism 63
Night Games 10
Nilsson, Maj-Britt 89, 205
No Exit (aka *Behind Closed Doors*) 100
Norstedts 201
Notini, Dag 207
Now About These Women see All These Women
Nykvist, Sven 25, 30, 37, 40–2, 91–2, 180, 185, 196

Oberhausen Manifesto 10
Oedipus complex: oedipal angle 66; oedipal fixation 66, 69; oedipal substitute 198

Olin, Christina 'Kerstin' 112
Olin, Lena 184
One Flew Over the Cuckoo's Nest 114, 126
Ord & Bild 46, 109
Other 63, 145; feminine Other 62; woman as Other 46

Palm, Göran 115
Paradise Place 69, 131, 153–4, 156
Paradistorg see Paradise Place
Paramount Pictures 1, 4, 171, 196–201, 206
Pasolini, Pier Paolo 108, 128
passion, En see Passion, A (aka *Passion of Anna, The*)
Passion, A (aka *Passion of Anna, The*) 15–17, 24, 28, 63, 67, 75, 77–9, 80, 91–2, 100, 157; *see also* humiliation
Passion of Anna, The see Passion, A
patriarchy: old patriarchal gender myths 46; patriarchal Christianity 56; patriarchal double personality 65; patriarchal glory 130; patriarchal hegemony 109; patriarchal ideology 47, 58; patriarchal society 113; *see also* Erik Bergman
Pawlo, Rebecca 184
Peer Gynt 52
People of Hemsö, The 183
Persona 1, 10, 13, 16–17, 24, 32, 39, 42, 48, 49, 53, 54, 57, 60, 63, 66, 78, 101, 103, 118, 149, 150, 158, 161, 164, 178, 183, 193, 195, 204, 214–16; Alma 54–8, 60, 63, 150, 161, 215, 216; Elisabet 54–8, 63, 66, 152, 155–8, 164, 178, 183, 214–5; *see also* feminism/women, idealism and womb
Persona AG 15
Phantom Carriage, The 60, 82, 168
Plath, Sylvia 71, 112–13
Poe, Edgar Allan 161
Porn Film, The see Porrfilmen

pornography: 108, 109–10; anti-pornography activism 110; fantasy of pornotopia 111; porno chic 110; pornography films 2, 108, 110, 171, 172; *see also* feminism/women
pornotopia 111
Porrfilmen 172
post-war: cultural boost post-World War II 41; post-war art cinema 118; post-war consumer 21; post-war nuclear age 112; post-war youth culture 183; *see also* World War II
Pram, The 10
Primalbladet 208
Primal Institute 114, 115, 214
Primal Revolution, The 175
primal scream 59, 116, 140, 144, 147, 151, 167–8, 186, 189, 193, 194, 196, 212–14; *see also Face to Face*
Primal Scream, The 3, 111, 112, 114, 116, 144, 145, 169, 215
primal therapy 3, 112, 114–16, 168, 205, 207, 208, 209–10, 215
Prince, The (screenplay) 176
Prison 100, 113, 120, 187
Private Confessions 147, 216
Psychiatrist, The (screenplay) 3, 112, 116, 117–18, 126–8, 134, 137–8, 140, 141, 143, 148; *see also Face to Face*
Psychology Today 114
Psykiatern see Psychiatrist, The

Rains on Our Love 1, 65
rape 46, 109, 128, 133, 134, 136, 137, 139, 158, 159, 186, 197, 201, 212; anal rape 67, 128; *see also Face to Face*
Raven's End 10
Red Riding Hood *see* Little Red Riding Hood
regnar på vår kärlek, Det see Rains on Our Love
Reservatet see Lie, The

Resnais, Alain 118
Return, The 151, 166–8, 193–4
Rhapsody: A Dream Novel see Dream Story
Riffe, Ernest 9, 61
Riten see Rite, The (aka *Ritual, The*)
Rite, The (aka *Ritual, The*) 22–5, 27, 38, 41, 42, 109; *see also* censorship
Rorschach test 200
Röster i Radio TV 38, 205
Royal Dramatic Theatre *see* Dramaten
Ruud, Sif 183

Salò o le 120 giornate di Sodoma see Salò, or the 120 Days of Sodom
Salò, or the 120 Days of Sodom 108, 128
sanctuary 53, 70, 78, 80–4, 86, 88, 97, 100, 104, 183, 184, 214, 216; bourgeois sanctuary 133, 154, 159, 194, 198, 211; homely sanctuary 131; sanctuary of the wealthy Western world 88; *see also* bourgeoisie, idealism and *Scenes from a Marriage*
Sartre, Jean-Paul 100
Såsom i en spegel see Through a Glass Darkly
Sawdust and Tinsel 8, 9, 62, 150
Scandinavian mythology 177
Scener ur ett äktenskap see Scenes from a Marriage
Scenes from a Marriage (film) 2, 4, 5, 58–61, 75 90, 100, 109, 110, 120, 131–2, 140, 144, 147, 149, 151, 154, 178, 181, 184, 204, 206; Marianne 34, 50, 85–99, 104, 126, 134, 144, 147, 178–9, 216; *Scenes from a Marriage* (TV series) 3, 7, 38, 40, 41, 42, 48, 50, 53, 71, 75, 77, 82, 85–8, 92–5, 99, 104, 138, 151, 154, 160, 201, 205, 207, 216; *see also* feminism/women, Erland Josephson, Liv Ullmann and Marianne Höök
Schein, Harry 9, 14, 25, 30, 31, 61, 89, 132, 152

INDEX 239

Schnitzler, Arthur 121, 127
Segelcke, Tore 181
self-theatricalisation 58, 78, 80, 84, 96
Serpent's Egg, The 110, 121, 211
Serpent's Egg, The (screenplay) 176
Seventh Seal, The 1, 49 , 184
sexuality: anal sex 128; graphic sex 109, 110; sexual abuse 67; sexual humiliations 121; sexual imagery 8, 109; sexual liberation 3, 109, 157, 184, 194; sexual passion 51, 69; sexual repression 56, 108, 110, 131, 157
sexual revolution 87, 101, 107–11
Shame, The 13, 14, 16, 22, 24, 27, 42, 75, 138, 183, 204
Shaw, George Bernard 51
Show 29
Sight and Sound 35, 203
Silence, The 8, 10, 18, 24, 47, 54, 57, 75, 108–10, 118, 143; see also censorship
sista äventyret, Det see Last Adventure, The
Sjöman, Vilgot 3, 11, 18, 22, 23, 39, 60, 61, 66, 108, 109
Sjöström, Victor 52, 60, 82, 168
sjunde inseglet, Det see Seventh Seal, The
Skammen see Shame, The
Skoglund, Erik 24
Skymningslandet see Twilight Land, The
Smiles of a Summer Night 7, 61, 66
Smultronstället see Wild Strawberries
Snakeskin, The (screenplay) 54, 149
Social Democratic Party 14
Sommaren med Monika see Summer with Monika
Sommarlek see Summer Interlude
Sommarnattens leende see Smiles of a Summer Night
Söndagsbarn see Best Intentions, Sunday's Children, The
Stangertz, Göran 185, 186
static camera 40, 87, 90, 95, 180

Stockholm 9, 11, 29, 52, 67, 69, 70, 76, 115–16, 119, 138, 143, 148, 171, 172, 174, 176, 207–8
Strindberg, August 25–7, 49–50, 59, 66, 71, 76, 79–80, 82–3, 88, 90, 96, 99, 127–8, 153, 183, 211
Strindberg, Göran 42
Strömberg, Mikael 155, 156, 163, 165, 173, 184, 190, 192, 197
Strongest, The 49, 153
Sullivan, Harry Stack 113, 146, 182
Sunday's Children 147, 216
Summer Interlude 68, 94, 109, 128, 147
Summer with Monika 102, 109
Svenska Primalföreningen *see* Swedish Primal Society
Sveriges Liberala Studentförbund 108
Sveriges Nationella Förbund (SNF) 60
Sveriges Nationella Ungdomsförbund (SNU) 60
Svensk Filmindustri (SF) 8, 14, 30, 31, 55
Swedish Film Institute 11, 14, 30, 126
Swedish Primal Society 114, 208
Swedish Radio 21, 26, 175
Swedish TV 22, 36, 37, 177
Sylwan, Kari 101, 103, 180, 185
symbolism: anal sex symbolism 128; Christian symbolism 101; colour symbolism 91; Little Red Riding Hood symbolism 191; multi-faceted symbol 177; religious symbolism 93; sex-and-death symbolism 128, 162
Szasz, Thomas 113

Taube, Aino 181
tax evasion affair 176, 202–6, 209
They Call Us Misfits 14
Through a Glass Darkly 7, 39, 63, 68, 69, 102, 178, 187
Thulin, Ingrid 30, 47, 67, 89, 94, 102, 103; *see also Cries and Whispers, The Silence* and *Wild Strawberries*

Thy Rod and Thy Staff 61
Till Damaskus see To Damascus
Till glädje see To Joy
Time 7, 18, 203, 204
Titicut Follies 113
To Damascus 49
To Joy 89
To Love 10
Törnqvist, Egil 49, 189
Touch, The 1, 16, 17, 29, 32, 36, 46, 75, 95, 210
traum 127, 167, 216
trauma 61, 116, 127, 128, 131, 167, 168, 189, 212, 213, 216; post-traumatic response 186; repressed traumas 188; traumatic memories 67, 161; *see also* childhood and claustrophobia
Traumnovelle see Dream Story
Trollflöjten see Magic Flute, The
Truffaut, François 11
två saliga, De see Blessed Ones, The
Twelfth Night 148, 171, 172
Twilight Land, The 151, 161–6, 187–193
Tystnaden see Silence, The

Ullmann, Liv 2, 16, 28, 30, 34, 35, 54, 55, 76, 85, 87, 89–90, 93, 102, 124, 138, 171, 173, 174–6, 178–9, 183, 184, 193, 194–5, 199–200, 204–6, 209, 213, 214; *see also Face to Face, The Lie, Persona* and *Scenes from a Marriage*
United Artists 17
Unto My Fear 182, 187
Uppbrottet see Breakup, The
upper-class: Djursholm 70, 76; Östermalm 120, 152; upper-class environment 70; upper-class residence 181; upper-class women 181, 192
Uses of Enchantment, The 189

Vargtimmen see Hour of the Wolf, The
Vietnam War 11, 13, 42, 56; *see also* New Left
Vildanden see Wild Duck, The
Virgin Spring, The 7, 68, 177
Visionen i svensk film 10
Vision in Swedish Cinema, The *see Visionen i svensk film*
Viskningar och rop see Cries and Whispers
vita sporten, Den see White Game, The
von Rosen, Ingrid 28, 76
von Sydow, Max 16, 112, 158
von Trier, Lars 211

Waiting Women 66
wallpaper 96, 187–8; *see Face to Face*
Wallpaper, The (screenplay) 187
When We Dead Awaken 215
While the City Sleeps 100
White Game, The 15
Who's Afraid of Virginia Woolf? 82, 88
Widerberg, Bo 10, 11, 13, 15, 18, 28
Wild Duck, The 29, 52, 53, 55, 77, 104, 132, 211
Wild Strawberries 9, 49, 52, 58, 60, 80, 89, 94, 100, 101, 104, 131, 146, 147, 152, 158, 184, 187; *see also* von Sydow, Max
Winter Light 10–11, 61, 66–7, 75, 78, 80, 92, 137, 216
Woman in the Window, The 118
Woman Without a Face 68, 120
womb: cold womb 67, 71, 80, 94, 103, 154, 159, 165, 194; mind/womb of a woman 54; morgue-womb 101; shared womb 54, 56; womb of hysteria 100, 160
Workbook no. 24 22
Workbook no. 26 99, 118
Workbook no. 29 117–29, 130–68, 172, 177, 211; *see also Face to Face*
Workbook no. 30 172

World War I 51, 154
World War II 8, 18, 23, 67, 107; *see also* post-war
Woyzeck 38

yummy film 211

Zauberflöte, Die see Magic Flute, The
Zetterling, Mai 10–11

GPSR Authorized Representative: Easy Access System Europe, Mustamäe tee
50, 10621 Tallinn, Estonia, gpsr.requests@easproject.com

www.ingramcontent.com/pod-product-compliance
Lightning Source LLC
Chambersburg PA
CBHW021941290426
44108CB00012B/926